The
WORKS
of the
LORD

Dr. Charles R. Vogan Jr.

Copyright © 1997 Charles R. Vogan Jr.
All rights reserved

Scripture taken from the HOLY BIBLE, NEW INTERNATIONAL VERSION, Copyright © 1973, 1978, 1984 International Bible Society. Used by permission of Zondervan Bible Publishers.

ISBN 978-0-6151-3934-0

Ravenbrook Publishers

A subsidiary of
Shenandoah Bible Ministries

www.shenbible.org

Contents

Introduction	1
What are the Works of the Lord?	27
The Lord's Works reveal him	138
His Works accomplish his will	209
The Lord's Works support his people	258
Remember the Works of the Lord	298
Conclusion	342

PREFACE

The works of the Lord surround us. It would take far longer than our short lifetimes to catalog them all and to study all of them in depth. He has shown his vast power and his profound wisdom in what he has done. His works truly teach us what kind of a God we have.

But his works aren't limited to the physical creation. Think in several dimensions for a minute: he made a world for us to live in, and then he started making a spiritual kingdom for his children to live in – a world that not only we can taste now but have hopes for being a part of for eternity. If this world required such amazing complexity for our short lives, just think of the unimagined size and complexity of a world designed to go on forever! It boggles the mind, to think of what God is capable of doing.

It doesn't make sense to be in the dark about God's works. We need to know a great deal about his work in this world in order to do our work every day; the sciences (both "hard" and "soft" sciences) are busy studying his works to make our lives easier and more productive (though they would never admit that God was responsible for this world!) But the Church is no less responsible to search out the works of the Lord in the spiritual kingdom, because here is a gold mine of information that would make our spiritual lives more productive. Without this information about what God has done, we are just as helpless before spiritual forces as a man is helpless before this world's elements when he doesn't understand them.

Therefore we have to look for and study God's works. There's no need to go to the library and try to find books on the subject, because we have all that we need in the Bible – God's written record of his works. We will find in the Scriptures all the information that we need about the subject. But we have to study it out; we can't just read the stories and think that we now know his works. Just like a scientist takes the data at hand and experiments and works with it until he discovers a useable principle, we have to work with the texts of the Bible and meditate and compare passage with experience until we discover what it is that the Spirit is leading us to see.

If we do our study in this way, we will find that God's works are like precious gems to us. They will be useable tools for our own works. They will be foundation stones for our lives. In other words, we can't hope to build our spiritual lives in a way that will outlast the fires of Judgment Day unless we lay hold of the kind of works that can't be destroyed by time or sin or the Law. We need lasting materials to form our future – and we will find them in what God alone does.

The result of a study like this, of course, is that we will come to know our God in a much deeper way. We can't help but appreciate him more when we understand what it is that he has been doing, and where he is headed in his work. We will draw closer to him in faith in his works, and we will hope for the goals he has in mind. We will learn how to work with him instead of against him – become "fellow laborers" with him. In short, we will throw our lot in with the Lord as he works to make the world that he wants to see here. We can't help but come to know him better when we study his works, and knowing him is what the Christian life is all about.

Introduction

The Works of the Lord is a subject that spans the entire Bible. I don't know if you ever looked into it before, but most of the authors of the Biblical books refer to the "works" or "deeds" of the Lord many times; and of course *what* the Lord did – which constitute his "works" – fills the whole Bible.

Dip in a few places and you will see what I mean:

For you make me glad by your deeds, O LORD; I sing for joy at the works of your hands. How great your works, O LORD, how profound your thoughts! (Psalm 92:4)

Great are the works of the LORD; they are pondered by all who delight in them. (Psalm 111:2)

They have harps and lyres at their banquets, tambourines and flutes and wine, but they have no regard for the deeds of the LORD, no respect for the work of his hands. (Isaiah 5:12)

LORD, I have heard of your fame; I stand in awe of your deeds, O LORD. Renew them in our day, in our time make them known; in wrath remember mercy. (Habakkuk 3:2)

And we know that in all things God works for the good of those who love him, who have been called according to his purpose. (Romans 8:28)

There are different kinds of working, but the same God works all of them in all men. (1 Corinthians 12:6)

For it is God who works in you to will and to act according to his good purpose. (Philippians 2:13)

Great and marvelous are your deeds, Lord God Almighty. Just and true are your ways, King of the ages. (Revelation 15:3)

There shouldn't be anything mysterious about the concept of working; we all work – even the laziest of us do something to get along. But the idea of God working is something we need to spend some time studying. Our tendency is to get so wrapped up with our own work that we don't even think about what God might be doing. Usually we only think about it when we need him to rescue us, or fill in with something we can't do ourselves.

But that, as we shall see, is an extremely short-sighted view of God. He is constantly working on things that we will never know about, on things that will outlast our own works. If anything, God's works are far more important – and therefore more worthy of study – than our own work.

What is God's work?

"Work" is exerting some strength, with a little skill, to bring about a desired effect. Or it may be a lot of strength with a lot of skill. Work can range anywhere from digging ditches to writing computer programs; the common element is that the worker is trying to reach a goal, and he uses whatever is at hand to do it.

There is also the material upon which someone works. A ditch digger works with the dirt; a cook works on food; a musical conductor works with the orchestra members. When the worker starts, his material isn't in the shape that he wants it to be in; when he's done, however, it's more to his liking. The goal, in other words, is to get the material that one is working with to a certain point.

This all applies to God's work, of course, but in a much more profound sense than it does to man's work. The power that he exerts is enough to fling out galaxies or to finely craft the elements of an atom; his wisdom is startling and far-reaching in its consequences; his goals are complex and yet simple, clear to a child and yet far beyond man's wisdom to understand.

And he works with all sorts of material. In Creation he worked with nothing, making it into a universe of material bodies and spiritual souls. Through Providence he moves vast forces in intricate ways in order to keep the world system running smoothly. In the Church his Spirit blows across the souls of men and they are fed and made strong and built into a spiritual Temple.

You can *see* the works of God. Because he uses materials, and because there are results from his work, we can often see what is going on. Little boys (and men, too!) like to stand beside a construction site and watch the workers use heavy equipment to do a lot of work; and we can do the same while God works. It doesn't occur to us that we *can* do this because again, we don't usually think in terms of God working; we imagine that he just snaps his fingers and things happen. But he usually *works* when he does something (not that he couldn't snap his fingers if he wanted to!), and work involves material and time and strength and wisdom and process. We can't see *all* of his work, but because he does much of it here in this world for our sakes we can very easily watch him work.

God works constantly. He is always busy on many, many jobs. If we knew the least part of what it takes to create and run a universe we might begin to appreciate the staggering amount of work that God does. Add to that the spiritual dimension, the enormous amount of work to address the sins of man and build the coming kingdom, and you will see that God is very busy. And yet, because of his special nature, this constant work 1) doesn't take his mind away from something when it needs his full attention, 2) doesn't tire him out in any way, and 3) doesn't even tax his abilities in the least. Nor is he under a special obligation to anyone to do all this work; he does it because he wants to, and he sets his own schedule for getting it all done in the way that pleases only himself.

God has purposes in his work. We will see those purposes as we study the matter further. For now, we can see that God does nothing aimlessly, nor is anything that he does a wasted effort. The least detail of God's work (and some of the details are unbelievably small and insignificant!) fits into the overall developing picture; only he understands how to do that. We talk about the complexity of government bureaucracies, but we can't even imagine the complexity of God's creation – the variations, the interdependencies, the sensitive balance of it all. If the smallest detail was out of place then everything would fail; but the works of God are dependable and sufficient down to every small detail.

So far we haven't been describing anything that we can't easily understand, except for the fact that God's work is infinitely beyond our capacity to do. Our work resembles God's work, except we work on such a smaller scale than he does. But there's one thing about God's work that makes it qualitatively different from ours, something that we can't claim about our own work even if we had the infinite wisdom and strength that God has:

Only he can do his work in this world.

This thought has more under the surface than you might think. Nobody else can do God's work. It's not true that, if we only had God's strength and wisdom, we could do the same kinds of things that he does. This is the way that Satan feels about himself! The devil would love to claim the glory that God alone has; the problem is, his claims are empty. He isn't God, and nobody else is either – because nobody else can do what God can do. The issue is this: there is only *one* God, and there are certain things that *only God himself can do*. Nobody else is allowed to try, under pain of usurping God's place in the universe. Just as the president of our country has certain duties that nobody else is allowed to assume – that's *his* job! – so, in a much more profound way, the works that God does are works that only he will do; he will never turn them over to another, nor could anybody else do them. If they did, they could lay claim to be equal to God.

This should become more apparent as we study some examples from Scripture and think more about it.

Characteristics of his works

God's works are easily distinguishable from the works of others. Thank God for these characteristics, because otherwise we could mistake man's works for God's works and start trusting in the wrong savior. Just as there are tell-tale signs in the work of a master furniture craftsman, the works of God witness to *his* presence, doing his work that only he can do. He leaves proof of his handiwork behind him like fingerprints.

But you should understand that these characteristics of God's works aren't obvious to everyone. It takes a sharp-eyed, experienced scout to pick up faint marks in the brush, signs that an animal or man had passed by some days previously. In the same way, it takes spiritual eyes and experience in the ways of God in order to see clearly the signs of his presence. Not everyone will be able to tell that God has been on the scene. It's not because he fails to leave the tell-tale signs, though; Paul tells us that it's *our* fault if we can't see God, not his fault:

> The wrath of God is being revealed from Heaven against all the godlessness and wickedness of men who suppress the truth by their wickedness, since what may be known about God is plain to them, because God has made it plain to them. For since the creation of the world God's invisible qualities – his eternal power and divine nature – have been clearly seen, being understood from what has been made, so that men are without excuse. (Romans 1:18-20)

What are those signs of God's presence when he works?

- ***They glorify him.*** "Declare his glory among the nations, his marvelous deeds among all peoples." (Psalm 96:3) When God does something, only he will get the glory from it. Glory, you will find in the Scriptures, means "who gets the credit." The Lord doesn't want anybody else to get the credit for what he does, because he wants to drive the point home to every human being that *only he can and must work his will out in this world.* You will notice that, whenever God is involved in something, all eyes and hearts turn to *him*, that people start thinking about their relationship to him, that they wonder what he thinks of them, that they get pretty concerned about finding out what he wants from them, and so on. In other words, God is suddenly uppermost on their minds. Now given the nature of sinful man, this *never* happens unless God personally visits us. A miracle, a truth forced into a hard heart, eyes opened to spiritual realities – these kinds of things wake people out of their sleep of death and make them sensitively aware of the presence of God. You can tell that God is close when people start talking about *him*. You can tell that God is *not* involved when man gets the credit in any way – when he presumes to pretend in any way that he can do what God does.

- *They are perfect.* "He is the Rock, his works are perfect, and all his ways are just. A faithful God who does no wrong, upright and just is he." (Deuteronomy 32:4) "Perfect" here involves several ideas – complete, morally acceptable, suitable – but we can sum it all up by saying that God's works will perfectly work out all the requirements necessary – God's requirements, that is. Nobody else can claim that. Jesus proved his own ability to live a sinless life, a life that was pleasing to his Father in all ways – morally, socially, politically, economically, religiously, because life is simply that big – and that sinless life was a good example of the perfect work of God. What are the requirements of God for any work to pass his muster? They are a multitude! Not only does that work have to pass the grade as far as the Law of God, but it has to fit into the overall plan of God's purposes in time and space, and it has to fit into the world of men and angels in such a way that the right things happen. Since only God is a sufficient judge of any situation, only God can do a work that perfectly fulfills the requirements of that situation. You won't find anything left undone, or done imperfectly, when God does it.

- ***They instill fear in men.*** "All mankind will fear; they will proclaim the works of God and ponder what he has done." (Psalm 64:9) Fear is a healthy thing, not the negative idea that many people make it out to be. Often people quote the verse that says "Perfect love casts out fear" to support the idea that we don't have to fear God; but that's a wrong interpretation of that verse. Godly fear – fear of God – is necessary for survival in God's world; fear of anything else in the world is what the verse is actually talking about. You will find, in the places where Scripture shows God coming close to men and women, that people always feared this God who came so close. Fear of God, in other words, is just this: being strongly aware that God is near, wanting to be found blameless in the sight of his burning eyes, suddenly inclined to do what he wants of us, painfully aware of our shortcomings in the light of his expectations of us, willing to forget about our own glory and start promoting his. The reason we fear him is that he sees to the bottom of our hearts, where nobody else can see; we stand naked in his sight, as the Bible teaches us. There is no escaping his scrutiny, therefore there is no excuse for our sin and every reason in the world to change and become what he expects of us.

- ***They are marvelous.*** "Praise be to the LORD God, the God of Israel, who alone does marvelous deeds." (Psalm 72:18) Just exactly how God does things remains a mystery to us. His works are beyond our comprehension – that is, in regard to emulating them. Science is based on the working premise that any discovery has to be re-do-able – someone else has to be able to duplicate the process or the discovery was probably no good. And man would love to be able to duplicate God's works; remember Simon Magus' request of the Apostles? (Acts 8:19) But part of the definition of the works of God is that *only* God can do them. Even if God would lay out before us the plans of his projects, and explain each little detail of how he went about doing something, we would never see it. It's beyond us. And for good reason, too – we are *not* God! We are only creatures who stand back amazed when God works in our world. There is no explaining how he does things; we can only praise him for them. So, if you can understand an action completely and how it happened then it wasn't God who did it.

- *They are knowable.* "Are your wonders known in the place of darkness, or your righteous deeds in the land of oblivion?" (Psalm 88:12) The point of this verse is that what God does is done out in the open in the full view of men. We *can* know the works of God; we *can* see him working in our world. He isn't far off somewhere letting the world run on its own, he isn't hesitant to stick his finger in our affairs because he might confuse us if he did. The philosophers are wrong who say that God is unknowable, who say that God has nothing to do with how our natural world works. He works in our world to the extent that we are fully able (if we had the eyes to see, that is) to observe and know his work.

This doesn't contradict the above point, because we can see and know about an action without understanding how it works. Take light for example; we use it, we see it and talk about it, but nobody has an earthly idea of what it is! That's true of all God's works that he does for our sakes; we can see them and take advantage of them (or feel their power!) without understanding how he did it. It is, after all, through his works that he becomes better known to us; it would be counter-productive to his purposes if we could never know them!

- ***They are good.*** "I will tell of the kindnesses of the LORD, the deeds for which he is to be praised, according to all the LORD has done for us – yes, the many good things he has done for the house of Israel, according to his compassion and many kindnesses." (Isaiah 63:7) This is a prime way of distinguishing God's works from anybody else's works. God does good for his people, not harm; everything he does will benefit them in some way. Not in ways that sinners would like to see, or the ignorant or the naïve, but in ways that God knows will help them. You have to remember the ultimate goals that God has for us, and the requirements along the way that have to be met. There are many things that we don't see or understand that God is taking care of for us, as well as the obvious needs that we can see. So when God works on our behalf, you can be sure that "in all things God works for the good of those who love him, who have been called according to his purpose." (Romans 8:28) We will see later how this gets worked out.

- *They fulfill his will.* "In him we were also chosen, having been predestined according to the plan of him who works out everything in conformity with the purpose of his will." (Ephesians 1:11) There are several important reasons why God does *only his will*. **First**, only he knows what needs to be done and exactly how to do it; how could he trust us to come up with a scheme that would reach eternal goals? **Second**, only what he wills is perfectly good. Everything we want is tainted with sin and ignorance. **Third**, who is running this kingdom, anyway? The name "Lord" means (if words go by their plain meaning anymore) that *his* will is done, not anybody else's. **Fourth**, we should be thankful, when we think about it, that he does his will and not ours; I believe that we all could testify to the fact that we would only make matters worse if we told God what to do. Now given these reasons, you can see why God just goes ahead and does his own will when he works in our lives, without stopping to ask us for our permission. In our right minds we would only want that anyway.

When you are looking for God's works, look for these characteristics. If you don't see them (and be tough – they are clear and God promises that they will be there amidst his work) then just assume that the work under question is *not* God's doing.

The importance of God's works

Or maybe we should ask the question, "Why should we study the works of God?" There are two reasons, one negative and one positive.

First the negative reason. *We have got to get our attention off ourselves.* We are too preoccupied with what *we* are doing, and we are giving almost no thought to what God alone can do. Not only are we taken up with the daily affairs of life, and deceived into thinking that more strength and know-how on our part will make life successful, but our spiritual existence is at stake as well. If we do good, and read the Bible, and go to church, and pray, and even "seek God's face," then we think we are doing well in our religion. That's just not true. Many Christians, let alone pagans, are deceiving themselves in this way. If God isn't unmistakably working in your life then it's *you* who are trying to make Christianity work and *you will fail*.

There are untold examples of this truth. Most of what goes on in churches today, even though done in the name of God, are the efforts of man and they will fail. Religious movements and institutions won't get the blessing of God just because they claim to do it in God's name! One has to differentiate between what man is called to do and what only God can do, and usually people don't bother to discern between the two. It's backward to do something and then pray God's blessing on it; one must start with God's work and pray that man's efforts will fit into it. And it's even more ridiculous to do whatever what one wants and hope for the best, especially if the stakes are really as high as we are about to see. If we insist on doing the necessary steps of salvation and spiritual growth ourselves, then God won't do it, and we will fail.

Second, the positive reason. *God's works are our only hope.* We have to study them if we want what the Bible promises us. Do you want to go to Heaven? Only God can get you there; you don't have a chance without him. Do you want a place ready for when you get there? "I am going there to prepare a place for you." (John 14:2) You wouldn't know what to do there if it weren't for his preparations and willingness to guide you. Do you want to grow spiritually? Only God can make you grow spiritually. "So neither he who plants nor he who waters is anything, but only God, who makes things grow." (1 Corinthians 3:7) You can't do any more about your spiritual growth than a branch on a tree can grow on its own.

The reason that you need to study the works of God is to find out what he is, in fact, doing in your life. Wouldn't it make sense to find out what he's doing so that you can arrange your life accordingly? After all, he has been giving you certain spiritual resources to make you grow – are the treasures of this life so important to you that you don't have time to take what God has in store for you? He uses certain means and methods to bring your life along the path he has called you to walk along – are you inadvertently fighting him, mistaking those means of salvation as irritations in life? "Endure hardship as discipline; God is treating you as sons." (Hebrews 12:7) How many times we have fought against our Father because we didn't realize that he was pruning the dead branches, tearing away our rags of filth, preparing us for Heaven!

If you want to know anything at all about what God is doing in your life, then start by familiarizing yourself with the works of God. The more you know about what he does in this world, especially in the lives of his people, then the better informed you will be about the direction that your own life is taking, and the less you will be deceived by man's works.

Discerning God's works

If you are interested in finding out more about God's works, you must start in the Bible. From there you will gain the principles involved and be equipped (theoretically) to go out into the world and pinpoint the places where God is working.

Notice I said "theoretically." There are several places where one can go wrong in this seemingly simple process. You should be aware that there are forces involved that are conspiring against you:

- *You've been trained not to see God's works.* "As for you, you were dead in your transgressions and sins, in which you used to live when you followed the ways of this world and of the ruler of the kingdom of the air, the spirit who is now at work in those who are disobedient." (Ephesians 2:1-2) What is that unholy spirit "now at work" doing? Deceiving and lying, that's what! He started in the garden of Eden, and he's still busy trying to pull the wool over our eyes concerning the truth about God. How long were you under his schooling? How much do you have to unlearn? It takes a while to shed the wrong ideas and replace them with the truth. Our enemy viciously ingrained them into our minds and it will take nothing less than the power of God to release their hold on us. Some Christians (maybe most?) keep wrong notions about things all their lives.

- *The works of others try to emulate God's works.* "For such men are false Apostles, deceitful workmen, masquerading as Apostles of Christ. And no wonder, for Satan himself masquerades as an angel of light. It is not surprising, then, if his servants masquerade as servants of righteousness. Their end will be what their actions deserve." (2 Corinthians 11:13-15) This is perhaps our greatest problem in discerning the works of God. Those people who are *not* in any way partners in God's work confuse the issue and look for all intents and purposes very Christian. How does one tell the difference? If a man claims to preach in Christ's name, can we justifiably challenge his claim? If someone at work or in school claims to be a Christian, shouldn't we give him or her the benefit of the doubt on the basis of their claim? Are there ways that we can tell that their claims are false?

This is an especially dangerous problem because the people involved are determined to be known as Christians – they are one of us. They won't make it easy on us and go start an obviously non-Christian cult somewhere! They are going to introduce their falsehood in the guise of Christian duty and worship, and then say that God initiated it. That's a tough one.

- *You aren't going to like what you see.* "They have harps and lyres at their banquets, tambourines and flutes and wine, but they have no regard for the deeds of the LORD, no respect for the work of his hands." (Isaiah 5:12) The context, if you check it out, is the awesome work that God has done to save and purify his people, the vineyard of the Lord. The passage is loaded with the purposes of God; his work carries themes of righteousness and holiness. But that's precisely what the Israelites didn't want to hear! They preferred another kind of religion, a religion that doesn't cost so much and emphasizes the pleasanter aspects of living with God.

You still have your sinful nature, like it or not. You will find that God's works will center on taking care of that sin once and for all. He will be dealing with issues that you would prefer not to bring up. He will be taking you out in the wilderness to spend time with him, when you would prefer to hobnob with your buddies in your favorite pastimes. He will give you tasks to do that you don't want to do. Expect this sort of thing; that's the way God works with us.

If you manage to get past these hurdles (which in itself will be a work of God!) then you should also be aware of helps in discerning God's works. Fortunately it isn't up to us to figure out how to overcome the impossibilities of getting into God's Kingdom so that we can get a close look at God's works. God promises to bring us there, and these are some of the ways that he has provided us to make it happen:

- ***Start with the Bible.*** "I will tell of the kindnesses of the LORD, the deeds for which he is to be praised, according to all the LORD has done for us – yes, the many good things he has done for the house of Israel, according to his compassion and many kindnesses." (Isaiah 63:7) *Who* will tell us? Isaiah will! And you will find that David told of the works of God – and Moses, and Joshua, and Elijah, and Jeremiah, and all the prophets, and Jesus, and Paul, and John. *This* is where you start if you want to learn something about what God has done – they saw it done.

Oddly enough, people don't tend to start with the Bible; they start with themselves. For example, their "testimonials" about what God "did for them" form the foundation of whatever they believe about God after that. But immediately they run into the problem of trying to justify what they experienced as a true work of God. What they often have to do is bend the truth around what they experienced, because what they experienced doesn't square with the *Bible's* testimony about God. This is backwards and never safe. If you start with the Bible and find out from reliable sources what God actually does, and how he really goes about things, *then* you can move to your own life and find out the times that the Lord worked in you *in those same ways*. You have to establish the principles first, then apply the principles to yourself. The trouble is that it's always painful to discover that there are things in one's life that God didn't do, that we made up and called it God's work. But that only points up what we are – we are still sinners and ignorant of much about God – and we should be anxious for God to do his work in our understanding as well.

- *Wait.* "I am still confident of this: I will see the goodness of the LORD in the land of the living. Wait on the LORD; be strong and take heart and wait on the LORD." (Psalm 27:13-14) This is perhaps the hardest part. One of the ways that the Lord works is through time; he usually doesn't do things immediately – he spaces it out over days or weeks or months or even years. We want to see results now, though, and when we fail to discern the form of God in our circumstances then we assume that God isn't there and off we go in some other direction instead.

Waiting on God to reveal himself is a particularly Christian trait, and it only comes by long, rigorous training. Did you ever go outside at night and look for shooting stars? If you have, you will know that you have to wait for quite a while before you will see one – if then. An impatient observer will never see that elusive, sudden streak of light across the sky. So the Christian. He can never expect to see the works of God if he is too impatient to wait on God's timely movements. He has to be expectant, ready for anything, and trained to spot the sudden swish of the Spirit as he blows across our world. In other words, he has to get used to sitting at God's feet and looking towards God, not the world or himself. When God has his full attention *then* he will show himself.

- ***Study what you see.*** "I remember the days of long ago; I meditate on all your works and consider what your hands have done." (Psalm 143:5) The word "meditate" in Hebrew is like a cow chewing its cud. You get the picture: one only gets good out of the works of God if one thoughtfully, slowly, exhaustively, thinks about it. There is much to learn there, and a quick, cursory glance won't teach you a thing about how God works in this world. You won't know any more about it than the pagans do if you don't stop and consider his work from all angles.

You have much to think about. **First**, find out *everything* he did. Often the details are spread

Introduction

across scores of people and hundreds of years. **Second**, relate what you are seeing with other ideas from other Scriptures; passages never contradict each other, rather they support and enlighten each other. **Third**, the obvious thing is to see if God is still doing such things – throughout history in other people's lives and also in your life. **Fourth**, what repercussions are there going to be on those who don't take God's works seriously? **Fifth**, can you discern a process, a method, a progress toward a goal, in what God is doing? Why is he doing this work? And you can ask many more such questions about the works of God.

- *Pray.* "Show me your ways, O LORD, teach me your paths; guide me in your truth and teach me, for you are God my Savior, and my hope is in you all day long." (Psalm 25:4-5) This is the bottom line if you want to learn anything about God. Face it: "God is in Heaven, and you are on earth; so let your words be few." (Ecclesiastes 5:2) You can't find out anything about God unless he reveals himself to you. Let him talk to you for a while. People have been reading the Bible for millennia and getting nothing out of it; you yourself have experienced the feeling of reading the words but not penetrating into the meaning of the passage. God has to help you understand it.

Our hope, notice, is in *him* – not ourselves. We depend on his mercy, on his forgiveness, on his willingness to come near, on his ability to open our eyes and hearts. He understands that we are but dust and ashes, and he will know how to present the truth to us in a way that will be clear to us. It's his promise, after all, to show himself to his people! That's what we depend on.

What can we do about his works?

There are some important "therefores" when we study the works of God. Hopefully you won't go away unchanged from this material! If you meditate on his works then you are going to come to some life-changing conclusions that you simply have to act on. The Lord expects you to see the point and live as if God really is real instead of a cold concept in a dead book.

- ***You stick to your work and let him do his.*** This is so important. We have got to learn that the things that we *have* been called to do is our work, but what God alone does is *not* our work. The trouble is that we are so accustomed to fending for ourselves that we usually aren't aware that we are usurping God's authority and trying to do his work for him.

    You can tell when things are out of order when you aren't getting anything out of life anymore. The feeling of emptiness hangs in the air; nothing you do really fulfills the longing in your heart for something solid. Relationships aren't working; church is a bore; a righteous heart and tongue are wishful thinking; you don't know which way to go. When you start running into dead ends in your life then it's time to do some self-examination and ask yourself some tough questions: Is God close to me? Am I aware of his presence? Or have I moved away from him? Have I taken over more and more of my life so that I don't need God anymore? Would it make a difference in things if I suddenly found God again, and he started doing his work in my life? If answers to such questions tend to point out your need for God then it's time you backed off from some of your business in the world and started waiting on God.

- ***Train yourself to spot them.*** Again we have to look at this concept, because it isn't one that sits well with the modern attitude. For some reason we are perfectly willing to go to college or vocational schools and spend time in training for a secular calling, but we aren't willing to spend time in training for spiritual skills. Every Christian thinks he's an instant expert on God! Everybody thinks that just being a Christian fully prepares them for the life of faith.

Paul, the greatest of the Apostles, disagrees.

> Not that I have already obtained all this, or have already been made perfect, but I press on to take hold of that for which Christ Jesus took hold of me. Brothers, I do not consider myself yet to have taken hold of it. But one thing I do: forgetting what is behind and straining toward what is ahead, I press on toward the goal to win the prize for which God has called me Heavenward in Christ Jesus. All of us who are mature should take such a view of things. And if on some point you think differently, that too God will make clear to you. Only let us live up to what we have already attained. (Philippians 3:12-16)

First we must start with this attitude: that we *don't* know it all. Some of your most cherished views just may be wrong, or lacking in some aspect. If you don't have a teachable spirit then you won't learn much about God's works.

Second, this subject has to become important to you – important enough to set aside time for it and expend some energy on it. Paul considered the things of God worth going after. If you want God to work in your life then you have to act like it. You have to familiarize yourself with his works, train yourself to spot them, learn their ins and outs – in other words, become an expert in the works of God so that when they do appear you can take full advantage of them.

- *Depend on God for his work.* This also takes some skill and patience, because it isn't natural for self-sufficient man to turn things over to God. For one thing, we are afraid of how God might handle a matter – he may expect us to give up our sin in the process! For another thing, God usually takes time and usually works through people and processes to do his work, and that makes us impatient. We like to get on with it, to not have to depend on others – not even on God. We are individuals to the core. God's ways are naturally aggravating to us and we don't like how he does things.

But it's crucially important that we start waiting on God to do what only he can do. And when he begins to work, accept the conditions that he lays down for you if you want to benefit from his work. For example, the modern concept of revival is exactly backwards from what it ought to be. If you want a revival, we are told, then simply get some of the leaders together to pray and plan, and advertise it all around, and collect a bunch of people together under one roof for a week of special meetings, and work on their emotions to coax them down front to make "decisions," and then go home – a job well done! But where is God in all this? Was there any step in the process for which he alone is responsible? What if he decides not to work within the framework of your schedule – which often happens, because many of the "converts" turn out not to be converted after all, which a little checking on their lifestyles will reveal. Revival, as the Scriptures tell us, comes when *God* decides to revive his people – it doesn't come at a preset time that man decides. God revives his people to life, not to hypocrisy; their lives are forever changed, not temporarily disturbed. If we would bother to study how God revives his people then that would go a long way to helping us work *with* him, not against him within the terms of our own agenda.

We have to learn how to depend on God completely for what he does. This often will result in strange behavior; others will wonder why we aren't in there doing our fair share of the work! But we will know that it isn't any use to try to do God's work for him; he simply has to come down to do it himself, and we are going to wait until he does. After all, only he can do a perfect job – which is what we want! Only he can do good. We take away from his glory when we jump ahead and try it ourselves. "No one whose hope is in you will ever be put to shame, but they will be put to shame who are treacherous without excuse." (Psalm 25:3) "Treachery" is you deciding to alter the plans without permission to do so. The person who honors God will wait on him to do his work.

Method for studying them

Here is how we will attack this subject. **First**, we are going to find out exactly what his works are. We're going to search the Scriptures and make lists of God's works and try to come up with a good idea of what it is that he does. This will help distinguish his work from anybody else's. **Second**, we are going to see how his works teach us about who he is and how he does things. The purpose of studying God's works is to learn about God! It's God that we need to know more about; his works turn us to him. **Third**, we are going to learn how his works accomplish his will. God's will is all-important; what he wants to do is much more important than what we want to do. We will find that his works invariably steer things into his purposes. **Fourth**, we will see how his works support his people. He does many things that we aren't aware of, but much of what God does in this world is directly related to getting us to Heaven. It would be most helpful to see how he does that. **Fifth**, an all-important subject: the art of "remembering" God's works. It isn't any use to study his works only to forget them again! There are important ways we can benefit from knowing and remembering how God works; we will study how to become experts in the works of God.

What are the Works of the Lord?

Every Christian has reason to praise his God. If for nothing else, he can tell the story of how the Lord reached down into a dark world and pulled him into the kingdom of life and light. Our own salvation is miracle enough to praise him; often we will "swap stories" when we get together and listen to how God saved others and we love to hear about it.

But prayer needs more than this initial experience to go on. You may have noticed that you start running dry on things to talk about to God if you only have one single experience to fall back on! If all you know about God is the first time you met him – the first salvation experience you had in Christ – then your relationship is going to be pretty shallow. It's like a boy and a girl who first meet each other; if their future consisted only of rehearsing what it was like on that first day then it will be a pretty shallow relationship. Fortunately life is a series of meetings, of experiences, that pull us into deeper experiences and more meetings, and all these together weave a fascinating past that enriches our present and provides hope and direction for the future.

Speaking of prayer, you will find that it is sort of like a sausage grinder. Prayer itself is the eternally revolving screw inside the grinder, and it simply goes round and round whether anything is fed into it or not. If you put meat in one end, though, the screw will pull it inside the grinder and turn sausage out the other end. We can say the same thing about prayer (if you don't mind the strange example!). Put in the "meat" of prayer – the works of God and the knowledge of God's nature – and prayer will work on that material until the "sausage" of prayer comes out the other side – faith and hope and love in this God. *If you quit putting fresh material into prayer, you will stop getting results from prayer.* Like a grinder that runs out of meat, prayer can run dry of results too – as you well know by now if you've been a Christian for very long. The key is to keep feeding prayer the material to work on!

That's where the works of the Lord come in. That's why David meditated on, considered, thought much about the works of the Lord – because such meditation lifted his eyes beyond this world – no matter what the problem – and encouraged him with its news about his God. The more he learned about God, the stronger his faith in God became. "For you make me glad by your deeds, O LORD; I sing for joy at the works of your hands. How great are your works, O LORD, how profound your thoughts!" (Psalm 92:4)

That's why we must start with the works of the Lord themselves. What is it that he has done? If we get these things fully in view (or at least touch the surface of the subject) then we can move on to how to get the most benefit from them. But first things first. Let's see what it is that God has done.

Creation and Providence

We start, of course, where the Bible starts – with the first thing that we know and see about God – with the fact that God created everything in the world.

As a matter of fact, it's extremely important that we start here. Creation is a fundamental doctrine for our faith simply because it tells us so much about God that we need to know; it separates the true God from the many false gods that populate men's minds. We start with Creation because:

We find out the agenda for the world. If you want to know the reason for things, start at the beginning. The way a thing is designed will tell you much about its purpose. For example, we know that a car is for transportation because we see that it has wheels. God doesn't do anything capriciously; he has a good reason for everything he does. And what he intended the world to be, from the very beginning, is built into the fabric of the world, to the extent that none of life makes any sense at all unless we know what he was planning to accomplish in Creation.

We find out who all this belongs to. He who makes, owns; and he who determines, rules. If God made everything, then he certainly has the right as well as the ability to determine the outcome of it all. Creation shows us what he wanted to see in the world in the first place; we see there what his purpose was in making things. The Lord rebuked Job for doubting his power and authority; he reminded Job that he was alone in the beginning, and he was the only one who decided how things were to be made and how they would operate. Therefore this is his world and he will do with it as he likes – who can challenge him?

We find out man's part in the scheme of things. Once you realize who is running the show then you can better see your own position in the situation. Creation tells us what we are doing here. Not only do we find out what God intended when he made us, but we also learn our right relationship with the world itself. There is much food for thought here.

At the very simplest level we can say that God made everything in the world. It would be easy to simply make a list of everything we see around us – all these things are his handiwork. But what we want to do is look at *why* it required God to make it all! The unbelievers aren't impressed with simple lists of created things; they can see the world too – but they don't make the obvious connection that we do and attribute it all to God. We have to go a step further and ask the question, 'Why is it necessary to believe that *God* created all this?' What is it about the world that shows unmistakable signs of the Divine presence and purpose? Can we see something here that the unbelievers can't see?

- **God made all the world out of nothing.** "In the beginning God created the Heavens and the earth." (Genesis 1:1) "By faith we understand that the universe was formed at God's command, so that what is seen was not made out of what was visible." (Hebrews 11:3) Here is the fundamental doctrine of Creation, and here is the most severe problem that unbelievers have with God the Creator.

The reason they have so much problem with this is because it describes a God that is clearly beyond our comprehension to figure out and control. In order to make the world out of *nothing*, God's power has to be entirely different kind than ours, and his wisdom must be unknowable. How do you create something out of nothing?! But God does it all the time – not only did he create the building blocks of the universe out of nothing, but he continues to call forth things from nothing. He creates life where there was only death; he creates light where there was only darkness. He creates love in a heart of hate. *We require some building materials if we want to make anything, otherwise we will get nowhere; but God doesn't require anything to build upon.* Nobody can add to the process because he doesn't need anybody's help. He prefers to work alone, and he knows that only what he does will last anyway. When God creates, he makes something where there wasn't anything before, or where the situation and existing material to work with would be an impossible situation. He does that all the time – out of necessity, I might add, because, though the need is great, nobody else can do it!

- ***God brought order out of chaos.*** "The earth was formless and empty, darkness was over the surface of the deep, and the Spirit of God was hovering over the waters." (Genesis 1:2) The Hebrew phrase for "formless and empty" is *tohu v'bohu* – תֹהוּ וָבֹהוּ – which can also be translated "without form and void." In other words, there was nothing at the beginning; God alone makes something out of nothing.

Even when he began creating the elements of existence, it required his constant power and presence to result in an organized universe. The raw materials by themselves will never align themselves into neat little rows and sit up and become aware of themselves. In order to get a clump of atoms to be self-aware, in order to get stars and galaxies and plants and animals and day and night and rain and snow, God has to plan out the course of matter and *force* it to take forms that suit his purposes – against its nature.

Scientists do know one thing: let matter and energy alone and they will eventually settle down into inactivity and disorganization, not activity and organization (a process they call *entropy*). Life doesn't happen by itself, and the complexity and necessities of life don't come about by chance; and that's why scientists still can't produce *proof* that evolution is true. Their studies have even forced them into admitting that it appears as though the universe came about with man in mind (!) – it's called the *anthropic* principle. In other words, the universe looks very much as if it's centered around man.

All this is no surprise when you know the truth about God. His business is to counteract the natural tendency of the world – the tendency to degeneration and entropy and settling down into nothingness. He makes patterns, and forces things into structure. He has it all planned out how to best arrange things to get the best results. He is the Organizer, the Planner, the Supervisor who brings success out of failure. He introduces understanding where there was only confusion; he plants purpose into those who are wandering aimlessly. *He will have design and purpose in everything he does* – he will always counteract the tendency of chaos and destruction, because they lead away from him, and he will always direct everything to *his* goals. It's characteristic of him to make sense of everything and make a beautiful thing out of chaos when nobody else can.

- *God made it all very good.* "God saw all that he had made, and it was very good." (Genesis 1:31) What a significant statement! Whatever God does, he does it in such a way that you must admit that it's good. "Good" means that a thing perfectly fulfills God's requirements, that it satisfies the maker and the user in some way. When God first made the world, he evidently saw that it would suit his purposes – and ours – quite well.

But part of the idea of goodness is that the thing that's good will itself be blessed – happy, self-fulfilled, productive – because it fits into the overall system perfectly. It's not without reason that the Scripture talks about the trees and the mountains "joyfully" praising God their Creator. When the animals were blessed, they were fulfilled and happy in the way God made them. When man got his calling and blessing from God, he felt the goodness of God's work in his life, which is why he made such a terrible mistake in throwing all of it away through sin. Man had it so good then! If he would have let well enough alone, and lived according to God's good purpose, and fit into the perfect creation around him, there would never have been trouble in his life. Whatever God does is supremely good and calculated not only to please him but to please us as well. The way he arranges our lives, the things he gives us to do, the relationships and people he provides for us, the purposes in life – all these can't be improved on, despite what our sinful hearts (and Satan!) tell us to the contrary. Whatever God does is *good*.

- *The whole creation obeys God.* "Have you ever given orders to the morning, or shown the dawn its place?" (Job 38:12) This passage in Job – from chapters 38 to 41 – is a fascinating study in how God made the world and all the creatures in it. The point of the passage is this: each creature, each aspect of the world, does what God designed it to do, and it does it very well. Each creature is specially skilled to do the duty that God gave it. Everything lives and moves in a way that God first determined for it ahead of time. It can't help but live that way; his instructions to it are etched into its brain beyond the reach of reason, into the instinct. Like a computer program, the commands of God are written into the creature's inner being, and it will live and die in total obedience to what God made it to be.

We of course don't know why God made some creatures the way they are, or why he made the world the way it is. He has his own reasons, certainly; but the point is that everything is following his wishes to the letter. Whatever he is doing must be a grand, unified scheme in which each creature plays its part and the whole depends on the parts. If one aspect of creation would be slightly off, then the whole thing would fail – hence the blind obedience, the urgency to obey, burned into every part of creation.

The only part that went wrong, as we know, is man – and his *disobedience* is what started the disaster. Look at the damage it has done already in God's beautiful world! If man were a fish or a rock he would have simply kept God's command and everything would be fine. But man himself wanted to be like God, in the ruling seat instead on his knee in obedience. And since God gave him the ability to obey willingly (which the rest of creation doesn't have), and he failed by wanting something other than God's will, when he broke God's command he brought the whole system down with him.

The difference between us and the rest of creation is that we have the ability (and now the inclination) to disobey God, whereas the other creatures don't. In either case, however, God expects strict obedience, even from man who can disobey. He made the rest of the world in a way that its obedience is certain; but with man alone he required obedience without forcing it.

• *God made man in his image.* "So God created man in his own image, in the image of God he created him; male and female he created them." (Genesis 1:27) We're not going to explore here *what* that image is, but we will observe that man was created to bear the image of God in the world. That means that the rest of the world should be able to see God in us! We should live such a life, and be such a witness, that reminds the world of God when they see us. We are, after all, God's representatives on earth, and we rule under his authority. What we say and what we do should be God's will itself, carried out perfectly in our daily circumstances. We should be doing exactly what God himself would do if he were here in person.

This has a lot of bearing on who we are, and what we are doing here, and what God expected of us from the beginning, and how far astray we've gone from the original blueprint for man. You can see that it isn't just that God *made* us; he made us *in his image* – a profound privilege and responsibility. It's also a deep mystery: how can we possibly represent God fairly in this world? How can we know God well enough to rule in his Name, to do his will here? What is there in a man that knows there's a God, that can commune with God, that can work so that God's perfect will is done? Man is like this because God designed him to be a citizen both of the physical world and of the spiritual world. Of all of creation, man alone can know God and can freely honor him by being like him – the Lord made us so that we can do this. The reason is that God has important work for us to do.

- **God never meant for creation to fulfill man's deepest needs.** "The eye never has enough of seeing, or the ear its fill of hearing." (Ecclesiastes 1:8) Man is like an earthworm: he gobbles up food and enjoyment and good times and bad times and love and hate and success and disaster, which all passes through him, and then he gets up the next day and moves along, hungry again, looking for the same things all over again. There is no end to his hunger – physical and psychological and spiritual. People wonder why the good times don't last, and success wasn't as sweet as one hoped, and money doesn't satisfy. The reason is because the Lord didn't make this world to satisfy the heart of man. Everything here is of a passing, temporary nature.

We can enjoy what God has made, but what he has made won't give peace and unending joy to us. We are more than creatures of our physical senses! If a plateful of supper was good enough for man to live for, what difference would there be between us and the animals? If God made man in his image, able to see and value the eternal things of Heaven, wouldn't it be cheap happiness to settle for things that disappear after one use?

As a matter of fact the Lord made us to be kings and priests in his kingdom, rulers over creation at his right hand, standing in and yet above the changeableness and shallowness of this world and satisfied only with his spiritual world. This is ingrained into our hearts – even the most wicked of hearts – and our lives are a continual search for the world that we were made for. It's a shame to see people waste their energy on things that won't satisfy them, and a double shame to hear them talk as if they were satisfied with this life alone. That's a bare-faced lie; death will soon force them to admit the truth when they have to give up this world and stand before God empty-handed in the end – ashamed of themselves.

Another idea that goes along with Creation is **Providence** – the doctrine that God takes care of the world he has made. Creation is one side of the coin, and Providence is the other; because what he started, he will finish. Some people think that God has nothing to do with the world, that it runs on its own now without him, and we are all left up to our own devices to get along in life. But the Scripture teaches the opposite – Providence shows us something about God that we need to know for our faith and daily walk.

Whether we know it or not, God is constantly busy providing for every creature's needs. The thing is on such a grand scale that we can't conceive of how much he is really doing for the world right now. If he pulled away his hand then everything – *everything* – would collapse; that's how much we depend on him.

> ***He keeps the world in existence.*** "He is before all things, and in him all things hold together." (Colossians 1:17) There's no one better to keep the world together than the one who made the world! He provides the laws of physical nature and sees to it that they are strictly followed. We can depend on the world operating the same way day after day, because the Lord built uniformity and purpose and pattern into it.
>
> This is one fact, however, that many people don't see. The laws that govern the universe look so self-sufficient that we may very well be misled about who is in charge of things in the world. Do the planets revolve around the sun simply on the basis of Keplerian theory? Does life happen anywhere in the universe – wherever some of the essential basic building blocks happen to exist? Does rain happen just because certain weather conditions exist? Or perhaps the fundamental question is this: are we really required to bring God into the picture in order to explain how the world operates?
>
> I believe so, because the Scriptures do just that. The Bible attributes everything that happens in the world to God's special intervention and direction. Even the rain is the result of his will. If science will admit it, there is a level where it's helpless to understand why things happens in the physical world; there's no explaining the

fundamental basis of existence and relationships, because God is totally responsible for it all. Whatever he does, nothing else can do – therefore it's outside of our understanding as creatures. Science also is obligated to stand back in amazement at God's unexplainable work.

He provides for the daily needs of every creature. "The eyes of all look to you, and you give them their food at the proper time." (Psalm 145:15) By design, God made all creatures totally dependent on him. They constantly have needs, and the drive to fulfill those needs take up their waking hours. He also designed the system so that *only he can fulfill those needs*. People are either ignorant or rebellious if they think that they can get what they need from any other source than God himself. Whatever God does is good – no other god (or source of fulfillment) can make that claim. Do you want what is good? Then you have only one place to go for it.

This truth also tells us something about God's intentions. It's interesting that the Bible specifically tells us that God *will* provide, that he *wants* to provide, that he takes special pains to provide – yet we don't think he really will. Why do we doubt him? Why do we work and sweat and worry and hoard and make life miserable for ourselves and others in order to improve our life – as if God won't give us what we want, so we have to get it ourselves? He takes care of his people! "I have never seen the righteous forsaken, or their children begging bread." (Psalm 37:25) The power and wealth of Providence is still a basically untried resource for many of us, because we don't realize that God stands ready to provide for us in all ways. It works just as surely as clockwork.

When you think about Creation and Providence – about how much God has done in the world and what he is doing right now – and especially about the underlying principles involved – you should get a whole new view on things. The world isn't a product of random occurrences and aimless wanderings; God is closely supervising all aspects of the world, which we should be glad of when we think about it.

THE MAKING OF ISRAEL

Creation wasn't the uppermost matter on God's mind when the world started. He of course knew how man would react to his first command in the Garden of Eden, and he could see the vast destructive force of sin on the entire human race in the future. When the sentence of death speeds from the judgment halls of God into the world of men, it's like scattering pins with a bowling ball; the ruin and destruction is awesome. His new world was in for some hard times.

But God doesn't take pleasure in the death of men. He began preparing for a grand rescue long before it was needed, because the thing that is closest to his heart is the work of mercy and grace. He loves to forgive, to restore, to bring from darkness into light; the Bible says that he *is* love because of what he loves to do.

This work of grace, however, is no small task. You will better understand the nature of the remedy if you know what sin has done to our natures:

Sin separates us from God. A sinner's typical reaction to anything about God is to avoid the subject. Religion, yes, because that can be a very interesting subject and we all have opinions about it. But don't talk to me about God – the God that the Bible talks about, that is.

This is a universal characteristic of sinners. Everyone avoids God in some way. Outright atheists are obviously avoiding him; but even Christians have their believing point beyond which they refuse to cooperate with him. What we prefer to do is to make up a story about God, one in which an imaginary "God" will allow us to believe and do what *we* want – and then we are happy with our created "God".

But what God expects of us all is to come to *him* – and we will find, the closer that we get to the real God, that he's everything that the *Bible* says he is. He is holy, and just, and good, and wise, and many other things that make us uncomfortable in his presence. As sinners, we prefer the darkness rather than coming to God.

Sin obscures the image of God. The Lord made us to reflect his glory in what we do and say; what happens instead, due to our sin, is that we dishonor his Name. We break his plain commands and then have the gall to claim his Name over what we do! Instead of seeing in us what God would do if he were present, what the world sees instead is something that God most definitely wouldn't do to his precious world.

By now the problem of sin and death has reached horrible proportions. We have seen, over the last several thousand years, what pure evil can do in every situation under the sun. It's hard to believe what's in the heart of man; it's no wonder that the earth groans under our feet, waiting for the Judgment Day when God's glory and justice will again be plain to see. Right now the only thing plain to see about God is that he will claim none of the works that are going on in the world! But that's hard to see too, because men do their evil even in God's Name and would like to drag him in as their partner in wickedness.

Sin leads to death. The Lord promised that this would happen – "for when you eat of it you will surely die." And it has most definitely happened! Death is the most certain thing that will happen to all of us, because it's driven by God's determined will. It's a terrible sentence that has the power to cut off everything that you enjoy and hold precious in life; it comes at times when it's least wanted; it seems pointless and counter-productive. But come it will, by the unstoppable will of God, and it exacts a revenge on man for his willful rebellion that lays us all low in the dust. We are all the target for God's ultimate weapon.

This is the situation that we are all in, without exception. Paul tells us that the spirit of rebellion has been "at work in us" to thoroughly ruin God's creation. (Ephesians 2:2) It has certainly succeeded! So the work that God has on his hands is to reverse the process of sin, to stop it dead in its tracks and reclaim the victims completely. *The end result must be total freedom from any trace or effect of sin.* The job was enormous, and certainly something that only God could do. Let's look at how he went about solving the unsolvable.

> ***He made a covenant of faith.*** "Abram believed the LORD, and he credited it to him as righteousness." (Genesis 15:6) This one verse is the key to the entire plan of salvation, all the way from Abraham's time to our own and to the end of time. With this one stroke of genius the Lord put our salvation on a firm footing, entirely avoiding the issue of man trying to solve the problem of sin on his own.
>
> Only the Lord knew what would be involved in the long run when he made this covenant of faith with Abraham. Abraham never realized, just like we ourselves can't possibly comprehend, the tremendous amount of work that God committed himself to when he made a bargain with Abraham and his seed.
>
> The basis of the Abrahamic covenant is this: the Lord promised to do whatever was necessary to save Abraham and his seed from their sin – by making them righteous to *his* satisfaction – and they were simply to trust him to keep his word. *I* will do the work of making you righteous, the Lord told him, because then I know it will be done right; *you* will let me do it for you and refrain from trying to make yourself acceptable to me. An easy bargain? Not for God! Before it was over he would submit his Name to great dishonor because of the sins of Israel, he would give over his own Son to a disastrous death, and many other things that continue to amaze the angels who know his magisterial glory in Heaven. It wasn't going to

be an easy bargain for Abraham and his children either! Although God would take care of the details of salvation, Abraham found that his sinful heart rebelled at the thought of trusting God to save him. We all do; we panic at the worst time, when we need most to trust God's miraculous and well-timed salvation and help, because of fear or self-will or greed or pride or something else that controls us.

What is amazing about God's part of the agreement is that he decided to work out our salvation like this – through our faith in him – and not through our own works. It would have been an easy matter for him to demand our complete obedience to the full extent of the Law; but then none of us would have been able to do that, and we all would have been destroyed in Hell, and rightly so. There's glory enough in the fact that God is the supreme Judge, but the cursed in Hell don't know God as the Father of love. So he set up a plan in which he himself would shoulder the burden of being completely righteousness – which Jesus did when he came – and of course that means a great deal of preparation ahead of time. Thus the whole history of Israel is simply God working out all the necessary details of salvation so that, when Jesus finally arrived, God would fit the last piece into the picture and *save his people from their sin.*

The amazing thing about Abraham's side of the agreement is that he accepted God's plan. Natural man just isn't interested in free grace, interestingly enough – you've seen that yourself when you try to share the Gospel with a hardened sinner. The idea of God making us acceptable to the Law's demands doesn't appeal to a sinner, for many reasons. But Abraham saw the wisdom in the plan and laid aside any desires for solving his problems on his own (he did slip once, however, but he evidently came back to waiting on God). He could see that *his own efforts would not do him any good*; only God can save. Paul calls Abraham "the father of those who believe" because this is the basis that all Christians are on with God: *he* saves, we trust him for it.

He made a nation of his own. "Has any god ever tried to take for himself one nation out of another nation, by testings, by miraculous signs and wonders, by war, by a mighty hand and an outstretched arm, or by great and awesome deeds, like the things the LORD your God did for you in Egypt before your very eyes?" (Deuteronomy 4:34)

You have to know a little bit of history to appreciate this allusion to Israel's beginnings. The descendents of Abraham – Jacob and his twelve sons and all their families – ended up living in Egypt due to the efforts of Joseph (one of the sons); they were able to live there in safety during a severe famine over that part of the world. Since Joseph managed to secure a comfortable place for them in Egypt, the clan stayed there instead of moving back to Canaan. For the next 400 plus years the little band of people grew to millions, to the extent that succeeding Pharaohs became more alarmed but also more greedy for the extra labor. It wasn't long before the Israelites were totally enslaved in Egypt, made to work on the Egyptian building projects and suffering under oppression from their taskmasters.

Now it was no easy matter to get the Israelites out of there. It's sort of like the problem that Soviet Jews had about getting out of Russia; but the problem back in those ancient days was far more severe. There was no international community to put pressure on Pharaoh for his cruel use of the Israelites! He wasn't about to throw away such an economic boon. And in order to make sure that the Israelites didn't get any ideas about an insurrection, he ruled them with an iron fist and ground their spirits into the dust.

Into the picture comes the Lord of Hosts. Through a single man – Moses – he confronts Pharaoh with a *demand!* Pharaoh laughs at Moses. Then the Lord starts unfurling his power against the proud king, step by step, crushing the spirit of Egypt until the arrogant nation finally pleads for mercy on its knees. The whole affair was out in the open, plain to see. The God of the Israelites defied one of the strongest nations on earth and pried its hands off his precious people, and then recorded the story in the Bible so that everyone down through history would know about it.

What are some of the things that God did here? *First*, he preserved his people through those 400 years. Usually a group of people, no matter how proud they are about their ancestry, begin losing their identity when they mix into a different culture. We can see that over and over again in our own country's history. But the Lord had other plans for the Israelites; the promise was to Abraham *and his seed*, not to the Egyptians. So the two peoples never mixed. They carried on their daily affairs together, but the Israelites always kept away from their pagan neighbors' homes and instead stayed to themselves. To the casual observer this must have been an amazing state of affairs, this situation of one separate nation within another and never mixing; but God was doing it.

Second, the miracles that he did to convince Pharaoh that he meant business are obviously works of God. It was a beautiful thing to see, the battle between God and a powerful nation. At first the magicians of Egypt emulated the Lord's miracles to prove to Pharaoh that God could be safely ignored. But soon they found that God was doing things that they couldn't do; suddenly they weren't safe anymore. Egypt found out that Moses' God was fully capable of tearing their nation apart at the seams. The last blow – killing all the firstborn of Egypt, man and animal – sent the nation reeling in shock, and finally broke their resolve to resist him.

Third, there was the story about the Exodus of Israel out of Egypt. That trip was not without its problems too! They came to a body of water that couldn't be crossed; and as they were pondering that the Egyptian army rode up behind them, determined to take them back to the Pharaoh. What to do now! But God again stepped in with a solution which was just what was needed: an impossible situation required an equally impossible miracle – the parting of the

Red Sea, and the army of Pharaoh drowning in the Sea. The helpless Israelites were amazed at God's awesome power and the bitter and humiliating blow that was laid on their enemies.

The picture that we get from all these stories is that God can and will start unleashing his power through nature to make his point if he has to. God made the world, and he knows how to effectively use it against man to get what he wants. And for the sake of his people he will most definitely unleash his power against his enemies in whatever way he sees fit.

He gave them a land. "Leave this place, you and the people you brought up out of Egypt, and go up to the land I promised on oath to Abraham, Isaac and Jacob, saying, 'I will give it to your descendents.'" (Exodus 33:1) Sometimes we use the expression "Easier said than done", and the Israelites probably thought this when God first told them what he had planned for them. They knew from a previous scouting party that it would be a tremendous undertaking, most likely impossible, to wrest the land of Canaan from the giants who lived there. They felt that they had better sense than God! But they grossly underestimated their God.

They also didn't understand the terms of the covenant. If they would have taken the time to check the fine print, they would have read the words "I *will* give it to them." They didn't have to worry about the success of the venture! God fully intended to strengthen them and give them victory so that every single pagan in Canaan would either be killed or driven out; nobody would be able to stand before the Israelites because God was fighting for them.

They got an immediate proof of God's intentions and abilities at Jericho. Clearly God could do the impossible, and they followed God into a rich land to possess it forever. Nothing could stop God from fulfilling his promise to them. Not only that, but the Israelites inherited a land of planted fields and sturdy houses and full orchards – something that the Israelites no doubt much appreciated. He also decided who would live where in the land, by dividing up the land among the tribes.

Over the centuries the Lord continued to preserve his people in Palestine – they were threatened from all directions. If it weren't for God's ceaseless vigil they would have been thrown out long ago. This points to the reason why God gave them the land in the first place. He wanted a people on the earth who would witness for him – who would show the world that God is indeed real and he works on behalf of his people in such and such ways. He wanted a place where people could come to him, a spot on the earth where they could be assured of finding him. The land would also be a visible proof that God takes care of his people. Finally, he wanted a place where Christ could come and work the final stages of salvation out, for all the world to see, in the midst of his people. The Lord was planning to do a lot of work in the future and Canaan was an important piece of the plan.

Of course it was impossible to take and hold Canaan – that's why it was a miracle when God did it for them.

He ruled over them. "For when I brought your forefathers out of Egypt and spoke to them, I did not just give them commands about burnt offerings and sacrifices, but I gave them this command: Obey me, and I will be your God and you will be my people. Walk in all the ways I command you, that it may go well with you." (Jeremiah 7:22-23) The Law that God gave the Israelites is perhaps the best known aspect of old Jewish history. Everyone knows about the Ten Commandments, and they've seen paintings of what it must have looked like when Moses came down Mt. Sinai carrying the two tablets of stone.

But what people don't often think about was that God was their *King*. The other nations had false gods who couldn't speak or rule their people, and the kings over them took advantage of their idol's shortcomings and ruled in the god's name – often with the result that their own word was taken as divine. But in Israel's case this wasn't so; their God *was* real, and God reserved the right of sole authority over his people. In fact, his rule over them extended to the smallest details – matters of cleanness, how to handle food, dealing with dead animals, what to do on the Sabbath day, and so on. He ruled their every action and every thought.

After a while some of the Israelites began to think that this was a sham, that Moses was deceiving them about God, and they decided to test the rules here and there. They found out in a hurry that it wasn't Moses who was running the show! Korah and his whole family dropped into a chasm in the earth when he dared to defy God's ways. (Numbers 16) The lot – a way of drawing the short straw – found out Achan and his sin against God. (Joshua 7) Nathan woke up one night and received a message from God for King David: the Lord knows your sin, and your son is going to die because of it. (2 Samuel 12) You see, the Lord was busy ruling his people whether they knew it or not!

The job wasn't an easy one; in fact, we would consider it quite impossible. To keep track of our own hearts is a job that no one of us can handle because of all the possibilities for error; the Law may have been on only two tablets of stone, but it has implications in every aspect of our lives, in ways that we would never have dreamed of. Now complicate that with millions of people across thousands of years, in different lands and mixed into various cultures, in contact with all kinds of pagan nations around the globe, and you can begin to imagine the job of ruling a nation in the way that God rules his people. He isn't satisfied with outward conformity, you understand; the obedience that he requires is a matter of the heart – the heart has to be perfect according to his standards.

The work involved is staggering. Can you imagine ruling over a people to the extent that God rules over them and doing the job so well that *there isn't one thing about God's Kingdom that a man can find fault with?* Surely the Lord works with perfection in this area.

He set up the Temple economy. "Make this tabernacle and all its furnishings exactly like the pattern I will show you." (Exodus 25:9) The Israelites built the Tabernacle – the "tent of meeting" where they used to meet with God in the wilderness – but God did the design work on the Tabernacle. He also laid out the plans for the Temple that Solomon later built in Jerusalem. The entire blueprint of worship for the Israelites was the brainchild of the Lord, not any man. It has two aspects.

First, only the Lord knows what is necessary in order for true worship to work. The complexity of the system is bewildering to the uninitiated. Since we don't know very much about God until he tells us, we aren't even aware of the requirements necessary when someone comes before God to worship him. We think that all one has to do is find him, say a short prayer, and end with the magic phrase "In Jesus' name, Amen." We couldn't be more wrong! And the sacrificial system is equally beyond our comprehension; all the offerings required and when they are required and why they are necessary requires a wisdom that we don't have.

All through history men have had a feeling that some sort of ceremony is needed when one comes before God. They have had at least some sense of the true situation, passed down to them from ancient times: that God is bigger (in some way!) than we are, that we are in trouble with God over sin, that we need some sort of sacrifice to appease him. Of course they've added more elements to the picture – almost all wrong – and the situation has gone from bad to worse. Nobody has a good idea of what to do in order to worship God correctly. And of course they can never find him and "appease" him at that rate.

Except Israel, and that's because God revealed it to them. They would have been just as much in the dark as their pagan neighbors if it weren't for the fact that God showed them clearly what to do. Some of the elements were familiar, but most of it was entirely new to them. It was all the result of God's plans and purposes and working it all out to perfectly fulfill the needs at hand, in respect both to himself and to them.

Second, it works. This is the amazing thing. The Israelites were fools if they thought that they could pray some words and have their sins forgiven, just like that, apart from God's direct intervention. *God makes our worship of him work.* The pagans couldn't claim answered prayer, a clean conscience, peace with God, a view of Heavenly things, a faith that transcends the world's problems. The Israelites could because their God made it all work.

They found, to their amazement, that God listened when they prayed. They discovered that a sacrifice made in faith moved God to forgive them and allow them to come close to him, even though it was all based on the sacrifice of animals. They loved him because they saw that he loved them. This was a real God who was fulfilling his promises among them! He worked miracles for them. He consented to live in their Temple (even though "The Heavens, even the highest Heavens, cannot contain you. How much less this Temple I have built!" – 2 Chronicles 6:18) so that they could find him and come close to him. The nations around Israel knew that the Lord, the God of Israel, was real.

And he was busy doing even more for them that they weren't aware of. None of us know the full extent of the work of the Heavenly Temple, but we will find out what has been going on when we get there. We will discover that the little bit that happened on earth was the visible outside to a vast system of ceremony that only God fully understands, but that all of God's children benefit from in some way. That's especially true now that Christ has come and fulfilled the Old Testament ceremony for us; but it was true for the Israelites in a very important sense: the worship that they offered God in the earthly temple was simply a shadow of the reality of what was really going on. An Israelite who had the faith to see that would realize that he was only touching the skin of the apple. He knew that God was doing far more than he understood or imagined. So he worshiped in the full assurance of faith.

JUDGMENT

The word "judgment" usually brings images to mind that aren't exactly correct. When we think of "judgment" we think of getting into trouble for something; we have in our minds the image of a judge who is handing down a sentence for a crime committed.

But that is less than half of the whole idea of "judgment." Judgment means this: *assessing a situation correctly*. And really the courtroom judge must do the same thing when he listens to plaintiff and defendant; he has to weigh the evidence for both sides, listen to the witnesses, listen to the lawyers' arguments, and then come to some decision about what really happened. That *decision process* is the judgment part; the punishment or rewards that he hands out are really based on the judgment that he made, and should be fitting to the case.

God is the supreme Judge over all of creation. He is the judge by right and by ability; *by right* because he made this world and it all belongs to him – everyone must play by his rules because we are in his court. And he is judge *by ability* because only he can fully know the complete situation of every creature in the world. Only he can decide what the fate is of every creature and be right in what he decides. Because of these two facts about God as judge, no one can challenge his judgment in any way; he has the right to decide our fate, and what he decides is far better than anybody else can come up with.

He has always been judging his creation, and he will continue to do so right up to the end. The Scriptures teach us that he works constantly at judging, and his work is so subtle and so extensive and so complex that we can only be amazed at how well he does the job.

There is a reason why he judges everything in the world: he wants everything to conform to his will, exactly, to the last detail, so that in all things he "works out everything in conformity with the purpose of his will." (Ephesians 1:11) It won't do at all to have a single thing out of line and ruining his plans. So he examines every single piece of the puzzle to make sure that it will stand the test of his standards. Everything that survives the coming day of fire *will* be pure and holy and upright and will reflect God's glory perfectly. Even our work – or should we say, especially our work! – he will put to the test to see if it passes muster:

> But each one should be careful how he builds. For no one can lay any foundation other than the one already laid, which is Jesus Christ. If any man builds on this foundation using gold, silver, costly stones, wood, hay or straw, his work will be shown for what it is, because the Day will bring it to light. It will be revealed with fire, and the fire will test the quality of each man's work. If what he has built survives, he will receive his reward. If it is burned up, he will suffer loss; he himself will be saved but only as one escaping through the flames. (1 Corinthians 3:10-15)

You will also remember from what the Lord told us that *only he* is able to judge aright. He told us, "do not judge, or you too will be judged" (Matthew 7:1), simply because we often jump to conclusions based on insufficient data – or more often, according to our sinful hearts. Only the Lord knows the full situation, and only he can see what is invisible to man. "He knew what was in a man" (John 2:25); therefore he takes the necessary steps to deal with man justly.

This last point teaches us how important the work of judging is in God's scheme of things. It's because of what he sees and decides that he acts the way he does. For example, in Genesis 6:5 we are told that "the Lord saw how great man's wickedness on the earth had become, and that every inclination of the thoughts of his heart was only evil all the time." *Therefore*, it says, based on this judgment of the situation, "I will wipe mankind ... from the face of the earth." (verse 7) His actions are based on his judgments. We often wonder why God does such and such. But if we could see the circumstances like he sees them and know the full story as he knows it then we wouldn't wonder anymore; his reaction would seem entirely fitting to the case. In fact, when we get to Heaven we will spend a lot of time reviewing his works that he did in our lives and praising him for his remarkable discernment and wisdom. His judgment always outlines the situation so precisely that his solution will inevitably answer the needs remarkably well, whether any of us understand it yet or not.

The thoughts and intents of the heart – "The Word of God is living and active. Sharper than any double-edged sword, it penetrates even to dividing soul and spirit, joints and marrow; it judges the thoughts and attitudes of the heart." (Hebrews 4:12) This is probably the first thing that hits people when they come into God's immediate presence. His eyes penetrate into and through us so that we feel quite naked in front of him – not only physically but naked of soul as well. We simply can't hide a thing from him! Saints and sinners alike bow down in front of him who sees to the bottom of their hearts.

Adam and Eve (Genesis 3:8) cowered in the brush when God came walking in the garden; they feared his penetrating looks and questions. They knew that they wouldn't pass the test. Isaiah (Isaiah 6:5) cried out in anguish when the Lord looked at him, because he knew he had sin stains upon him just like the other Israelites had. Peter (Luke 22:61) caught a single look from the Lord Jesus, on the night he betrayed him, and spent the rest of the night weeping bitterly because of the pain of that judgment. John, the Apostle whom the Lord loved, fell down on his face "as though dead" when Jesus turned his "eyes like blazing fire" upon him. (Revelation 1:17) You can find many, many more examples of people in the Bible who felt stripped and bare in God's presence and didn't like the feeling a bit.

The truth of the matter is that God is always watching us like that; we just aren't aware of it all the time. If we were, then we wouldn't get a thing done! But even when we can't sense his presence, that shouldn't make us feel like we finally got away from him. "Where can I go from your Spirit? Where can I flee from your presence?" (Psalm 139:7)

You are on center stage: the spotlights of Heaven are aimed at you and every whisper that you utter echoes through the halls of the King of glory. Your actions are studied, your thoughts are studied, your likes and dislikes are analyzed, your attitudes about everything are made the topic of divine discussion. You are like a medical specimen on the operating table that the doctor knows like the back of his hand – you have no privacy at all.

The Lord won't allow you to have any privacy. It might seem unfair that *everything* you do is put to extreme scrutiny like this; but you have to understand where he is coming from. You are the one thing in creation that has the ability – in fact, you've already done it to some extent – to foul up the works. You are a loose nut in the machinery of the world. Your potential for evil and destruction is enormous, and the fact that you were created in God's image means that you can desecrate God's Name in the process. He's *got* to keep an eye on you! If for no other reason than to protect everything and everyone around you from your wickedness. To take his eyes off you is like turning one's back on a drunk; one may very well be responsible for what the drunk ends up doing if one lets him go.

But it isn't only a negative reason that God keeps us constantly in his sight. He studies our motives and thoughts in order to sanctify us too. This also is a full-time job, because thoughts run through our brains like a wildfire through dry brush. Paul said that "we take captive every thought to make it obedient to Christ." (2 Corinthians 10:5) Where does Paul hope to get the insight on what to take captive, and how to take it captive, and what to do with it once he's got it captive? He has to get this wisdom from God who knows all of Paul's shortcomings.

This is where the Word comes in. Many people may think that the Bible is simply an old book that we can safely ignore. But for those who have dared to open its pages, unbeliever and Christian alike, it's the judgment of God that penetrates our hearts. Its words pin us to the wall with the truth about us, like no other book can. I know of non-Christians who are afraid to read the Bible – they know that when they read it, it will convict their hearts of something and they don't want to go through that experience. It describes man's heart so well! It calls a spade a spade; it opens our hearts and minds and describes what is there, for all the world to see. People can't sit through a sermon for that reason: the Word of God is so penetrating, so potentially embarrassing, that they often feel the preacher is talking about *them*!

But for us who are being saved, it's the wisdom of God and the power of God. The Word will tell us what we need to know about ourselves, and what God intends to do in order to save us. We *want* to know the truth! We want a right judgment about ourselves. That's why the Word is so precious to us; it's our salvation. It shows us where we are going wrong, why we are going wrong, what it will take to heal us, how we can better relate to others and to God – isn't that what we want to hear? "Come, see a man who told me everything I ever did. Could this be the Christ?" (John 4:29) Thank God for his judgment of me!

He judges by the standard – "He will judge the world in righteousness; he will govern the peoples with justice." (Psalm 9:8) The standard that God judges by is his Law. You will not find a fairer piece of legislation by which to rule a kingdom. It perfectly glorifies God and his nature in its requirements, it demands no more and no less from us than what is our duty as God's creatures, and the penalties and rewards that it lays out are entirely fitting to each case.

You know the feeling when you see a judge in a courtroom giving out an unjust judgment. If he allows a criminal to go free, the community cries out in protest! And if the innocent is condemned, the wheels of justice are set in motion to overturn the bad decision in higher courts. We have these strong feelings about the judge's judgements because *we measure his decision against a standard to see if he did justice by that standard.* If a judge openly defies a standard that we all accept, then something has to change – either the judge has to go or he must be made to change his decision. We will not give up our standards; our lives are based on certain values and we all must conform to those values. The judge is the highest appeal to those values, and the courtroom is the place where things will be put to right and the values will be upheld. "When the righteous prosper, the city rejoices; when the wicked perish, there are shouts of joy." (Proverbs 11:10) This is because the people can see their values at work providing justice and protecting them from the wicked.

You've probably seen a plumb line work. A builder hangs a weight on the end of a string and lines it up along the wall that he is building. Since gravity pulls the plumb straight down, he can tell if his wall is straight – he simply compares the wall with the string. He *knows* the string is right, and therefore he can judge if his wall is right too.

The Lord judges the world by his Law because his Law is *right*. He simply compares our hearts and our actions with the straight Law. Since he knows that the Law will say only what is good and holy and true, he can easily see – and so can we! – if we measure up to the "righteous requirements of the Law."

The reason he's so interested in the Law, by the way, is because it's the perfect and complete description *of his own nature*. The Law is simply a description of God and his kingdom. This explains why the Law is so high, so perfect, so unattainable for us sinners. When Jesus told us to "be perfect, as your Heavenly Father is perfect" (Matthew 5:48) he was pointing us to the matchless perfection of God for our standard. No other standard will suffice; man's rules and regulations are not enough to satisfy God's tough requirements.

Think of it this way: the Lord is very particular about his environment; he likes things just so. He is offended by sinners; their unholy ways are repulsive to him. Whereas we can live in a moral pigsty and not seem to mind at all, he can't tolerate the atmosphere of sin. "Your eyes are too pure to look on evil; you cannot tolerate wrong." (Habakkuk 1:13) "Such people are a smoke in my nostrils, a fire that keeps burning all day." (Isaiah 65:5) Whatever God wants and does and thinks and says is the only standard of excellence – all of creation either must conform to his holy nature or be destroyed as so much worthless trash. That's hard for us to think about, especially since we value ourselves so highly and we consider whatever we do as valuable. But we've shown how well things turn out when we are running things – with sin and death as a result! – and now it's God's turn to apply *his* standard to our lives and get what he wants – justice and life.

He works on the conscience – "At this, those who heard began to go away one at a time, the older ones first, until only Jesus was left, with the woman still standing there." (John 8:9) This story tells us that Jesus bent down and began writing in the dust. It doesn't tell us what he wrote, but he never did anything that was pointless. There is a Scripture that may very well give us a clue:

> O LORD, the hope of Israel, all who forsake you will be put to shame. Those who turn away from you will be *written in the dust* because they have forsaken the Lord, the spring of living water. (Jeremiah 17:13)

If this is what Jesus was doing, evidently he penetrated the heart of every man there when he wrote their names in the dust. They couldn't bear up under the shame that they felt in front of him; their own hearts convicted them without Christ having to utter a word. He – and they – both knew their past histories, their own times of sin and rebellion towards God.

Conscience is the inner knowledge of what is right; it's the moral counterpart of instinct in animals. God burned it into our souls so that it would always be there, guiding us in his ways according to his truth. It's *his truth* that is right, not our own opinions. We have minds that can work out solutions, but we need the Divine programming in our consciences to guide us in the right direction in the first place. Paul tells us that every human being was made with the Law of God etched in the heart: "the requirements of the Law are written on their hearts, their consciences also bearing witness, and their thoughts now accusing, now even defending them." (Romans 2:15) It may be that a person turns a deaf ear to his conscience or, what is worse, he will deceive himself intentionally so that he can silence his conscience So what little guidance is able to seep through to his heart will be undependable. The Bible calls this the "searing" of the conscience – deceiving oneself so that one no longer hears the truth from inside the heart.

Conscience can be a terrible master. God wisely made us with this very human characteristic because it will often keep us in line when nothing else will. We find ourselves doing what is right even when nobody is looking – why? Simply because it's what we *should* do! But if we sin against our conscience then the hard part comes. Our conscience won't let us alone; the awful deed stains us like blood on our hands, and we feel like everyone knows what we did, or at least they will soon know. A man can live with all sorts of physical punishments better than he can live with the terror of the conscience. "A rebuke impresses a man of discernment more than a hundred lashes a fool." (Proverbs 17:10)

Most people live within a few seconds of the lashings of an offended conscience. You don't have to speak to them much about God, about their past history of sin, before they begin to wilt inside. They try to avoid the subject of their own sinful hearts and they move on to other safe subjects. That's the conscience at work. Just a whisper from God's Law and they run like hunted criminals. "I will make their hearts so fearful in the lands of their enemies that the sound of a wind-blown leaf will put them to flight ... because of their sins." (Leviticus 26:36,39)

People often take God to task for his seemingly severe approach to sin. Can the Lord really be concerned with every little detail of our lives like this? Is he really offended with the smallest sins? Isn't it contrary to his basic nature of love to get so angry when we commit a little sin – a "venial" sin as they call it? But they are ignoring one big reality when they question God like this: they have already committed enough sin to sink a battleship. It's not the case that someone has only done one little sin; rather he has added a new sin (little or big) to a lifetime of rebellion and willfulness and immorality. We're looking at a single tree and wondering why God takes notice, when he's looking at the whole forest sitting there.

When the last day comes and God summons each of us before him to give an account, it's this lifetime of sin that will be staring us in the face. Right now we have a little memory problem; we don't remember *everything* we ever did that God might have taken offence at. But on that last day the Lord will take the blinders off our eyes and we will be able to see, just as clearly as he can see, the whole embarrassing mess in our hearts and minds. We will be struck dumb; we won't have anything to say. Our own conscience will testify to us that God was right all along, that we are just as bad as he told us we were, that we did indeed pass by many chances to change our ways, that when he came close to us in our lives we simply tuned him out, and many more things that we don't want to think about right now. And he will say, I told you about all this before now.

> Now we know that whatever the Law says, it says to those who are under the Law, so that every mouth may be silenced and the whole world held accountable to God. (Romans 3:19)

There are witnesses – "On the testimony of two or three witnesses a man shall be put to death, but no one shall be put to death on the testimony of only one witness." (Deuteronomy 17:6) This is straight from God's Law, and we can certainly expect the Lord to live by that law himself. It's the way he does things! And we will find this out when we stand before his judgment seat at the end of time.

God is sufficient witness in himself for anything that happens. We want more than one witness in our courts of law, because one witness may have the story wrong or he may even be trying to deceive the court. But two (independent) witnesses make a strong case; if they both agree on what happened, then we can be pretty certain that it happened that way. But who can see all things like God? How can thousands of witnesses add anything to the testimony of God? His is the perfect testimony that nobody can improve on.

But he is going to have witnesses anyway. Judgment is a serious matter with him, and if we're going to have to face an accusation of having sinned against the Lord of Heaven and earth then he is going to have other witnesses there at our trial. It's very uncomfortable how he brings witnesses out of the woodwork like this! People we know and people we don't know are going to testify that yes, they saw us do such and such sin; and yes, they have their own gripe against us for the way we treated them (or ignored them, whatever the case may be). As the trial goes on we are going to realize, perhaps for the first time, that the life that God gave us affected many others, and there were people who depended on us for important things, and we failed them as well as God. The enormity of our responsibility is going to hit us between the eyes when God calls all these witnesses against us. Even the earth and the Heavens will mount the witness stand: "This day I call Heaven and earth as witnesses against you that I have set before you life and death, blessings and curses." (Deuteronomy 30:19)

  This examination reminds us of our first duty that God gave us – to fill the earth, subdue it, and rule over it in God's Name with his image on our persons. Where does it stop? How much am I responsible to do in my life? Who is my brother, that I have been accountable to him? Was my every step, my every word, a burden to others, a cross in their lives, that I was never aware of? How much of this would I have avoided if I had taken God more seriously in life?

  The role of witnesses in God's judgment is a very serious matter to him. He is busy collecting all the evidence that will relate to each one of our cases. In Revelation 6:9-11 we read about the witnesses who have been killed for the Lord's sake – and God has them under the altar in Heaven, waiting until the time is right to bring all the details out in the open. Notice that the testimony will work two ways: these witnesses will testify against those who had them executed, and their executioners will be forced to witness in their favor to exonerate their names. We know this last fact will occur by what another passage tells us:

> Live such good lives among the pagans that, though they accuse you of doing wrong, they may see your good deeds and glorify God on the day he visits us. (1 Peter 2:12)

Judgment is a very public affair; God isn't the only one who is interested in the results. Just as we haven't lived in a vacuum all of our lives, we will have to answer to more than God at the end of time. What we have done and said, even though in secrecy, "will be proclaimed from the housetops" (Luke 12:3) so that all the universe will know. So it's a very involved, complex affair that God is preparing as the Judge of all men; that last day will show how well-organized and prepared the Lord is for uncovering the truth about everyone.

Fitting reward, fitting punishment – "Your eyes are open to all the ways of men; you reward everyone according to his conduct and as his deeds deserve." (Jeremiah 32:19) Man has always known, deep down, that this is a "do good and you will live" system he lives in. The social sciences make fun of primitive societies that try to appease their gods with sacrifices and other such useless activities; but those primitive peoples are simply addressing the pain of conscience (just as we moderns do in our own ways) and trying to buy righteousness for themselves. They know that there is good and bad waiting for us all, and this life is the door into one or the other.

God does have good and bad waiting for us. He told us clearly what those options are in the Bible and in the history of his special people Israel; he expects us to take all this seriously because he takes it all very seriously. He has been busy preparing the full extent of those options ever since the world began, and we will finally see his work at the end of time when he calls us to one or the other. Why don't we take it just as seriously? We seem to forget that there is another world, even when we claim to have an interest in the matter. This world takes up so much of our time and energy that thinking about what is to come next seems like being "too Heavenly minded to be of any earthly good!" But this is a poor showing for a people who have been called into God's kingdom. "No eye has seen, no ear has heard, no mind has conceived what God has prepared for those who love him." (1 Corinthians 2:9) We should be fascinated with the subject.

You'll remember that God is building a house to live in, which will be fully manifest only at the end of the world. (Revelation 21:2-4) He is busy working now to lay stone upon stone, life upon life, testimony upon testimony, in order to have a people all of his own. When it's done then the old earth and the old Heavens will pass away and the great preparations that God has been making for the eternal joy and peace of his people will finally be made plain. This will be the reward of the saints: to be so close to God that he will live *in them*.

Jesus reminded his disciples that he wasn't going back to Heaven to relax now that the hard times were over; he was going back to work on their reward. "I am going there to prepare a place for you." (John 14:2) What all he is doing, and why it takes all this time to prepare, we can't possibly imagine. But perhaps this will help: remember when your parents or someone close to you would make you wait for a present? The longer it took the worse was the waiting! But when they finally brought it out to you, you could see that the extra time was necessary – they put a lot of effort into making it what would make you perfectly happy. That, dear Christian, is what Jesus is up to right now. Imagine the infinite power and wisdom of Christ put to the task of coming up with a reward that will make you happy! Can you conceive of what the Lord of Glory will come up with if it took him these 2000 years to create it?

The Lord is also busy preparing the just reward of the wicked, only that won't make them at all happy. Does the Lord prepare disaster for the wicked? He organizes and plans even this to the smallest detail! To some, unfortunately, he is going to say "Depart from me, you who are cursed, into the eternal fire *prepared* for the devil and his angels." (Matthew 25:41) What, do you think, did he prepare for the devil and his angels? An unquenchable fire, a worm that doesn't die, torment to cause weeping and gnashing of teeth. We don't know much more than that (and who would want to look inside?) but again we have to realize that Hell must be an awesome place because it took no less than God to come up with it.

The Bible gave us hints all along that God was working on something in eternity. The symbolism of the Temple, for example, wasn't meant to confuse the Israelites; they weren't supposed to look at the blood of bulls and goats and think that this animal sacrifice would really cleanse their hearts from sin. The picture pointed to the reality that God was putting together in the Heavenly Temple. Just about everything in Israelite history points to a spiritual, eternal reality that God was building. Did they inherit the Promised Land? Canaan was only a symbol of the promised land that God was preparing – "for he has prepared a city for them." (Hebrews 11:16)

Finally, the Lord told us that he works in concert with us on this project of rewards and punishments. It's characteristic of the Lord to work out things so that we get what we asked for. The pagans will get what they ask for and no more; they didn't want God in the first place, and that's precisely what they are going to end up with: *no God*. The problem is that they didn't anticipate how terrible that would be! They built for themselves a life that leaves God out of the picture, and at the Last Day the Lord is going to take the final step back and leave them to themselves in misery. Only then will they discover that God gave them the rope to hang themselves.

Christians, on the other hand, will find that their works precede them into Heaven. The process is twofold: *first*, God prepares works ahead of time for us to do, works that need doing, and gives them to us when the right time comes. (Ephesians 2:10) *Second*, we do them. We don't always, you'll understand, and that's where our sense of responsibility and obedience come into the picture. *Third*, these works lay the bricks of our future glory. The Lord takes our good works, done in faith and obedience, and creates a beautiful reward and testimony out of them. (Matthew 6:20)

So much for the judgment of the Lord. His honor rests on his ability and wisdom to judge everything in righteousness; it should be no surprise, then, that we find him hard at work on this matter of judgment. If we can't appreciate the full scope of his work in this area now, we will at the end of the world. Like watching an artist who unveils his work at the pre-appointed time, we will become witnesses of his amazing work on Judgment Day.

THE COMING OF CHRIST

The biggest event in the history of the world, in the unfolding of God's kingdom, was the coming of Christ. It was thousands of years in the making, and when he came there were all sorts of prophecies fulfilled and new things were started. There were high hopes in this One who was to come; the Jews were looking for a Messiah who would finally bring in God's righteous kingdom, subdue the nations, make Jerusalem the center of worship, and fill their lives with good things. It was such a glorious affair that one would be surprised if the Jews weren't there in masses waiting for him, ready to crown him king and give him the key to the city.

But it never transpired that way. In fact, the Messiah came and almost nobody took notice. A few shepherds, some foreign kings, and a couple of old Jews were the only ones who welcomed him. The king of the land sent an army to kill him! Finally, hidden away in an obscure village, this Promised One grew up and readied himself for a ministry that would bring him dishonor, hardship, misunderstanding, dislike, and eventually death. His years of work would fall to the ground, apparently to no avail. For all the expectations that everyone had in this man he certainly ended up a nobody!

There's a more profound loss involved here. The coming of Christ was the main event that God himself was looking forward to. All his other work takes second place in importance to this. This is the work that he wants to be remembered by; this is what he points *us* to, so that we will, in amazement, praise him for his glorious works. He put more skill and wisdom into this work than anything else he has ever done; he put his heart into this one, his only Son, and for the sake of sinners shouldered the burden of pain and death – a work that made the angels stand in awe. And though it was so important to God that Christ should come, it went by almost unnoticed among men. The most important thing that he had ever done and they ignored it! Added to the burden of the work itself was the calloused indifference of the world.

The problem is even more extensive and serious than this. God openly prepared for Christ's coming long before the event itself happened. Through thousands of years of history he laid the foundations of the Incarnation, and taught Israel about the Messiah. He promised results from their long centuries of labor and waiting: salvation, freedom from the enemies of our souls, a righteous kingdom, and so on. They could easily see what God was leading up to – it would someday all culminate in the person and work of Christ. Did they take notice along the way? Did they appreciate the fact that their religion was not a matter of "eating and drinking, but righteousness, peace and joy in the Holy Spirit"? (Romans 14:17) Did they patiently put up with the temporary trials, knowing that it would result in the salvation of their souls? Did they look past the animal sacrifices and believe that the Lord was putting together a sacrifice that would finally and completely cleanse their hearts of sin? Did they have any discernment about what God was really doing on a spiritual level when he worked with them on the physical, symbolic level?

Usually they not only had no idea what God was really doing, but they couldn't have cared less if someone told them. In fact the prophets did tell them!

> For when I brought your forefathers out of Egypt and spoke to them, I did not just give them commands about burnt offerings and sacrifices, but I gave them this command: Obey me, and I will be your God and you will be my people. Walk in all the ways I command, that it may go well with you. (Jeremiah 7:22-23)

This was only like water on a duck's back; they paid no attention to him. They showed where their hearts really were – on the things in this world, not with the Lord's kingdom. They couldn't make the distinction between secondary matters and primary matters, and so they missed the Lord's real work that was going on. Jesus made a pointed observation about the Jews in his own day, that their attention (as was their fathers') was also on things in this world and not on what God was really doing:

> Woe to you, teachers of the law and Pharisees, you hypocrites! You build tombs for the prophets and decorate the graves of the righteous. And you say, "If we had lived in the days of our forefathers, we would not have taken part with them in the shedding of the blood of the prophets." So you testify against yourselves that you are the descendents of those who murdered the prophets. Fill up, then, the measure of your sin of your forefathers! (Matthew 23:29-32)

He went on to say that he would send prophets to them too, and they would kill his prophets because *they still could not discern the work of God.*

> O Jerusalem, Jerusalem, you who kill the prophets and stone those sent to you, how often have I longed to gather your children together, as a hen gathers her chicks under her wings, but you were not willing. (Matthew 23:37)

These passages show us how God feels about this most important work of his. Of all the works that he does, he wants the salvation of men to be most prominent – he wants us to see what he is doing and get interested in it ourselves. The work involved in sending Christ into the world to save sinners was a tremendous upheaval in Heaven *and* earth, and like a flaming torch the cross of Christ is now held high for all men in all times and in all countries to see clearly and come to. It was the most complex and most delicately balanced of all his works. It's the center diamond in the works of God, the thing of which he is most proud, certainly the most profound mystery of the acts of God. If we don't know about anything else that God has done in this world, this one thing we must know, because upon it the Lord bases our entire future and well-being. God is satisfied in

Christ: "You are my Son, whom I love; with you I am well pleased." (Luke 3:22)

Let's look at a little bit of the preparation and labor that God invested in the coming of Christ.

>***Preparation through the Jews*** – "And who is like your people Israel – the one nation on earth that God went out to redeem as a people for himself, and to make a name for himself, and to perform great and awesome wonders by driving out nations and their gods from before your people, whom you redeemed from Egypt?" (2 Samuel 7:23) At the beginning of the world, man knew something about God the Creator; but after that time the peoples of the world hadn't the faintest idea of who he really was. Not only did the little knowledge that they did have of God become obscure, they never did know about the side of him that had to do with salvation. As far as they were concerned God looked like all the other gods of the nations – pretty useless.
>
>But through Israel the Lord showed how precious his works are for us. Here we find out what he is prepared to do in order to save his people! It turned into a book, as a matter of fact: the story of the Savior, the God who saves from sin and death, the Lord of all the earth who isn't like other gods. This God delivers from the enemy, this God rules with a Law, this God forms a nation out of his people and puts them in a good land, this God fights the battles with their enemies, this God punishes for sin, this God forgives sin and imparts holiness. The whole story of how God saves is there in the history of Israel.

You can see, therefore, the importance of the nation Israel. It was in their special world that God worked out the details of the salvation process; long before Christ came to implement it on the spiritual level, the Jews had learned it on a physical, symbolic level. They found out, long before the rest of the world did, about the special concepts of salvation, the ways that God goes about it, the results that God is looking for, and many other details that we are now familiar with in Christianity. They have already heard about Heaven and grace and forgiveness of sin and living by faith. They know more about the Son of God and what he came to do than we probably do – it was all in the promises and teachings of their prophets.

Why did God work out all this material ahead of time in such great detail? One reason was that there would be at least *one* reception committee when Christ came! The Jews of all people would surely recognize their God when he came to save men's souls. "He came to that which was his own" (John 1:11) – to the Jews first, because salvation was their history, their privilege, their foundation. This was their God. Something should have clicked in their heads and they should have done some studying, comparing the ministry of Christ with their Scriptures. The two were one and the same – here was their God come to make good on his past promises to them.

Preparation of the Temple system – "It was necessary, then, for the copies of the Heavenly things to be purified with these sacrifices, but the

Heavenly things themselves with better sacrifices than these." (Hebrews 9:23) Here is the heart of the Old Testament system; and for those who can see it, it's the heart of the work of Christ as well. The Lord put a great deal of work into the Temple system because it represented the way that man will find peace with God, which is the most important thing about our relationship with God.

Usually people get bogged down in the passages that describe the Tabernacle – in Exodus and Leviticus – and just skip the whole thing and move on to the history sections. But when the Lord takes such great pains to describe every detail, this should throw up a red flag for us: here is something that we should pay attention to. He's walking us through this house that he built, showing us not just things that look pretty but things that he attaches great significance to. It's not his fault that we don't get the point right away!

The different parts of the Temple represent profound realities in the system of salvation. For example, the Lord directed Solomon to use an enormous amount of gold and silver in the Temple – he literally covered the walls with tons of gold, and many of the articles in the Temple were covered with it too. Gold awes the mind with its beauty, and staggers the imagination with its great value. So also the salvation that Christ gives his people: it is of immense value, and we see it correctly when we are overwhelmed with its dazzling light and fabulous richness. This is wealth that the world can't give us. But there's another idea in the use of so much gold: it's a heavy metal, and the Hebrew word for "heavy" also means "glory" – the glory of the Lord is a "heavy" presence that we not only can feel but overwhelms us when we come into his presence. Remember when Solomon first opened the Temple for worship services?

> Then the Temple of the Lord was filled with a cloud, and the priests could not perform their service because of the cloud, for the glory of the Lord filled the Temple of God. (2 Chronicles 5:13-14)

The reason that God takes so much time describing the Temple in the Old Testament is because it's the central image of the most important work he wants to accomplish. The Temple was the site where sin was dealt with, where men and women found their God and became reconciled with him. The other nations wished they could have it so good! Only to the Jews was this privilege given. When they lost the Temple during the destruction of Jerusalem, they lost the heart and soul of their religion and literally pined away in Babylon until they had a chance to return and build it again. For while the Temple stands, God's promise stands:

> Now my eyes will be open and my ears attentive to the prayers offered in this place. I have chosen and consecrated this Temple so that my Name may be there forever. My eyes and my heart will always be there. (2 Chronicles 7:15-16)

Pay attention, then, when God talks about his Temple. You will see this again when Christ comes to fulfill everything that the Temple represents. God is intensely interested in the work of the Temple.

Preparation of revelation – "These are the Scriptures that testify about me." (John 5:39) Not satisfied to simply work out the history and the Temple system among the Jews in order to prepare for the coming of Christ, the Lord also created a written revelation that would explain what he was doing. The importance of this written revelation can't be overstated: with history and events, there must also be interpretation. And rather than let man form his own opinions on what God might be up to, God himself is going to carefully and completely explain everything so that we will be able to know the truth of what's going on.

The Bible is so important to the Church, and yet we often don't appreciate its worth – especially the Old Testament. We Christians especially tend to miss the point about how necessary the Old Testament is for explaining about Christ's person and work. The Jews know – or at least they ought to know – how the Old Testament describes Christ because the whole system of salvation was first worked out in their history. But history is not only a recital of events, it's the interpretation of those events too; the one telling the story is going to tell it in such a way that the facts fit his purposes. God wants us to learn the *right* lessons from what happened to the Israelites. So he tells us the story from *his* point of view, and he draws conclusions based on *his* perspective on things, and he points out how he thinks we need to react to this story. And if you get his point while you are reading all this, you will notice that he's leading up to his great work in Christ in the New Testament!

The Old Testament is so full of Christ that it's simply amazing to think that it was all written long before Christ ever came. It's obvious that it's a book written with Christ in mind; God was preparing the Jews for the Lord Jesus, whether they knew it or not. They could read about where he would be born, what kind of man he would be, the work that he would be doing, the very words of his teachings, the results of his labors, the end of his life, and the resurrection and the ascension. They would have known all about the nature of the salvation that he was bringing to man, the very fulfillment of their own symbolic system. They could have grasped the crucial nature, the central position, of the Lord Jesus Christ to all the work that God had done and ever will do. All this is spelled out in the revelation that God gave them.

You will find much of this *only* in the Old Testament. A lot of what God did in Christ is described only once – in the Old Testament – and it isn't repeated in the New again. We see it *done* in the New, but unless we have already studied the doctrine for it in the pages of the Old then we won't understand what we see. Notice how the Apostles approached both Jews and Gentiles in their preaching: they pointed to the life and works of Christ, and described the meaning and importance of it all by quoting the Old Testament and teaching out of there.

His birth and growing up – "The virgin will be with child and will give birth to a son, and they will call him Immanuel – which means, 'God with us'." (Matthew 1:23) There are two central doctrines about Christ, and this is one of them. Christians everywhere have always believed in and cherished the incarnation of Christ because it forms the foundation for all his work on behalf of men's salvation. The phrase "the person and work of Christ" reflects the two important facts about him: that he is God (his person), and that he saves men from their sins and makes them new (his work).

This incarnation was a special work of God that men clearly saw. It was *miraculous*, first of all, in that a baby was born to a woman who had no relations with a man. The baby was formed in her womb by the direct act of the Spirit of God. And it took place over *time*, secondly, because the Lord Jesus didn't just appear out of Heaven and begin his ministry. He started life the same way that we all do: nine months in the womb, a birth, growing up under the care and authority of his parents, learning and experiencing. And thirdly, it accomplished the *will* of the Father in that Jesus was and became the Savior that his Father had in mind from long ago. He wasn't born in a palace, and he didn't enjoy the praise of men; he was the son of a poor carpenter and had "no beauty or majesty to attract us to him, nothing in his appearance that we should desire him." (Isaiah 53:2) He learned the ways of his Father and he learned the heart of man, all in the school of real life.

> Although he was a son, he learned obedience from what he suffered and, once made perfect, he became the source of eternal salvation for all who obey him and was designated by God to be high priest in the order of Melchizedek. (Hebrews 5:8-10)

It took thirty plus years to do this work of bringing the Messiah into the world and preparing him for his short earthly ministry, but it was a work of perfection that only God himself could do. Jesus would have to be able to handle a crushing burden, a work load that no other man had been able to accomplish. This on top of having to fight off the Pharisees (the religious experts – Jesus himself had no formal training!), encourage the broken-hearted, and train the disciples to carry on after he left. It's no wonder that people were amazed and said, "Where did this man get this wisdom and these miraculous powers?" (Matthew 13:54) God did a good job of preparing Jesus for everything that happened.

The ministry – "The words that I say to you are not just my own. Rather, it is the Father, living in me, who is doing his work." (John 14:10) Jesus was always careful to disclaim any originality in what he did or said. This may seem strange to us because we feel that if anybody has the right to do exactly what he wants, Jesus certainly does. But he wasn't at all interested in doing his own will; that wasn't why he came. He came only to "do the will of him who sent me." (John 6:38) It's because he wanted exactly what the Father wanted anyway; there was no difference of opinion, and they saw things exactly the same way.

It was critical that Jesus and the Father wanted the same thing. After all, what was uppermost on God's mind was to fulfill everything that he had been getting ready for during the past 2000 years. He wanted to culminate this salvation process now! And since he laid out all the details in the history of the Old Testament, he wanted to make sure that everything in Christ's life would go according to plan *and not otherwise*. So the Father was in total control over Jesus' entire life – from the words he spoke to the miracles he performed. There was nothing left to chance, nothing left to the whim of man. This had to happen exactly according to plan in order to work, right up to the bitter end.

Whatever Christ did, he drew attention to the fact that it was the Father doing it through him. This was God's work, he claimed, not just the work of another man. Here is what you people have been waiting for – take hold of it and believe on it. "My Father is always at his work to this very day, and I, too, am working." (John 5:17) What did Jesus mean by this statement? Was God off somewhere in the universe doing some mysterious thing that didn't involve man?

> I tell you the truth, the Son can do nothing by himself; he can do only what he sees his Father doing, because whatever the Father does the Son also does. (John 5:19)

Understand, then, that everything that Jesus did is what God wants to do in men's lives. Do you want to learn about God and his works? Then study what Jesus did – *this* is what God is doing and what he wants to do. There isn't anything else he's interested in doing for you. Christ is the whole picture of what God has in store for you. Start with the Gospels and list the works that you find: coming close to you, identifying with your being human, counseling you with wisdom, rebuking you for your sins, protecting you from those who judge you, healing body and soul, forgiving sin, guiding you to a fuller knowledge of God the Father, teaching you to pray, getting you together with others who are like-minded, walking with you along the way, building you into the Church, and so on.

Jesus also pointed out the fact that he was doing things that *only* God could do – which was a testimony to the kind of work he was doing. "For the very work that the Father has given me to finish, and which I am doing, testifies that the Father has sent me." (John 5:36) You will look in vain for such things from other men. No wonder that we are told "Salvation is found in no one else, for there is no other name under Heaven given to men by which we must be saved." (Acts 4:12) There is no other Counselor like Christ, or other Savior, or other Lord, or other Teacher, or other Captain, or other Rock, or other Brother. Only he can do the work of God in our hearts.

The death and resurrection – "That power is like the working of his mighty strength, which he exerted in Christ when he raised him from the dead." (Ephesians 1:19-20) We tend to think that God simply snapped his fingers and Jesus got up and walked out of the grave. But that shows our ignorance of all the powers that were involved.

What put Jesus in the grave in the first place? Our sin! Just think about that for a minute. We treat our sin so lightly, as if it were of little importance, but it has a tremendous power for destruction. Through the requirements of the Law, sin has the power to kill – even Christ, who is life itself, laid down under its power (willingly, we must admit) and died. The Law demands *death* because of sin; what Christ suffered was nothing less than the full power of death and separation from God the Father. The state of things, because of sin, was terrible.

But the Father has strength even stronger than sin and death. He can overcome *anything* that sin can do; he can reverse the damage, no matter what was done, and pull out of smoking ruins a beautiful new creation. From the unspeakable tragedy of a dead Savior, the Father can reach down and lift up a living, triumphant Savior.

He not only can do that, he can lift up Christ so completely out of death that sin no longer has any power over him. Never again will sin be able to affect his life in any way. This is the really awesome thing about the resurrection that hasn't hit us yet in its fullness. We are so used to sin that we've grown accustomed to its being around all the time. We don't understand what life is like where there is only righteousness, only the will of God done, only love and obedience, only praises to God, only life and joy and peace. Such a life is beyond us now – but Christ has that life. That's the kind of life that God gave him at his resurrection; a different kind of life than we know. It has a power that completely overcomes sin and all its effects.

You can see, of course, why it takes the power of God to get such a life. We've never been able to accomplish it. In fact, we've never even entertained the possibility of such a life because we've consistently failed to come close to such a thing in our own efforts at "doing good." God's display of power was startling in how it so completely achieved what it has taken mankind countless millennia to vainly attempt.

The ascension – "And seated him at his right hand in the Heavenly realms, far above all rule and authority, power and dominion, and every title that can be given, not only in the present age but also in the one to come." (Ephesians 1:20-21) Here is a doctrine that we almost never think about, and certainly we underrate it as one of the works of God. But it rates as perhaps one of the most important things that God has done in Christ; without it we have no salvation.

When God raised Christ from the dead, he gave him the life that would characterize all of God's people. But when God raised Christ into Heaven and seated him at his right hand, he started the process of giving out that life to all of his people. The Resurrection was the making of the

Second Adam; the Ascension was the making of the Church of God.

Now that Christ is in Heaven, he's in a position to send his Spirit to Christians everywhere in the world. While he was on earth he was limited in his scope of ministry: the crucifixion hadn't happened yet, the basis of the covenant – the sacrifice of the Lamb – hadn't been formed yet, and the Spirit was not yet a universal reality in the Church.

> But I tell you the truth: It is for your good that I am going away. Unless I go away, the Counselor will not come to you; but if I go, I will send him to you. (John 16:7)

Now that he rules over the Church from the vantage point of the throne of God, he's in a position to completely guide and bless her. This is a tremendous asset for the Church, to have Christ in the position of universal power.

The ascension also represents Christ's position of power over the entire world. Remember the prophecy in Psalm 2?

> I have installed my king on Zion, my holy hill ... Ask of me, and I will make the nations your inheritance, the ends of the earth your possession. You will rule them with an iron scepter, you will dash them to pieces like pottery. (Psalm 2:6,8-9)

He was once the scorn of all nations; they ridiculed him and put him to death. But now it's his turn. God has "placed all things under his feet" (Ephesians 1:22) and Christ is even now forcing the world and everyone in it to conform to his overall plan of salvation. Those who will be saved, he will save; those who will not be saved, even they will play their parts in the drama, in the contexts of nation and culture and everyday life that surrounds the Church. We wonder sometimes if the Lord has everything under control when life gets alarming or confusing; but he does have it under control, and he won't allow anything to overcome his people.

The glorification – "Therefore God exalted him to the highest place and gave him a name that is above every name." (Philippians 2:9) There is a note of irony in this statement, especially if you know anything about the life of Christ when he was here on earth. When he was here he was despised, not appreciated; men spit at him and mocked him and dared to put him to death. Even the disciples wondered how he could take such abuse if he was the Son of God. The angels positively marveled at it.

If there has been any man in history who has been misunderstood it has been Jesus Christ. For all the forewarning and careful teaching that the Jews had, they didn't recognize him when he finally came. The Romans didn't see anything but a common criminal. The Greek philosophers considered his story a ludicrous fable. The Crusaders thought that Jesus was calling them to make war on earthly enemies. The Moslems, for their turn, thought he was a good prophet but nothing like their own man Mohammed. The Hindus place his image on the shelf alongside their millions of other gods. Modern Americans use him for an excuse to make merry on Christmas. Thousands of cathedrals and tens of thousands of churches have been built in his honor, and many of them sit empty or nearly so. The crude and the not-so-crude use his Name as a common curse word. Even born-again Christians will only appreciate his work to get them "saved", and then they run off after other subjects and projects that are more interesting; they know almost nothing about him. In all this, people have little realized the direct importance that the Son of God has in their lives.

Well, this will change. God has already started the process of glorifying his Son: "And now, Father, glorify me in your presence with the glory I had with you before the world began." (John 17:5) The work of the Church is (supposed to be, at any rate) to hold up the name of Jesus Christ and show the world the unutterable importance that he has in everyone's life. And as the end approaches, the process will become even more intense; the day will come when …

> … at the name of Jesus every knee should bow, in Heaven and on earth and under the earth, and every tongue confess that Jesus Christ is Lord, to the glory of God the Father. (Philippians 2:10-11)

Jesus will be *the* topic of discussion on Judgment Day. God's work through him will be the one thing everyone will want to know more about. Unbelievers will realize that they missed the boat entirely when they ignored *him*. Christians will realize that they are what they are only because of *him*. For the first time in human history, men and women will come to see the Christ for what he really is: the pinnacle and the capstone of all God's work among men. "The stone the builders rejected has become the capstone." (1 Peter 2:7) Some will discover that they weren't saved simply because they didn't come to God through Christ, and others will discover that it was because they depended solely on Christ that they were saved.

> Now to those who believe, this stone is precious. But to those who do not believe, "The stone the builders rejected has become the capstone," and, "A stone that causes men to stumble and a rock that makes them fall." They stumble because they disobey the message – which is also what they were destined for. (1 Peter 2:7-8)

Now this is an awesome thought. It should make you stop and wonder at God's works – that God is going to bring everyone's attention to Christ one day, to make us all realize that there has never been and there will never be anything more important than knowing him.

Hopefully this little bit of review has enlightened you on how much God has done in the area of salvation. If we can liken his work to a crew working on a skyscraper, all the other work that God has done has been like putting up fences and clearing the ground around the area; the work he did in Christ is the skyscraper itself. It has been a tremendous, glorious work, with far-reaching implications for every living person, and it should get much more of our attention than it does.

BUILDING UP A KINGDOM

While men are busy with everyday affairs, building cities and making money and formulating laws and waging war, the Lord is doing something "on the side" apart from most of men's activities. It's a quiet work that hardly anybody notices; it's out of the way of man's busy life, off to the side where hardly anybody looks. But to God it's the most important of works in this world, far more important than anything that man is involved in. We think that what we do is important, but in the end we will find out that we have been mistaken: this work of God – the building of his kingdom – will turn out to be the "dark horse" of history, the place where the really important work was going on and yet nobody realized it.

When Jesus came he announced the coming of the "kingdom of God" – "The time has come – the kingdom of God is near. Repent and believe the good news!" (Mark 1:15) People should have taken him more seriously. It did indeed come, though not many paid attention. It started with his firm foundation, grew into a spiritual foundation at Pentecost, and started spreading like wildfire through the Roman Empire. Soon it turned into an overwhelming power that brought the mighty Roman State down to destruction. If you trace its growth through the centuries you would be impressed at its **scope** – over all the world and in every tribe and nation – and you would be impressed by its **tenacity** – it has survived countless episodes of persecution from God's fiercest enemies – and you would be impressed by the **wisdom** behind it all – there's a mind far wiser than ours that's building something that will outlast the world.

Is God interested in building his kingdom? What was uppermost on Jesus' mind when he lived here on earth? You can find out by the prayer that he gave us. Prayer, especially when *he* prays, represents the deepest convictions and hopes of the human heart. It deals with subjects that are of *primary* importance. And he told us to say this:

> Our Father in Heaven, hallowed be your Name.
> *Your kingdom come*, your will be done on earth as
> it is in Heaven. (Matthew 6:9-10)

As far as Jesus was concerned, the kingdom of God was of primary importance. It's right up there at the head of the list – the *first* thing to ask for. So rest assured that God takes his kingdom building seriously, so seriously that everything else gets second billing in comparison.

Thank God, though, if you can see his kingdom at all. Not everyone can see God's works in his kingdom; they have too much of this world in their eyes and they don't have any idea of what God is building up. The kingdom of God is perhaps the most mysterious of God's works, simply because it's another world from ours.

> The knowledge of the secrets of the kingdom of
> Heaven has been given to you, but not to them.
> Whoever has will be given more, and he will have
> an abundance. Whoever does not have, even what
> he has will be taken from him. This is why I speak
> to them in parables: "Though seeing, they do not

see; though hearing, they do not hear or understand." (Matthew 13:11-13)

This is one area where we need to ask God to open our eyes to the reality of the thing. We can easily grasp matters of morality and relationships with others and church organization and spiritual duties; but when God calls us to step into another world – not *this world*, but his *spiritual* kingdom – we need help. We will never see it, and therefore will never appreciate his labors, if he doesn't open our eyes to his kingdom. "I tell you the truth, no one can see the kingdom of God unless he is born again." (John 3:3)

These are some of the more important characteristics of God's work in his kingdom, things that we should be aware of and able to discern:

> ***It is a kingdom.*** "The LORD is King for ever and ever." (Psalm 10:16) This is the fundamental idea of a kingdom – that there is a *king* in charge over things. We modern Americans know next to nothing about such a thing; our land started out as part of a kingdom, but we soon shook off the shackles of the King of England and made our own way. But Christians find that they've entered into a new world, at least in this respect, when they enter the kingdom of God – and we don't usually understand what's going on there. In God's world there is no democracy or aristocracy or anarchy or communism – only the King.
>
> What is a king? A king rules over a people and the land. He lays the law down that everyone has to obey – and he judges cases where the law has been broken. He lives in a palace and has servants waiting on him. He collects taxes and

deals with other kingdoms, sometimes calling on the men to form an army and, with himself at the head, meets the enemy on the field. His heirs will rule the kingdom when he is gone.

So far we can agree that this is the world's idea of a king, because this is usually what the kings of the world have been like. But we must go further than this if we want to understand the true nature of a king – and therefore of God as King. Consider *first* that his Law defines what is right and wrong for everyone– and therefore has to be perfect. If a king rules capriciously (one day this rule, the next day a contradictory one) then the kingdom will soon come apart at the seams. His subjects need a reliable standard by which to guide their lives. A king who rules in righteousness and wisdom will have a happy kingdom.

Second, he is ultimately concerned about the welfare of his subjects. He certainly has the power, and he is in the position, and it ought to be his will, to bless the people and improve their living conditions. He takes care of them in many ways, for example by protecting them from enemies and providing public improvements and stabilizing the economy so that each man can work and provide for his own.

Third, a king knows his subjects. This is so important, because unless he knows their hurts and grievances he can't know how to help them. Unless he knows their abilities he can't utilize their labors to the common good, and if he knows their failings then there won't be any unpleasant surprises in store. A good king will get close to his people, and they will get close to him, and the kingdom will prosper accordingly.

Fourth, the king enjoys his kingdom. He is in charge, after all, and he's making sure that the work that goes on will achieve the results that he wants. When they do then he is pleased. He appreciates his subjects, he enjoys the atmosphere of the work place, he basks in the praises of his people, his projects are succeeding, everyone is prosperous, the kingdom's reputation is getting around to others, and all in all it's a happy place to be. The king enjoys such a life just as much as his subjects do!

These are all true of God as king. His Law is a perfect guide that adorns God's people like a ring of fragrant flowers:

> See, I have taught you decrees and laws as the LORD my God commanded me, so that you may follow them in the land you are entering to take possession of it. Observe them carefully, for this will show your wisdom and understanding to the nations, who will hear about all these decrees and say, "Surely this nation is a wise and understanding people."
> (Deuteronomy 4:5-6)

This Law of God is matchless for its ability to order our lives with precision and perfection; it controls and governs a nation so that all things are righteous and holy, and all the requirements of the king are fulfilled. The Law never changes – what was right and wrong in the past is still right and wrong, and it will be that way in the future. We have a never-changing standard to rule our lives by.

Is God concerned with our welfare? "Cast all your anxiety on him because he cares for you." (1 Peter 5:7) He provides what we need in this world and what we need for the spiritual world. He heals and teaches, he leads and counsels, he feeds and rebukes, he watches over us when we sleep and carries us when we're unable to walk on our own. God is so personally involved with each of his people that earthly kings are put to shame; they can't match the deep involvement, the caring love, the attention to all the little details of our lives, that characterize God's work.

And the Lord knows us intimately.

> O LORD, you have searched me and you know me. You know when I sit and when I rise; you perceive my thoughts from afar. You discern my going out and my lying down; you are familiar with all my ways. Before a word is on my tongue you know it completely, O LORD. (Psalm 139:1-4)

Since God knows us so completely, since we have no secrets from him, we can trust him to be a king to us in a way that nobody else can be. He knows what's good for us and what we need; so what he does in our lives is going to be remarkably accurate in targeting our needs. And when he calls us to active duty in his kingdom it's because he knows what we can do (there are no such things as volunteers in God's kingdom – those whom he calls to work are the ones who must do the job, because only they *can* stand in the gap and do what's necessary).

Finally, the Lord enjoys his kingdom. "The vineyard of the Lord Almighty is the house of Israel, and the men of Judah are the garden of his delight." (Isaiah 5:7) God's labors bear fruit, and his people become his chief source of happiness. He enjoys spending time among them. He loves us like children, and with the heart of a Father he gathers us around his knees to bless us and love us. As a matter of fact, he is planning to live with them – and that takes a good deal of interest in someone, as you know if you have ever lived with anybody over a long period of time!

It's a spiritual kingdom. "My kingdom is not of this world. If it were, my servants would fight to prevent my arrest by the Jews. But now my kingdom is from another place." (John 18:36) Here is the Lord's own testimony of his kingdom and the difference between it and "this world."

There are several places in Scripture that talk about "physical" versus "spiritual." The two worlds are different, but they aren't found in different parts of the universe. Many people mistake the spiritual kingdom with a place up in the sky, out in deep space, perhaps beyond all the galaxies somewhere; and the physical world is everything on this side of that far-away Heaven. But that can't be right, because the Bible talks of the spiritual world right here amidst the physical world. "The kingdom of God is *near*." (Mark 1:15) "Offer your bodies as living sacrifices … which is your *spiritual* worship." (Romans 12:1) "You do not lack any *spiritual* gift." (1 Corinthians 1:7) "If we have sown *spiritual* seed among you ..." (1 Corinthians 9:11) "They all ate the same *spiritual* food and drank the same *spiritual* drink." (1 Corinthians 10:3-4) "And you who are *spiritual* ..." (Galatians 6:1) From these passages we can conclude that there is a spiritual world, and spiritual realities, that surround us here in this world.

But they are not the same – the physical and the spiritual worlds. Someone can be very much alive physically, and aware of and living fully in *this* world, and know nothing about the spiritual world.

> The man without the Spirit does not accept the things that come from the Spirit of God, for they are foolishness to him, and he cannot understand them, for they are spiritually discerned. (1 Corinthians 2:14)

In fact, someone may know *of* the spiritual world without actually being in it. There are a lot of people in this predicament; they know about God, they know about the Law, and they know about some of the issues of spiritual life and death, but they don't want to deal with it – they stay well back from the edge of this dreaded kingdom.

> This is the verdict: light has come into the world, but men loved darkness instead of light because their deeds were evil. Everyone who does evil hates the light, and will not come into the light for fear that his deeds will be exposed. But whoever lives by the truth comes into the light, so that it may be seen plainly that what he has done has been done through God. (John 3:19-21)

All this is to say that God is working on a spiritual kingdom. The point is that he can do a tremendous amount of work, with a lot of comings and goings and impressive results – and nobody notices because they don't have the spiritual faculties to be aware that anything is going on. It's happening right under their noses and they still can't see it!

God's kingdom is of a purely spiritual nature. It would make an interesting study to find out exactly what the "building blocks" of a spiritual kingdom are; for now, we will look at only a few important items in the inventory. *First,* the key to the spiritual world is the Spirit of God himself. A lot of confusion can be avoided if we center on the work of the Spirit when we refer to "spiritual" things. "Spiritual" doesn't mean anything more or less than whatever the Spirit of God is doing. And what does the Spirit of God do? He brings us to the reality of God, the immediate presence of God. He makes us see the hidden world that this physical world obscures. He parts the curtain of the flesh and walks with us into the throne room of the King. "The Spirit searches all things, even the deep things of God." (1 Corinthians 2:10) Without the Spirit we will never see God.

Second, spiritual realities are actually things about God himself. The Bible constantly refers to God being the very thing that we need spiritually. He is our "refuge" and our "rock" and our "righteousness", and hundreds of other names. When we talk about the strength to live the Christian life, it's God's strength that we really want – not anything that this world offers us. When we want spiritual wisdom – "spiritual words" – it's nothing less than God's wisdom and God's words that we want. You see what God is doing by all this. He is building *himself* into the work so that the whole thing depends completely on him. There's no use building a house from inferior materials! You may as well use the best tools and premium supplies so that it will last and do what it was built to do. Only God, and what he is, can satisfy the needs of the hour.

Third, the work is done in a spiritual way. "Not by might nor by power, but by my Spirit, says the Lord Almighty." (Zechariah 4:6) God scoffs at the way men go about doing work in this world. He does it entirely differently, in ways that we are convinced will never work, and he always succeeds. We terribly underestimate the effectiveness of the spiritual means that God uses to work his wonders:

> For though we live in the world, we
> do not wage war as the world does.

> The weapons we fight with are not weapons of the world. On the contrary, they have divine power to demolish strongholds. (2 Corinthians 10:3-4)

Mighty empires have learned to tremble at the sound of the Word of God, and to fear the legions of humble saints. And well they should, because the people of God have learned how to rely on God's spiritual power and wisdom to overthrow the physical strength and wisdom of this world.

It's an unshakable kingdom. "Therefore, since we are receiving a kingdom that cannot be shaken ..." (Hebrews 12:28) The image of this passage is like shaking a pine tree with snow on the branches; the more that you shake it, the more snow comes off, and you can see more of the green of the tree. This entire passage from Hebrews – 12:25-29 – is talking about the difference between this world and the spiritual kingdom of God. It calls *this* world the "created things" that God will one day "shake" off like snow; it says that the *spiritual* kingdom of God is what "cannot be shaken" and it will remain when this world is gone.

There are some profound truths in this concept. *First*, this world isn't God. Some people don't know that yet. They look to the world for all their fulfillment, as if nature and meat and drink and jobs and sex and fun and excitement is all they need in life. They are dead wrong, and unfortunately they won't find out how wrong they are until God takes it all away in the end. *The world and everything in it is doomed to destruction.* To depend on it in any way is like putting your feet on a slippery rock: when it goes, so will you. (Psalm 73:18-20)

Second, notice who will do the shaking. God will one day undo everything he made in this world. The world of Genesis 1 is going to be torn down again – by its Maker. Does this say anything about his intentions about the purpose of this world? Did he make it to last? Does he share our opinion that we can make a righteous kingdom in this world? Is this where he wants us to build our treasures, our future? Look at it this way: he has already started to pack his belongings, and the house we are living in (the earth, with all its furnishings, and all the circumstances of our lives) is showing signs that he is getting ready to move out. And when he does he's going to burn the place down behind him! I would think that we too ought to be packing for the Big Move, and not be so foolish as to fix up this old place when he has no intention of staying here himself.

Third, only the spiritual world is unshakable. Things last there. God speaks words of comfort and you are comforted forever. God enlightens your mind and the wisdom deepens, enabling you to see more of the truth and to get a better understanding of the Almighty. Spiritual love doesn't cool off like physical love; it wraps around you and holds you and draws you close to God and your brothers and sisters. We only get glimpses of such a life here, because things in this world separate us too often from God and his world, and from our brothers and sisters in the faith; and we have to be content with the hope that *someday* we will come into this world of unmixed and unending joy. That's our hope. That's why we are so willing to let go of this world and all its transitory shadows and empty promises.

It's a virtually unnoticed kingdom. "The kingdom of Heaven is like yeast that a woman took and mixed into a large amount of flour until it worked all through the dough." (Matthew 13:33) If you've ever watched someone make bread you will appreciate the picture that Christ gives us here. At first the yeast doesn't seem to add anything to the dough; there is a faint smell of yeast, but nothing happens when you mix it in. Over an hour or two, though, you begin to see what is happening: the dough balloons out to several times its normal size! This is how God is working now in his kingdom, and his work is the yeast that has been added to our lives here in this world. At first we don't notice anything; but *time* shows results: we always grossly underestimate the power that God unleashed in our lives as we watch the process of spiritual growth.

Jesus also used the picture of a mustard seed, which is one of the smallest seeds that you can plant. At first nobody is impressed; but over time the seed turns into a plant that's not only large but useful. (Matthew 13:31-32) He's making a point that almost everyone misses at first until it hits them later on. *The work of God is always unimpressive at first.* Nobody takes notice. Nobody appreciates the fact that the powers of Heaven have been unleashed in this world and that someday the powers of this world will come crashing down as a result. In order to build a strong building you must start with a few good stones – and those stones may look pretty unimpressive lying there on the bare ground all by themselves. Building takes time, and skillful building takes even longer. But we are too impatient to wait; we want impressive beginnings, expensive and brassy kick-offs, a work that can assure us at the beginning that we've really got something here. People are careful: they don't want to invest in something that's going to fail. But God gives no such assurance; he gives no sign that anything will succeed; in fact, he usually will wait until the conditions are the worst possible that they could be before he begins. The only thing that he offers us in the way of assurance is that *he is doing the work*. That should be enough, but it usually isn't and we turn away looking for something more promising to solve our problems.

For example, how did God make man? From the dust of the earth! An unimpressive beginning for the future ruler of the world! Joseph – the son of Jacob whom his brothers sold as a slave to Midianite traders and who ended up in Egypt on the bottom of the social scale there – in time became the second most powerful man in Egypt for the sake of his people's safety and well-being. Whom did God choose to rule his people Israel? David, the youngest of Jesse's sons, and a surprise choice to everyone including the prophet Samuel. When the political situation in the Middle East hit the boiling point, and Sennacherib's armies showed up in force at Jerusalem's doorstep to finally destroy her, Hezekiah did what nobody would have expected him to do (pray!) – and the supposedly overwhelming enemy was laid low in the dust as a result. And the greatest example of God's strange way of using humble beginnings to bring about earth-shattering results has to be the story of Christ himself.

Did anybody think, at the beginning of these and other examples, that God was taking the right course of action? Did they share in his expectations of success when he started with such unpromising materials? Only a faithful few did, if that; almost everyone else took no notice until the work of God suddenly became so huge and overwhelming that they were swept up into its powerful reality as either its victims or the ones blessed by it.

> The hands of Zerubbabel have laid the foundation of this temple; his hands will also complete it. Then you will know that the Lord Almighty has sent me to you. Who despises the day of small things? Men will rejoice when they see the plumb line in the hand of Zerubbabel. (Zechariah 4:9-10)

Men of discernment will rejoice, that is. Some people know that what God does is never small – it's nothing less than the strength and wisdom of God entering into our lives, and soon things will begin to change. There is no power or wisdom on earth that will stop it or prevent its progress, even though it might look as if God's work can't overcome the circumstances that oppose it. Don't underestimate God's work!

It's a perfect kingdom. "He will wipe every tear from their eyes. There will be no more death or mourning or crying or pain, for the old order of things has passed away." (Revelation 21:4) Sometime you ought to read these last two chapters in Revelation. They describe the new world that God is building right now, that won't be fully revealed until the end of time. Much of it is symbolism, but the symbols point to deep realities that answer fundamental needs in our lives. The overall point of the passage, I believe, is that this kingdom is going to be perfect – in contrast to the world that we live in now.

"Perfection" is a powerful word. In respect to God's kingdom it refers to the fact that everything that *must* be done, *will* be done. All the problems will be solved, the future will be assured, the past will be fully judged, and the present is right on course with the overall plan. In order to have a world like that, the Lord is working right now at building a kingdom from the ground up that won't look at all like this world. We have failed in our attempt to create a perfect world, but he won't in his. He's using stones that will last this time, souls of righteous men made perfect, his own truth to found everything on, his own Son's blood to make everything holy, his own will to guide the future of the kingdom. Instead of relying on, or reusing, anything in this world, he's starting over with materials from Heaven to build a kingdom that John describes as shining "with the glory of God." (Revelation 21:11)

Man has tried over and over again to build a utopia here on earth. The first recorded instance is in Genesis 11:1-9, when they built a city and "a tower that reaches to the Heavens." But their efforts were doomed to fail; they used materials that are entirely unsuitable for making something last forever – in this case, "brick instead of stone, and tar instead of mortar." We are limited in what we can do because the only building materials that we have available are things of this world, things of weakness that were never intended to last forever anyway. Add to that our inclination to sin, and our ignorance, and you can see why we are always doomed to failure when we try to build a society of justice and peace and happiness. We can't do it.

God, however, is doing that very thing right now. He's using building materials that have already proved their worth for saving from sin and death. He's using the Stone that satisfies, the Rock that gives water in the desert, the cornerstone that keeps the rest of the building in perfect alignment, the foundation that supports the whole building. He's building everything on the perfect Son of God and filling the whole building with his presence. It can't fail! The long-sought-for goals of life and righteousness and peace and joy and love will finally be realized, because God is doing this thing right.

The point here is that the Lord is going to succeed where we have failed, simply because he does things only in perfection.

THE LAST DAY

We've already looked at the judgment of God, and that it will be part of the program of the Last Day. But there's more to the Last Day than simply judgment. One gets the idea from reading the Bible that what happens in this world isn't everything that's on God's mind; there's an undercurrent in history that's sweeping all of us along to that Last Day, the day when things will be fully revealed and we will see and understand much more of God's work and ways than we do now. There's a sense of expectation in the Scriptures about this Last Day.

Many people nowadays don't believe in a Last Day. Modern science has influenced the mind of modern man in such a way that he thinks the world has a life of its own, a destiny of self-fulfillment that only eons of time and continual self-development will reveal. He thinks that history is man's story, and we have yet to see the potential that is in him.

People who believe such things couldn't be more wrong. We live in a borrowed world, and we are breathing God's air and eating his food and are living under the shadow of God's unfolding plans. This is *his* world, not ours; he designed it with certain things in mind, and when he accomplishes what he wants with it then he's going to wrap it up and get rid of it like a worn-out coat. (Hebrews 1:10-12) The universe has no other destiny than what God makes of it. History is "his story" – the story of God and his world and his creation man. We should rewrite all of our history books with this in mind, because we've gotten it all wrong so far. Nations rise and fall because it suits his purposes, and civilizations prosper or wither up because he wants them to. Time is *not* open-ended, and history is *not* cyclical (in the sense that it simply revolves around on itself, forever repeating itself) because God never does the same thing twice. This is all a master plan of his, and each moment is a building block in the kingdom of God. We are all in his hand, and the weavings of time are bringing us together into the final work of God that he has been aiming at all along.

The Last Day is the capstone of all his work here. It will make everything plain to us. It's a day of expectation, a day of excitement, like the day a baby is to be born. The Lord is making arrangements right now for that day, and working hard to make the Last Day a day that everyone will remember. It's on the Last Day that his plans and ways and work will be fully revealed and understood by everyone, and his glory will be most fully seen. No wonder he's looking forward to it! No wonder that he's working now to prepare for it. And we can see, if we have eyes to see it, his work of preparation for the Last Day.

The culmination of his work here. "Then the end will come, when he hands over the kingdom to God the Father after he has destroyed all dominion, authority and power. For he must reign until he has put all his enemies under his feet. The last enemy to be destroyed is death." (1 Corinthians 15:24-26) Remember that God takes his work very seriously. The lives of his children are at stake! A good father will throw himself into saving his children if they are in danger, and God our Father knows far better than we do what trouble we sinners are in. When he undertook to rescue us from sin and death, he did it with the love and determination that only a father has.

This passage tells us what he's busy doing right now – destroying everything that has ever set itself up against him. He's setting up his own kingdom where justice prevails, and he's creating a new race of people who will never again succumb to the temptations of sin. We've seen all this before. But what we need to understand is that God really is moving the program on to the finish. It often doesn't look as if he's winning! It usually looks as if the world wins instead of God, and there doesn't seem to be much progress spiritually. Just when we think that the Church has managed to stagger to her feet, something or someone comes along and knocks her sprawling into the dust again. But if you read between the lines, if you have eyes to see, you will find that God is making sure that the victory is his. He's not going to lose this fight.

He leaves little clues laying around that alert us to the fact that he's still in control and the kingdom is growing. The pagans think they are winning; the world is gloating even now about the apparent death of the modern Church. But saints have a way of coming out of the fire stronger than they went into it. For example, take the case of King Solomon. He started out as the favorite son of David, hand-picked by the Lord, and he pleased the Lord mightily by asking for wisdom instead of worldly things. And it looked as if all the predictions about the Son of David were coming true in him. But as he married women from other nations and his heart inclined toward the false gods that these women brought with them, he fell out of favor with God and he started his downhill slide into sin and misery. God's man failed again! But now, after the damage is done and there doesn't seem to be any way of redeeming the situation, Solomon comes back to God's Word and finds a deeper meaning there. Because he lived through the fires of failure, he could write a book like Ecclesiastes. So the failure resulted in a powerful and lasting testimony on the emptiness of this world's pleasures and pastimes – a most valuable book indeed for the rest of us.

The Church itself is a good example of the gradual building of the kingdom. Over the centuries there have been an embarrassing number of fights and quarrels and splits and factions in God's Church, and the world is quick to point to the lack of love in the Church that our Lord warned against. But a longer look will show what has come out of this unpleasant mess: the lines are getting sharper and sharper as to what the truth really is. The only useful feature about heresy (but one that we should appreciate) is that it makes the truth all that much clearer to see. Doctrinally we are much further ahead than the early Church; we have the same Scriptures, but the "false brothers" over the centuries have done us the service of making our understanding of the Scriptures much more certain. (1 Corinthians 11:19)

Little things like these, that hardly anybody notices, show that God is still busy on his project of saving people, and he's getting closer to the end. It isn't safe to predict just how far along he is right now, because we are notoriously short-sighted when it comes to God's works. We don't know if he's about done or whether he has a few centuries to go yet! But the progress ought to be encouraging to us for no other reason than that he's most definitely getting closer to his goal of completing the plan of salvation.

Unveiling the great work. "… into an inheritance that can never perish, spoil or fade – kept in

Heaven for you, who through faith are shielded by God's power until the coming of the salvation that is ready to be revealed in the last time." (1 Peter 1:4-5) What God is doing is still a mystery to the world. Some of us have been given little glimpses ahead of time, and we know what his goal is and something about how he's going about it. We've also been given assurances that he will most definitely finish all his work – nothing is going to stop him. But the whole picture hasn't been seen by man yet, nor by any other creature in the universe. The Lord is keeping it under wraps, like an artist covering his masterpiece, until the Last Day when he will uncover it at last for all to see.

He's careful, as a matter of fact, to keep it under wraps. Who would have thought that a poor man like Jesus would be the Savior of the world? Who would have guessed that his words were "more precious than gold," that we should have taken him much more seriously? Only a few guessed the truth about him; he was determined to "put aside his glory" and stick to the work that he came here to do. The result was that he came and went, and made a big impression on the world, but the total number of saved has only been a small part of the world's population. Unbelievers are still mystified by his humble appearance and his apparent present silence in Heaven!

But that will change. The reason that people haven't seen the glory of Christ is because the Father kept that glory hidden, and is still hiding that glory in many ways, until the Last Day. Then he will take off all the veils that stand between us and Jesus Christ and "every knee will bow ... and every tongue confess that Jesus Christ is Lord." (Philippians 2:10-11) In fact, since Christ is the center of God's work to save us and also to judge the wicked, the major event of the Last Day will be this great unveiling of the Lord Jesus. Many Scriptures tell us of this. The Lord puts great importance on ceremony, because through it he can show what is precious to the Father and how we need to come to Jesus for everything we need. That day will be the highlight of the ceremony of unveiling God's works – he is looking forward to the ceremony of the revelation of his Son with a great deal of anticipation.

Speaking of the coming Judgment Day, Paul says that "This will happen when the Lord Jesus is revealed from Heaven in blazing fire with his powerful angels." (2 Thessalonians 1:7) What was hidden will be hidden no more – to the great distress of unbelievers. Peter refers to the fact that, for now, the glory of Jesus is veiled from human eyes; but "though you have not seen him, you love him; and even though you do not see him now, you believe in him." (1 Peter 1:8) Their faith will prove well founded at the day of the unveiling – "you, who through faith are shielded by God's power until the coming of the salvation that is ready to be revealed in the last time ... when Jesus Christ is revealed." (1 Peter 1:5,7) That will be the day that people everywhere will find out that what they heard about Christ really is true, and they should have taken him more seriously.

There is another thing that God is keeping under wraps right now – judgment.

> But because of your stubbornness and your unrepentant heart, you are storing up wrath against yourself for the day of God's wrath, when his righteous judgment will be revealed. (Romans 2:5-6)

There is trouble brewing right now, and most people aren't even aware of it. In fact nobody knows what God has in store for the Judgment Day. We tend to forget what we do from day to day, unless we let our consciences prick our hearts from time to time. We just don't keep accounts of how we've sinned against God. But he does. Every sin deserves – and will get – the wrath of an offended God; the Law and God's honor will be avenged to the last "jot and tittle." And on the other side of the coin, every act of righteousness and faith gets recorded and a "treasure" is stored up for that person who did it. "God is not unjust; he will not forget your work and the love you have shown him as you have helped his people and continue to help them." (Hebrews 6:10)

But for now all this is hidden. The Lord doesn't write big letters in the sky identifying who his faithful children are – and therefore the world, and even other Christians, may be totally unaware of how blessed and honored these special people are in God's sight. It's rare when God says to a man, "You who are highly esteemed!" (Daniel 10:11) We have true saints in our midst and most of us couldn't pick them out. There are also the damned among us, and they live such successful and pleasant lives that we are fooled about them too. God knows their end, however; we will be surprised at the "good" people who will be missing from the great Banquet at the end of time.

When that end comes, the Lord will slip the veil away from all his work and everyone will immediately understand what he has been doing. The whole thing will make sense then. We will see, which we can't see now, the strong foundation that he has built in Christ and the flimsy waste of the world's appearances that's only worth throwing away. There won't be any more misconceptions, no more longing looks back at the world (like Lot's wife) because everyone will see what the world really is. God's kingdom will shine like the sun, radiant with the person of Christ, and nobody will be fool enough to think that there was any comparison between the two kingdoms.

The war is over. "I will take away the chariots from Ephraim and the war-horses from Jerusalem, and the battle bow will be broken. He will proclaim peace to the nations. His rule will extend from sea to sea and from the River to the ends of the earth." (Zechariah 9:10) Gradually God's kingdom is extending over all the earth. You may say that it doesn't look as though it is! But there are millions from all over the world who will testify that they've come under the banner of the Lord of Hosts. Men and women from every nation, tribe and tongue, from every age in history. The ranks of God's army are swelling every day with new recruits. You may not see many of them; but with a few here and a few there, over the years and in every land, the gradual membership in the Church is growing to an amazing degree.

But the process has been nothing less than a full-scale war. We all started out as sworn enemies of God, determined to fight him and his ways to the death. And he was just as determined to win us over to his side and tear the hands of his enemies away from our souls. It's been a bloody fight, with pain and hardship and wins and losses on both sides. Yes, the world and the devil "win" many times – they manage to keep millions of sinners under the burden of sin, ignorance, and therefore death, which God never did want to happen. And God does "lose" many times, apparently giving the field to the enemy and leaving the Church helpless in a wicked and powerful world.

But the end times will show what really went on in this fierce struggle for men's souls. God never did lose control of things; the "wins" of the enemy will turn out to be hollow victories (after all, what consolation will it be that they have damned souls to share their misery? The rich man saw nothing good in that – Luke 16:27-28) And the "losses" of God will turn out to be stunning strategic maneuvers that brought great blessings. God doesn't really lose! And the devil never really wins! A careful eye will sometimes see that even now, although we have to confess that there are many situations that we don't understand how God will ever redeem his honor and bless his people out of what is going on. Faith knows that

God will win – he *is* winning – and there's no question as to the outcome of things.

But we won't always be at war. The day is coming when we will lay our weapons down beside the Lord's weapons, because there will be no more need of them. That's the goal that God is working toward right now. He is skillfully forcing his enemies into a corner where they can't get out. When the time is right, he will make the last move and they will be trapped – and doomed. Their end will be swift and sudden and entirely just. Just pray that you aren't in that corner when he moves in for the kill!

The end result will be that God will rule over all the universe to the praise and glory of every creature in the universe. He is king now, but few men bow to him as king. But in that day they will all bow to him. The wicked will bow to take their punishment, and the righteous will bow to receive their reward and their eternal life with him. There won't be any more breaking of his Law. Everyone will obey him, everyone will honor him (after their fashion, that is – those in Hell will be a continual witness to his justice), and his will shall extend over the whole kingdom as it should have done in the beginning of time.

> For to us a child is born, to us a son is given, and the government will be on his shoulders. And he will be called Wonderful Counselor, Mighty God, Everlasting Father, Prince of Peace. Of the increase of his government and peace there will be

> no end. He will reign on David's throne and over his kingdom, establishing and upholding it with justice and righteousness from that time on and forever. The zeal of the LORD Almighty will accomplish this. (Isaiah 9:6-7)

Notice the last sentence. This refers to the fact that the Lord is right now working hard to bring an end to this war and establish the eternal kingdom of Christ. And when God wants to do something, it's going to get done! And it *is* getting done!

The highest glory. "Praise be to the LORD God, the God of Israel, who alone does marvelous deeds. Praise be to his glorious name forever; may the whole earth be filled with his glory. Amen and Amen." (Psalm 72:18-19) This is a prayer that David lifted up to Heaven, with the hope (and prophetic insight) that it would someday be fulfilled.

Glory, as we've seen before, means "who gets the credit." God wants all the credit, of course, because he's responsible for this whole matter of Christianity in the first place. If it works, it's simply because God does it! We can't claim any of the credit, and we don't want other people to think that our strength or wisdom saved us or blessed us.

At least we *shouldn't* want other people to think so; too often we fail to draw their attention to God, and instead we focus on ourselves. We do like to think, once in a while, that we aren't complete fools and we have a bit of savvy about life. Yes, God is involved in our lives, we say; but look at how diligent I am! Look at how careful I am to stay holy. Look at my good intentions to others who need help. Look at my willingness to help in the church. Look – at *me*.

Now you would expect the unbelievers to talk like this, but not God's own children. They of all people should realize that "only God is good." (Matthew 19:17) Only he has wisdom. Whatever we have is borrowed from God. If it weren't for him we would die! "All who go down to the dust will kneel before him – those who cannot keep themselves alive." (Psalm 22:29) It's foolish for us to think that we can live a minute apart from God's direct intervention in our lives.

Therefore, we owe him the credit for everything. We ought to be drawing people's attention to God, not to ourselves. We ought to be pointing out what it is about God that so blesses us and lifts us up in times of trouble. Others should be getting a lesson on the works of God, and they should know something new about God after they've been around us.

Is this happening? Sad to say, it rarely happens. God almost never gets credit for things. But there's no need to feel sorry for him because he's storing all this away for the Last Day. He is determined not to miss out on a single bit of his credit! That day will be an amazing sight when he unrolls the annals of history for a complete analysis and holds up every single thing that he was responsible for. He will then get the glory for it all. Everyone will know then that he was guiding everyone's lives to the last detail, and all of history too.

The fullness of time. "... to be put into effect when the times will have reached their fulfillment – to bring all things in Heaven and on earth together under one head, even Christ." (Ephesians 1:10) There's an important characteristic about how God works, one that we too often ignore but we can't afford to ignore. That is this issue of *time*. He almost never does things immediately – that is, in split seconds. He almost always works over periods of time, some short and some long. It's not as if he can't snap his fingers and the thing would happen! He can do anything he likes in that regard. But what he prefers to do, as a matter of fact, is to stretch his work out over intervals of time.

There are reasons for this. One important reason is so that we have a chance to see him at work. If he did snap his fingers the action would be over long before we could get our eyes on it! How much praise would he get from us if we hadn't any notion of what he did? Another reason is that he's using these periods of time, the slow development of circumstances, to test and strengthen our faith. Peter says that trials "have come so that your faith – of greater worth than gold, which perishes even though refined by fire – may be proved genuine and may result in praise, glory and honor when Jesus Christ is revealed." (1 Peter 1:7) A third reason that he takes his time doing things is so that we will have a chance to see, believe, and get ourselves in line with his will. What if he impatiently did everything in split nanoseconds and, disgusted with us because we didn't immediately respond, destroyed us all? Thank God that he is more patient than that! "The Lord is not slow in keeping his promise, as some understand slowness. He is patient with you, not wanting anyone to perish, but everyone to come to repentance." (2 Peter 3:9)

So when he works in this world, expect it to take time. The thing unfolds gradually. At first the world presents insuperable problems, and the stakes are high. Then as God moves in slowly, he begins to do the impossible: a piece here, a stepping point there, some light coming on, a little hope, another setback, more work and pushing back the enemy, and then the final success when he breaks through with his healing grace. It's marvelous to watch the Master at work. He's always in control, always at peace about the situation, and always sure of where he is going even if nobody else is.

This means one thing for us: *wait on him*. He'll get there; just give him time. He knows best what you need and when you need it. This is like a giant and complex tapestry that he's weaving; he's not only trying to get you saved but many others as well, and some of those other people interconnect with your life. It's all a very complex affair and you have to give him time to make the right moves when the time comes.

We will all realize at the end of time how wise it was to wait on God. We will see then, at

What are the Works of the Lord?

the unveiling of his works, that every step along the path of our lives was necessary and well thought out. The lives of all human beings, the history of all nations, the powers of the air and the ground that we walk on, will testify to the awesome wisdom and power that God displayed in bringing it all into a harmonious whole at the Last Day.

Time, then, will be done with. He will have accomplished his purposes and there won't be the need to hold anybody in suspense any more. His blessings will become immediate blessings (instead of withheld ones) and his will shall be done immediately (instead of delayed responses). There won't be a gradual unfolding of his glory because we shall all see his full glory. But none of this is true right now, because this is still the era of time in God's scheme of things.

A whole new mode of existence. "'There will be no more death or mourning or crying or pain, for the old order of things has passed away.' He who was seated on the throne said, 'I am making everything new!' " (Revelation 21:4-5) When it comes to describing what it will be like to live after the end of time, we simply have to drop back to a lot of negatives: no more death, no more tears, no more sin and suffering, no more darkness. Since we've been living in this world all of our lives, it's difficult (sometimes impossible!) to imagine what a completely different world would be like.

Maybe you've been like me and gone outside and looked up into the clouds. Maybe you have imagined that day when Jesus will show up again in those clouds, there where the whole world can see him, and he will call us up through the air to the Judgment throne of God to receive our just rewards. That will be a terrifying day, a thrilling day, a day that is beyond our comprehension. And God will call his children to his feet and transform them into citizens of the Heavenly Jerusalem. What will that be like? What will we feel and think? I'm afraid the story stops here because mortal man doesn't have the words to express the glories of Heaven.

Whatever that existence will be like, that's what God is putting together right now for his people. Life may be sheer drudgery in this world, but rest assured that you have a home in Heaven where Jesus has gone ahead to prepare it for you. (John 14:2-3) Whatever it is, it will far outweigh anything you had to put up with here. "For our light and momentary troubles are achieving for us an eternal glory that far outweighs them all." (2 Corinthians 4:17)

Words may fail us when we want to know what it is like in Heaven, but the Word doesn't fail to encourage us with the hope of that life. "No eye has seen, no ear has heard, no mind has conceived what God has prepared for those who love him – but God has revealed it to us by his Spirit." (1 Corinthians 2:9-10) We can read about what it's like to live with God, and what he intends to bless his people with. We can also taste (a far cry from the feast that awaits us there, but precious nevertheless) the reality of the presence of God, though we find that our feet are still firmly planted in this dark world. In many ways God is preparing us for that new kind of life.

It's a shame that we don't take it more seriously. Too often we live as if *this* world is more important, that our affairs here require our constant attention. That's a serious misconception. "If only for this life we have hope in Christ, we are to be pitied more than all men." (1 Corinthians 15:19) Our home is *not* here. "They are not of the world any more than I am of the world." (John 17:14) Our attention should be on the *next* world, not this one.

> They admitted that they were aliens and strangers on earth. People who say such things show that they are looking for a country of their own. If they had been thinking of the country they had left, they would have had opportunity to return. Instead, they were longing for a better country – a Heavenly one. Therefore God is not ashamed to be called their God, for he has prepared a city for them. (Hebrews 11:13-16)

Such is our hope. It gives the child of God great encouragement to know that his Father is preparing this strange and wonderful life for him. Things will be different there, and they will be satisfying, and they will be eternal. The Lord has the wisdom and the ability to bless far beyond our comprehension – he "is able to do immeasurably more than all we ask or imagine." (Ephesians 3:20) And that's precisely what he is doing right now: preparing that "immeasurably more" for his people.

SCRIPTURE

We need to look at one last thing about the works of God – the Bible itself. It's nothing less than a miracle that we have the Word of God in our hands. You may not know about the history of the book itself, but it has been through millions of hands over thousands of years – and still it claims to be the very Word of God. How such a precious treasure from Heaven has survived the ravages of time and men's sins makes a fascinating story, but we can only tell a little bit of it here.

The Scriptures are the truth of God put into the words of men, so that they can have the opportunity to know the Lord. **Knowledge** is the key word; in order to understand something and take advantage of its benefits, one must first start with learning all about it. The Bible is just that – a source book for data on God. But it's more than just data, because as you read it the Spirit brings you into God's presence and you become convinced of the truth that you are reading. The spiritual words take on spiritual shape, and your faith takes hold of the hope offered to you in the words. So the knowledge that the Bible gives you is *spiritual knowledge*: facts that draw you to God, that impress you with his reality, that convey the necessary wisdom and strength to obey God and trust him. These words do what God sends them to do: they save the soul and woo the heart away from the world toward Heaven. They have a cutting edge that trims the sin from our souls, and they strengthen feeble arms and weak knees.

The words of men don't have the same effect that the Word of God has. Nobody was ever saved or helped spiritually apart from the Scriptures, because God speaks creative and healing and saving words that meet our deepest needs. Touch the hem of *this* garment and you will be healed of whatever is wrong with you, even when dozens of "physicians" of this world haven't been able to help you.

With such a power to save, it isn't any wonder that God has worked hard to preserve the Bible for each succeeding generation. He wants to make sure that we have within our reach the necessary truth to understand him. He will never leave himself no witness on the earth, even though it may be difficult for us to find with the world fighting us the way that it does. Somewhere, through someone, he preserves his truth; you can count on it. Even in the worst circumstances of history, there have been a faithful few entrusted with his precious truth who have stood in the gap and kept the truth pure for the next generation. And if you read about what many of them had to suffer in order to preserve the truth, you might be surprised that the Bible has survived at all – but it's all due to God's careful diligence.

> ***Preserve the truth for his people.*** The reason that God has been personally involved with progress of the Bible over the millennia is so that he might keep his truth intact for each generation. This is precious treasure! Men can live by these words – live forever, in the Temple of God, in holiness. These words are a sure guide to the commandments of God – what he expects from men, and what they must do if they want to please him. These words guide a sensitive soul through the darkness and the traps of this world. These words shut the mouths of the enemy. These words record what God has promised to do for us, like a signed contract that we can claim in our need. For as potentially life-changing as this book is, it's a

mercy that God is determined to preserve it for all of us. It is the same truth in all ages.

So you will find that the Lord will go to great pains to preserve his truth. You will find that, though the Bible has had a checkered history, the truth has always remained the same over thousands of years. You can see the same God in Genesis as you will find in Revelation. You will read about the same ways of God in the modern German Bible as you would in early Coptic versions. The words are different from language to language, and there are many existing Greek and Hebrew manuscripts around that don't exactly match each other, but the same God with the same characteristics and the same demands are in all of them. God has preserved his truth in such a wonderful way that the Bible is the best-preserved ancient document in the world.

People often scoff at the idea of taking the Old Testament seriously because they don't think that it truly portrays the Father of our Lord Jesus Christ. But the miraculous preservation of the Old Testament is a testimony against that. God wants us to read the Old Testament because it *does* teach us faithfully about him; he kept this book intact in order to preserve the *truth* about him. You will find the writers of the New Testament relying heavily on the teachings of the Old because they believe it to be what it claims to be – the very Word of God. And what they believed in, we can believe in too because we have the *same book* that they read and trusted.

This brings up another point, that the truth doesn't change over the years. It's remarkable how men have come up with ignorant notions about how God changes, how his truth changes from generation to generation. "Just get the spirit of the text for our time – the literal words were only for those older generations," they tell us. But that again is easily disproved by the fact that God preserved his Word exactly the way it was in the past, and he presents this "ancient" document to *us* so that we might accept it with childlike faith. What Moses knew God to be, that is the same God that we have.

Original revelation. The Church has always believed in the complete trustworthiness of the original revelation of God – the words spoken by God to the Apostles and prophets. It came in different forms and in different situations, depending on where you read in the Bible. Moses received much of God's revelation on Mt. Sinai, and he wrote most of it down later. Zechariah had visions. The Apostles watched and heard Jesus when he lived with them and later wrote down what they had seen and heard. Paul received his revelation directly as he was writing letters to the churches. John saw visions on the Isle of Patmos. In all cases, though, the men involved heard the very words of God – either by ear or in the heart – and that's exactly what they passed on to others.

The point is that what those men first heard was really the Word of God. There are many today who don't believe that; they think that God was certainly involved in some sort of learning experience with the men in the Bible, but it isn't necessary to say that these are words directly from Heaven. They feel that, just as those older generations found a way to "express their faith" in God, we can do the same in our own time, in our own ways – and not necessarily as the Bible says it either. *That's dead wrong.* The Lord knows what men will come up with when he lets them try to figure things out on their own, especially with matters that deal with the spiritual world. They'll come up with no good! Their hearts are inclined toward evil, away from God – even the best of men can't be trusted to write something down that the whole Church down through thousands of years will learn from. So the Lord took great pains to get the truth *as he himself sees it* into the hands of the Biblical writers. He used different methods of doing that, and a writer may not have been fully aware of how God was directing his thoughts; but we can rest assured that the Lord was fully satisfied with the results. The Scripture is exactly what God would have said if he would have come down here personally, gathered us all around, and – speaking in our language – explained his truth to us all.

Preservation. Unfortunately we don't know the exact words of the original revelation now. Through the thousands of years of copying and translating, our text has changed slightly. And we no longer have the original manuscripts in our hands; they've been lost or destroyed and we have no hope of ever finding them again. That's probably just as well, because people would probably worship them if we did. But the differences in the existing manuscripts are so slight that we can still trust them completely as the

Word of God. A "the" missing here, a couple of words turned around there, a vowel that may or may not be right – that's all that the problem about textual evidence is. Actually the Bible is in a better state of preservation than any other ancient book of literature; Homer's *Iliad*, for example, which we also don't have the original for, is hopelessly varied in all its surviving manuscripts; they differ significantly from each other.

But that's characteristic of the way God works in this world. Whatever he does, he brings together the spiritual *and* the physical in a way that the spiritual overrides the obvious defects of the physical. We can see that in all sorts of places. In this example, we believe that the Bible is truly the Word of God even though it's recorded in human words, been written on paper, been copied and tampered with at times, stuck on dusty bookshelves and ignored or mistreated, and translated into many languages of men.

When you consider the history of the Bible you have to stand amazed at God's wonderful Providence in preserving its accuracy. Some of these books go back almost 4000 years! They started out as family stories, got written down at some point, and were copied and recopied and recopied countless times. Cities burned, peoples were destroyed and deported to other lands, accidents happened – all the major and minor circumstances of a people and their land occurred time and time again through millennia. The books passed perhaps through the hands of hundreds of thousands of people. Copyists got tired, bored, or careless, and some (especially in the New

Testament times) weren't necessarily interested in the work that they were doing.

"Books" were actually dried sheepskin, strips of papyrus reeds glued together, or stone or clay tablets. "Pens" were slotted sticks dipped in homemade ink. They didn't have the luxury of printing presses, remember! It took a long time to copy a single book of the Bible, let alone the whole thing – and even then you would only have one copy. Then you would have to start again to make another copy. It was very difficult and tedious work.

But usually the men who made the copies of Scripture were very careful about what they were doing. Providentially the Jews were especially careful with the Old Testament – which is good, because it had to last for a longer time than the New Testament. They even got down to counting letters to make sure that the books they finished were as accurate as possible!

Now consider what God has done in this matter of preservation. Through the difficult work of making books in the old days, through the various ways that books were taken care of (or not taken care of!), through thousands of years and many lands and cultures, the Lord brought a single book through all these experiences for our personal use today. The feat is simply staggering. We don't appreciate what we have in our hands – the time and work and blood and skill and tears and prayers and care that this single book represents.

Translation. Translation is a tricky business at best. We don't speak the original languages (for better or worse!) and therefore we need to have the Scriptures translated into the language that we use. You realize, I hope, that the Old Testament was first written in Hebrew and the New Testament in Greek. English is a fairly recent invention! The languages that the Biblical writers wrote in are long gone to us, and now we have this awesome job on our hands of putting eternal truth into English.

It's not at all easy. There are two elements to a language that one must keep in mind while translating: the literal meanings of the words, and idiom. All languages are a mixture of the two. The "literal meaning" is precisely what the word means, which can be difficult to discover when one is dealing with a language that isn't spoken anymore. The "idiom" in a language is the way people put words together to make meanings different from the literal meanings of the words involved. For example, if I would say "Let's run down to the store" I probably don't mean that we should literally *run* nor is the store necessarily *down* from us. It's just the way we say things; it's a meaning that is different from the literal words used. A good translation will take both things in mind when dealing with Greek and Hebrew passages, because both elements of language are there.

All in all, translations have been fairly good throughout history. There have been a few bad ones; most are all right but with a few questionable areas; and some have been superlative. But there has always been something deeper running throughout the translation of the Scriptures – the presence of God's Spirit overseeing the process. In almost any Bible that you pick up you will be able to read the truth of God in a way that he will truly speak to your soul.

Every translation will show you what God's commands are, in a way that you are responsible for what you heard. Every translation will show you the person and work of Christ so that you can believe and be saved. Some translations may provide more stumbling blocks as far as exact doctrinal formulas, but they will nevertheless get the sense of the truth of God through to you. Do you think that's an accident? NO! God is working in his Church in many ways, and the translation of his Word is one important way. He wants to make sure that men and women hear the truth in their own languages – and his truth is simple enough that a translator would have to be deliberately twisting the passage in order to obscure God's meaning, at least when it comes to matters of faith and practice.

This doesn't mean that you can fully trust any translation that you pick up. If you don't have a translation that you feel comfortable with, get a more experienced Christian friend to recommend one to you. My point is that we needn't be alarmed by the wails of the purists who complain about a particular translation's weak points. Most likely your translation is successfully presenting you with God's truth. If you have need of a version for exacting scholarly work, then you shouldn't be relying on translations anyway – you should be using the Greek and Hebrew originals!

Defense against attacks. Satan, from the very beginning of the world, cast doubt on God's Word. "Did God really say …?" Well he's been at it again in our own generation, and it looks as if he has managed to convince many people in the Church that the Bible isn't as dependable as past generations naively thought.

God doesn't need defending; he's big enough to take care of himself, and he will when the time comes. But when someone is spreading lies and you have people around you who might believe those lies, it's time to stand up and call that liar down. And that's precisely what we have on our hands right now. Even Christians are saying that some of the Bible is untrustworthy, that it doesn't really mean what it says. That's a sign that the enemy has slipped into our midst and is turning the minds and hearts of God's people away from his truth.

Our particular problem started with German liberalism, which spread like wildfire through Europe and England and finally to our own shores. It prides itself on being rational, on being sensible, and it holds man up as a responsible creature who can think and act on his own. They tell us that we don't have much need for the Word of God, and it certainly is embarrassing to bring this ancient and outmoded book into the picture. Let's carve out our destiny "with God's help" according to the image of goodness and justice that's in our own minds. We know what we need; we don't need to be told.

You may not realize it but this clever attack has shaken the modern Church to her roots. It was well-timed – it exactly coincided with man's new powers in science which offered him a rational explanation of the world and tools to put everything to the test. Now our generation doesn't need God at all! Everything in life can be explained in terms of our own understanding and analysis, including religious affairs. The faithful few in the Church have been struggling usually unsuccessfully against this massive tidal wave of unbelief. What has usually happened, with a few exceptions, is that the defenders have themselves turned their weapons over to the enemy and ceased to fight; they see no reason to, and their own arguments appear silly now.

But even though the situation is alarming, this is still no problem to God. He's seen this kind of thing before and he can handle our modern unbelief just as easily as he handled massive problems in other times. What he will do is not argue the case with the unbelievers, but simply put a childlike faith in the hearts of his people. They will once again believe in the simple meaning of the Bible! This is all that it will take to turn the tide; the enemy will become furious when we lift up the "shield of faith" (Ephesians 6:16) and he will have to shift tactics completely. (There's no rest in this war!)

Keep your eyes open for this sign of God's working. When he awakens Christians' hearts to the need for taking the Bible seriously and they actually start living by what the book says, simply trusting God to do the impossible, then things will begin happening. It will certainly take an act of God to get people to trust in the Word for a change! But when they do, the promises of God will come true and we will see the power of God working in our lives again. We will be able to testify that, indeed, what God has done in the past, he has begun to do in our day as well. (Habakkuk 3:2) The Bible will once again become a precious resource to us.

The Lord's Works reveal him

As soon as a human being is born, he or she finds out that life is a learning process. We don't have to learn everything – some things, providentially, are built into our instincts or we would die immediately! But there is much to learn in this life if we want to take advantage of the opportunities around us. So growing up is a continuous school, in which we learn how to please our elders and how to use the world to our advantage and how to fit into society.

Unfortunately our educational systems stop at a certain point. Since school quits after the twelfth grade, people get the idea that they can stop learning then. Some go on to college and perhaps get graduate degrees; but still they get to the point where they are satisfied with how much they have learned and then they stop. Maybe they feel that they've paid their dues, that they don't need to learn anymore, that it's time now to use what they've learned and finally put together the life they've been dreaming about all these years. Some studies have discovered that the majority of college graduates never read a book again in their lives!

Aside from the fact that this mentality doesn't fit in with the real world, it has unfortunately infected the Church. Children learn, but adults are done with learning. The year or so after someone becomes a Christian was a time of accelerated learning, but soon the old attitude of "I don't have to study now" takes over and he settles down satisfied with the little he knows already. Sermons are OK as long as they don't demand too much concentration and thinking. The kind of Bible studies that we like are "discussion groups" – no studying, no thinking, just throwing ideas and opinions around. The end result of all this, as you can imagine, is that the pool of spiritual knowledge in an average group of Christians is about the equivalent of a second grade level of education.

As you know, a second grade education isn't enough to make it in the physical world. Neither is it sufficient in the spiritual world. We need constant information and we need continuous training in order to survive the battle for our souls. We've got to learn as much as we can, and we've got to use what we learn, or we are going to be at the mercy of powers who are not at all friendly to us. Christians despair too, and live in "great frustration, affliction, and anger" (Ecclesiastes 5:17) simply because they've stopped far short of the study and learning that it takes to live the successful Christian life.

This is a long introduction to the point of the present lesson: that we need to study God himself. Knowledge of God will enable you to ...

> ... live a life worthy of the Lord and may please him in every way: bearing fruit in every good work, growing in the knowledge of God, being strengthened with all power according to his glorious might so that you may have great endurance and patience ... (Colossians 1:10-11)

The more we study him, the clearer this Christianity business gets, and the better able we are to glorify him with whatever we do and say. The Bible teaches this fundamental truth over and over again. God knows that we need to know more about him; he shakes his head over our broken and senseless lives and says ...

> My people are destroyed from lack of knowledge. Because you have rejected knowledge, I also reject you as my priests; because you have ignored the Law of your God, I also will ignore your children. (Hosea 4:6)

The knowledge that we need to have about God isn't far away or hard to get. You don't need a degree from college; you don't have to have an IQ over 120; you don't have to offer sacrifices on an altar to please him. The material that you need to study is actually all around you, free for picking up and examining!

> For since the creation of the world God's invisible qualities – his eternal power and divine nature – have been clearly seen, being understood from what has been made, so that men are without excuse. (Romans 1:20)

Paul is including everyone here, the young and old and the wise and ignorant. Anyone can begin learning about God – at least, the data is there, even if they don't feel inclined to begin studying it. When you get done looking through creation for information about what God is like, you can move on to the recorded history of his acts and learn a tremendous amount about him –

> We must pay more careful attention, therefore, to what we have heard ... This salvation, which was first announced by the Lord, was confirmed to us by those who heard him. God also testified to it by signs, wonders and various miracles, and gifts of the Holy Spirit distributed according to his will. (Hebrews 2:1,3-4)

Here are whole libraries of data about God and his works. John once said that "Jesus did many other things as well. If every one of them were written down, I suppose that even the whole world would not have room for the books that would be written." (John 21:25)

It's plain to see, once you get into study mode, that the works of the Lord reveal who he is. They tell us all sorts of things about him. We can learn doctrine about God – simple statements about his nature, like "God is Spirit" – but to see that doctrine plainly in something that he does in this world has a way of impressing it on our minds and bolstering our faith in him. God has always had witnesses of his works for a good reason: witnesses tell us what they saw him do, and they interpret that work for us so that we can see what our God is like.

What we want to do now, then, is to find out what it means that God's works reveal him.

HIS WORKS REVEAL HIS PRESENCE

It's one thing to talk about God from what you've heard; it's another thing entirely to talk about him from experience. The difference between a Christian and a non-Christian is that the Christian has met Jesus personally; he knows that Jesus lives, that Jesus is the King, simply because he has met him. Christ is no storybook character to us! We talk to him when we pray; he speaks to us from his Word; he guides our steps in our lives; he rebukes us through our consciences for sinning against him and others. As Paul describes it, we are "alive to God in Christ Jesus." (Romans 6:11) Conversion put the Spirit of life in our dead souls and now we can know God and sense his presence. God's world shouldn't be a mystery to us anymore.

But it too often *is* a mystery to us. Our sin and our ignorance of God's ways still make the picture fuzzy. You would think that simply being a Christian enables us to know everything about God and what he's doing – but that idea underestimates the power of the dark world that we are living in and the degree of training we've already had in the ways of sin. We can't expect to live all of our lives in the dark and then, once we have our eyes open to see light, understand everything in God's spiritual world. This learning and training phase is going to take time.

So we need to find out how we can tell when God is near. He's different from anybody else, you know; when he's close by, men fear and mountains melt and angels worship and enemies run away. His presence is like a perfume lingering in the air, a telltale evidence that he's near. He leaves footprints wherever he goes, footprints of a nature that nobody else can make; with a little bit of training and experience we can identify his tracks and can tell what he has been doing.

What do we mean, then, when we say that his works reveal his presence?

> **He does exist!** "'Surely the Lord is in this place, and I was not aware of it.' He was afraid and said, 'How awesome is this place! This is none other than the house of God; this is the gate of Heaven.'" (Genesis 28:16-17) Jacob was shaken to his roots. He had heard about God from his father Isaac, but now he just saw this God face to face and God had spoken directly to him. Suddenly the old stories took on an unexpected reality.
>
> This is probably man's deepest problem. His isolation from God is tragic and devastating.

Adam certainly was made with the ability to know God as easily as he could feel cold and heat, but when he fell into sin he carried all of us into a dark, black kingdom where none of us can see out into God's light. We have lost that original spiritual sense, the "sixth" sense of the soul, and the result has killed us. We can take up the deadly ways of sin and never give it a single thought, whereas the angels shudder at the thought of angering God in any way. We've immersed ourselves in death, always deceiving ourselves into thinking that "this is really living!" We will gladly trade the riches of eternal Heaven for the worthless baubles of this world. We are blind fools, lost in our own darkness and resentful of anybody who tries to help us out of our screwed up lives.

So the first thing on God's agenda when he comes to work in our world is to make us aware of the fact that he is real. It comes as such a shock, it's so contrary to our previous experience in the world, that it's appropriately called "being born again." He forces us to see him, to become aware of him, to fear him. He calls us to him like a subject to his king – this king that we've heard about from far away places but now he's come here to our home – and his voice penetrates into the darkness of our hearts where no light has ever been before. Anybody who has ever seen God has never forgotten the experience.

A few examples from Scripture. At 80 years of age, Moses suddenly found himself face to face with the God that he had learned about when a child. God was beginning a work that would save Israel from the oppression of Pharaoh, and Moses was going to be instrumental in that work. But God never gives his work over to humans to do; he wants to do it himself, and that means that he's going to come on earth to do it. "So God looked on the Israelites and was concerned about them." (Exodus 2:25) He drew Moses into the wilderness and through the burning bush spoke directly to the man. "At this, Moses hid his face, because he was afraid to look at God." (Exodus 3:6)

Solomon had instructions from his father David on how to build a Temple for the Lord, and he utilized thousands of people and pulled resources from other nations around Israel in order to do the job right. It was seven years in the making. When they were done, the priests gathered together to offer sacrifices to God and Solomon prayed on behalf of all the people that God would own the work that they had been doing. He knew his God, of course; he was careful to do everything in strict accord to God's instructions in the Law and from his father David. Then the Lord answered Solomon's prayer – and showed the people that this temple and what was going to happen in it really was a work of God himself – by showing up in person at the ceremony!

> Then the temple of the LORD was filled with a cloud, and the priests could not perform their service because of the cloud, for the glory of the LORD filled the temple of God. (2 Chronicles 5:13-14)

He also showed up in person before Solomon in a vision. (2 Chronicles 7:12) It confirmed to Solomon that God really was involved in the setting up of the Temple.

Just one more example. When the disciples and Jesus were crossing the Sea of Galilee in their ship, a storm came up and threatened to capsize them into the water. In alarm the disciples woke Jesus and begged him to do something to save them. I don't know what they expected him to do, but his next act startled them!

> He got up, rebuked the wind and said to the waves, "Quiet! Be still!" Then the wind died down and it was completely calm. He said to his disciples, "Why are you so afraid? Do you still have no faith?" They were terrified and asked each other, "Who is this? Even the wind and the waves obey him!" (Mark 4:39-41)

They were suddenly aware that they were in the presence of God.

Whenever God works in this world, he's going to make sure that people know it's really him. There won't be any mistaking him when he does show up in person; there's only one God and there's no way to hide him. Deists believe that God runs the world by proxy – that is, he has others do his work for him. But what a surprise they get when he shows up personally to do the work himself! That gets people's attention! It charges the atmosphere right away; we get the feeling that things are going to happen now, like breaking loose a logjam and getting on with the job. His presence gives hope to the faint-hearted and makes sinners fear for their lives. Even a despairing and defeated army will suddenly come to life when their general comes to personally lead them back into battle.

The miraculous happens. "John the Baptist sent us to you to ask, 'Are you the one who was to come, or should we expect someone else?'" (Luke 7:20) These disciples of John the Baptist was asking Jesus if he was the Messiah that the Old Testament predicted. The Jews had been putting all their hope in the Messiah who would come, and people were starting to wonder if Jesus was the one. Hear his answer to their question:

> At that time Jesus cured many who had diseases, sicknesses and evil spirits, and gave sight to many who were blind. So he replied to the messengers, "Go back and report to John what you have seen and heard: The blind receive sight, the lame walk, those who have leprosy are cured, the deaf hear, the dead are raised, and the good news is preached to the poor. Blessed is the man who does not fall away on account of me." (Luke 7:21-23)

Here's proof, Jesus said, that I am the Messiah: I do the miraculous. I do the impossible. No man can do what I do. You know that God is at work among you by what you see and hear.

God has always majored on the impossible. God isn't interested in doing what man can do, because the job to be done is far and away more than man can handle. Sin must be dealt with, death must be destroyed, hardened hearts won over to the Lord's side, a spiritual kingdom to be made out of sinners – this is all clearly out of the range of man's capabilities. In fact, the disciples once despaired of any of these things actually happening because they saw the immense and seemingly unsolvable problems that were in the way. "The disciples were even more amazed, and said to each other, 'Who then can be saved?'" (Mark 10:26) But Jesus immediately answered, "With man this is impossible, but not with God; all things are possible with God." (Mark 10:27)

You know that God is involved in something when things work against all odds. Joseph hadn't a breath of a chance when his brothers sold him as a slave, bound for Egypt. Who would have thought that in a few years the boy would be ruling the country under Pharaoh, and that he really would be the salvation of his family as his childhood dreams predicted? Only God could have done that. Who would have thought that the mighty fortified city of Jericho would collapse at the mere sound of the shouts of the Israelites? That was a sign that the Israelites' God was fighting for them. Who would have imagined that David, a shepherd boy out on the hills behind Bethlehem, unknown to the outside world, would one day be the king and the forerunner of the Messiah? God alone brings the right people out of the woodwork when the time is right.

God has done even more amazing things. He literally pulls victory out of defeat. When Jesus died on the cross, his enemies knew that they finally had seen the end of him. There was no way that this "troublemaker" could ever hurt them again. But they didn't know much about the miraculous power and wisdom of God. Not only did Jesus' death buy the redemption of God's people, not only did he rise from the grave never to die again, but he rules now over those who nailed him on that cross. And consider the testimony of the Apostle Paul:

> But we have this treasure in jars of clay to show that this all-surpassing power is from God and not from us. We are hard pressed on every side, but not crushed; perplexed, but not in despair; persecuted, but not abandoned; struck down, but not destroyed. We always carry around in our body the death of Jesus, so that the life of Jesus may also be revealed in our body. For we who are alive are always being given over to death for Jesus' sake, so that his life may be revealed in our mortal body. So then, death is at work in us, but life is at work in you. (2 Corinthians 4:7-12)

In spite of the terrible persecution of the Christians, all the way from the Apostles to our own day, the Church of God continues to grow and thrive. You would have thought that the combined efforts of centuries of determined sinners would have stamped out all traces of Christianity and the Bible by now. But the impossible continues to happen, because God is doing this.

In fact, Abraham found out that the definition of faith is just that: *trusting God to do the impossible*. When God promises us something (in Abraham's case, a son) it's always in context of our total inability to do it ourselves (Abraham and Sarah were too old by scores of years to have children), and he considers our faith in him to do it anyway as righteousness – he's very pleased with us, in other words, when we wait on him for his miracle.

It answers the need. "Don't be deceived, my dear brothers. Every good and perfect gift is from above, coming down from the Father of the Heavenly lights, who does not change like shifting shadows." (James 1:16-17) Compared to what man gives, God's gifts are the only valuable things in the entire universe. They are worth more than whole worlds; a man would do well to "sell all that he has and buy" what God has to offer. (Matthew 13:46) Now just imagine, if the things of God's kingdom are so amazingly valuable, the staggering thought that God *gives* all these riches to his children. Free! And he doesn't hold back the most of it, only giving us a little bit and keeping the rest for himself; it's all ours for the asking.

Men have gone in search of many schemes to satisfy life's difficult problems. They've looked everywhere for a way to live forever, a fountain of youth that will erase the stains of age and pain. They ponder deep mysteries and try to solve the questions "Who are we, and what are we doing here?" They amass wealth, undertake great projects, and become greater than all who have gone before them – and still there is something deep in the heart that isn't satisfied. The basic needs haven't been met yet. One of the surest signs that God isn't providing for you is that what you have in life isn't helping the problems in your heart.

God, however, gives in order to satisfy. When he heals an old wound, there aren't any scars and there aren't any bad memories. When he dries your tears, he doesn't want to see you crying anymore! The woman with a twelve year hemorrhage found this out when she turned to Jesus for healing. All the doctors that she had seen weren't able to help her; but simply by touching the hem of Jesus' robe her body was completely healed. She got exactly what she needed from him. (Luke 8:43-48)

The things of this world can't satisfy. We eat and drink three times a day, and then we are right back at it the next day. "All man's efforts are for his mouth, yet his appetite is never satisfied." (Ecclesiastes 6:7) Thirst and hunger are driving us to spend most of our days getting food and drink to survive; it's amazing how much work we do every day just in order to stay alive. But when God fills us with food and drink, we won't need to find it for ourselves anymore. In fact, we will be forever filled with the food from Heaven when he feeds us. The woman at the well found this out when she offered Jesus a drink of water. He told her that "Everyone who drinks this water will be thirsty again, but whoever drinks the water I give him will never thirst. Indeed, the water I give him will become in him a spring of water welling up to eternal life." (John 4:13-14) God takes away our hunger, our craving, by filling us with the rich food of Heaven.

You may have all that you can ever want in this world. You may be rich and prosperous; you know that disaster can't touch you and you and yours can spend the rest of your lives in comfort. But you know, surely, that a day will come when all that you own will disappear and you will stand before God poor, blind, and naked, without a cent to your name. There is only one kind of treasure that will survive time, and that will enrich you in the Day of Judgment – the riches of God. Jesus warned us about trusting in momentary riches in this world:

> Do not store up for yourselves treasures on earth, where moth and rust destroy, and where thieves break in and steal. But store up for yourselves treasures in Heaven, where moth and rust do not destroy, and where thieves do not break in and steal. (Matthew 6:19-20)

Only a fool would think that the good things of this world can compare favorably with the things that God gives. If you were really wise, you would ask God for Heavenly treasures, as Solomon did, and let God decide if you can be trusted with worldly wealth. (2 Chronicles 1:7-12) God gives better things than material wealth: "If you, then, though you are evil, know how to give good gifts to your children, how much more will your Father in Heaven give good gifts to those who ask him!" (Matthew 7:11)

You know that God is working when the problem is completely solved, or the battle is really won, or the mind finally lights up with understanding of the truth. And you know that you've gotten something from God when it's a down-payment on eternal riches: a robe of righteousness that will cover you on Judgment Day, the Spirit of adoption that causes you to call God "Abba, Father," the love that forgives others and draws you and others together as brothers and sisters. These things of God are precious and worth "more than gold, yea, than much fine gold!"

A spiritual work. "Peace I leave with you; my peace I give you. I do not give to as the world gives." (John 14:27) In case you have the idea that God's primary business is to give out bags of groceries or A's on tests or new cars in the garage, you haven't been reading between the lines. God's primary concern is to build his *spiritual* Temple. What he wants to give you is the spiritual blessings of that Temple, and the spiritual gifts to adorn the Temple.

He does give out physical gifts to people, but that usually confuses us. He seems to give them out indiscriminately! Both the wicked and the righteous benefit from his food and air and daily necessities. The rain falls on the just and the unjust alike. Jesus healed lepers whether they appreciated him or not. Thousands ate bread and fish from the hands of Christ, and later they helped drive iron spikes through those hands. It seems as though physical blessings aren't necessarily tied to spiritual blessings; a man can be abundantly blessed with things in this world and yet be a candidate for Hell.

God does take care of his people in physical ways, but again we can't go on appearances. Sometimes he lets his special people beg for bread at the doorstep of the rich, like Lazarus with his sores. (Luke 16:19-31) Sometimes he leads his people through suffering and hardship, as he did the Apostle Paul. (2 Corinthians 11:16-33)

Christ told us to ask for spiritual blessings instead. It's no use, he said, to focus on physical necessities because "your Heavenly Father knows that you need them. But seek first his kingdom and his righteousness, and all these things will be given to you as well." (Matthew 6:32-33) God is primarily interested with your *soul*, and only secondarily with your body. Your soul needs saving; he can raise your body from the dead, but he won't do it if you are still a sinner at heart.

There are many places where this truth comes out by the way he dealt with men. Creation is a classic example. God made a material world, filled it with physical creatures and with humans who were no less physical, told us to increase and rule the world in his image, gave us food to eat and work to do, and then stepped back waiting for *spiritual results.* Proof? He expected Adam and Eve to obey his command about not eating the fruit from the tree of the knowledge of good and evil. He expected men, even after they fell into sin, to do good to each other – not kill each other as Cain did his brother Abel. He expected men to be peaceable and God-seekers, not "that every inclination of the thoughts of his heart was only evil all the time." (Genesis 6:5) He kept expecting spiritual results from this physical world!

More examples. The Old Testament Temple was the pride and joy of the Jews. By it they had a system of accessing God and getting forgiveness of their sins. Beside the fact that the whole purpose of this very physical Temple was to deal with spiritual problems, the Temple itself represented the Temple in Heaven. The writer of Hebrews calls the Jewish Temple a "shadow" that symbolized the reality. What God did in the earthly Temple was really like the forward of a book; the real story of forgiveness, the blood that cleanses, the sacrifice that satisfies the demands of the Law, the candlelight of Truth, the mercy seat of God, lay behind the physical veil until God felt it was time to bring it all out.

David was God's man even when Saul was ruling the Israelites. When he finally came to power, he became the symbol of unity of all the tribes of Israel. He took authority over the worship of God and instructed the priests about how to do their jobs. He ruled over the people according to the Law of God, which stabilized the society and forced everyone to orient their lives around the will of God. David was another of the Jews' pride and joy. But was God simply interested in David as a local ruler over a little country in the Middle East? Most certainly not! He used David as a pattern for the Messiah to come! What David was to the nation, Jesus is to his people – point for point. The Lord laid the foundation for the job description of the Messiah in the kingship of David, and the Jews knew that. Though God worked on a physical level, he had spiritual blessings and realities in mind for those of us down the road – realities that would reach out beyond the borders of little Israel to include the whole world.

Even such a simple little thing as providing food for you is fraught with spiritual implications. God isn't just interested in satisfying your physical hunger; he knows that you need far more than that to reach Heaven. "Man does not live on bread alone, but on every word that comes from the mouth of God." (Matthew 4:4) You should look at the food on your plate and realize that the Lord gave you this physical blessing so that you would have the strength to serve him "as living sacrifices, holy and pleasing to God – which is your spiritual worship." (Romans 12:1)

Another example. You should pray for the rulers and for peace in the land not because you fear the physical evils of war or social unrest (don't we all?), but so that "we may live peaceful and quiet lives in all godliness and holiness. This is good, and pleases God our Savior, who wants all men to be saved and to come to a knowledge of the truth." (1 Timothy 2:2-3) Note God's ulterior motive for peace: spiritual results, not physical well-being.

The authority of God. "So is my Word that goes out from my mouth: it will not return to me empty, but will accomplish what I desire and achieve the purpose for which I sent it." (Isaiah 55:11) God isn't used to being disobeyed; he is, after all, the King of kings and the maker of all creation. When he gives a command he expects everyone to take notice and do what he expects of them. The angels all understand this very well; they live only to do his wishes, and they know full well what will come of disobedience. The world understands this, too, in its own way: what God told the creatures to do, they are doing; the way that God made the rocks and trees and mountains to exist, there they stood just as he spoke and will continue to stand until he undoes his command. In fact the Word of God has a power all of its own. What he commands, happens, because the command itself is an act of creation.

The only creature who has fought against the system so far (aside from Satan and his followers) is man. When God speaks, we ignore him. When he commands, we rebel. When he leads, we head the opposite way. It's no wonder that he's so put out with us.

The Lord isn't going to let this situation continue for long. He *will* have the last word!

He's constantly busy "destroying all dominion, authority and power" (1 Corinthians 15:24). God raised Christ …

> … far above all rule, authority, power and dominion, and every title that can be given, not only in the present age but also in the one to come. And God placed all things under his feet and appointed him to be head over everything for the church, which is his body, the fullness of him who fills everything in every way. (Ephesians 1:21-23)

So expect to see this happening when he works in the world. For example, remember the time when a Roman centurion came to ask Jesus to heal his servant? The centurion touched the essence of Jesus' healing ministry when he gave this remarkable testimony about the nature of God's work:

> Lord, I do not deserve to have you come under my roof. But just say the word, and my servant will be healed. For I myself am a man under authority, with soldiers under me. I tell this one, "Go," and he goes; and that one, "Come," and he comes. I say to my servant, "Do this," and he does it. (Matthew 8:8-9)

Jesus was amazed. Here was a Gentile who understood more about the works of God than most Israelites did! He knew that Jesus was here to take authority over all the principalities and powers, and to take authority over all the evils of sin, and to take authority over sinners themselves. He knew the Master had come.

Things usually go from bad to worse when we try to solve problems our own way. Not only can't we get other people to cooperate with us, but sometimes animals prove pretty stubborn too! Balaam found this out the hard way when he tried to force his donkey along the road to Moab, in order to curse the Israelites for them. When the beast finally refused to move a step further, and even spoke to the man and took him to task for beating him, Balaam's eyes were opened and he saw the reason for his donkey's reluctance to move:

> Then the LORD opened Balaam's eyes, and he saw the angel of the LORD standing in the road with his sword drawn. So he bowed low and fell facedown. (Numbers 22:31)

The Lord had come and taken matters into his own hands; he controlled the donkey completely and had every intention of telling Balaam exactly what to do too.

You can tell when the Lord has arrived because things start happening: logjams break up, people cooperate for a change, and mountains fall and valleys rise to make a straight and level path for the King. There are no problems when the King shows up. "When a man's ways are pleasing to the LORD, he makes even his enemies live at peace with him." (Proverbs 16:7)

HIS WORKS REVEAL HIS NATURE

Ever since we lost contact with God in the Garden of Eden we've been in a fog about who God really is. We can't put him out of our minds because we are made in his image, after all, and there's just too much about us that brings the subject back up. How do we explain such things as value, meaning, conscience, right and wrong, and purpose except in terms of God and what he made us to do? So something in our inmost nature makes us return to the big question: what is God like?

We have to find some satisfactory answer to this. Every generation, every race of man has come up with an answer of some sort, right or wrong – usually wrong. They've made idols that represent what they think God is like and then worshiped those idols. Now they weren't fools; they knew that an idol is simply stone or wood and that it symbolized God. The problem is that the description of God that they came up with was all wrong. They made up what they wanted God to be like – someone who allowed sin, who could be manipulated to give them whatever they asked for – and then built an idol to represent this god. *We aren't any different in this respect.* We don't make stone idols and put them on our shelves, but we do make up a mistaken picture of the real God. The god that we create in our minds is often not the God who is described in the Bible. Ask any average person on the street what he thinks God is like and you'll probably get a whole lecture of ridiculous answers. He's just as much an idolater as the primitive tribes in the wild.

Paul tells us that we don't have any excuse in this area. We all ought to know far more about God than we do, because …

What may be known about God is plain to them, because God has made it plain to them. For since the creation of the world God's invisible qualities – his eternal power and the divine nature – have been clearly seen, being understood from what has been made, so that men are without excuse. (Romans 1:19-20)

Would you be able to analyze creation and the works of God and come up with a fairly complete description of God? You ought to be able to! Again, this is why the Scriptures talk about pondering, meditating on the works of God. A lot of things about God may not be immediately obvious from his works, but only by working it out carefully can you put the whole picture together and come up with the truth about him.

Let's run back through the history of the works of God and see if they tell us about the nature of God.

God is Spirit. "God is Spirit, and his worshipers must worship him in Spirit and in truth." (John 4:24) In other words, God is not identical to anything in this world. He isn't the "spirit of the age" or the "spirit of nature;" he isn't the ground of being, the underlying reality of the world. He's totally apart from the world; he's the Creator of the world, the One who existed before the world existed. He exists in a different way than the world does: he is God, and nothing else is God.

Remember he told his people not to make any idol of "anything in Heaven above or on the earth beneath or in the waters below." (Exodus 20:4) You can't represent God with anything in this world because he isn't like anything here. He is something completely different – Spirit, whereas created matter is atoms and physical energy. Even our spirits, and the spirits of angels, are created things and not self-existent, life-giving Spirit like God.

How do we know that he is Spirit and not of the same stuff that the world is made of? Because when he comes into this world he makes things go contrary to their nature! If God is really what the unbelievers say he is, then he is simply the God of rain, the God of food and plenty, the God of war, the God of physical comforts, the God of the land. All of man's idols look to things in this world and call them God. But that doesn't describe what happens when God comes into the world. For example, when God appeared to Moses he spoke out of a burning bush – an impossibility, a strange thing that didn't fit with the makeup of the bush at all! Later he came down to Mt. Sinai and the mountain shook, smoke poured from its top, lightning flashed, trumpets blared – so many strange things that showed that something unearthly was close to the earth and disturbing the natural status of physical reality. The Israelites were terrified.

Miracles happen when God touches this world. Axe heads float in water, a few loaves of bread are enough to feed thousands of people, mud smeared on the eyes cures blindness, striking a stick on a rock opens up a fountain of water in the desert, donkeys talk, strong city walls collapse simply when people shout, wine turns into water – the list can go on and on. Spirit and physical just aren't the same! God shows his complete control over the world when he works with it; he can make it do whatever he pleases, usually something that's completely unlike what it was designed to do. For example, how in the world can you explain Jesus *and* Peter walking on top of water? The only explanation is that we're dealing with something – someone! – who is not of this world.

We also have to remember that the Spirit ushers us into a different world than the one we live in; he pushes apart the curtains of this world into God's spiritual world and shows us that there's a reality that's apart from, and much bigger and more lasting and of more value than, this world. We find this too when we study his works. For example, we discover that Abraham had a deeper understanding of God's promise than we may have realized. He knew that the promise of a son was only the tip of the iceberg; something much bigger was afoot in God's kingdom: "For he was looking forward to the city with foundations, whose architect and builder is God." (Hebrews 11:10) He could see beyond this world into the spiritual Temple in Heaven where his Seed (Galatians 3:16) would minister salvation to the nations.

One last example. Jesus healed and preached and fed people for three years, and most people could only see a man like themselves who "went about doing good;" in fact, that's all that most people ever see, even in our own day. But Peter saw a reality that shook his world view:

> "But what about you?" he [Jesus] asked. "Who do you say that I am?"

> Simon Peter answered, "You are the Christ, the Son of the living God." Jesus replied, "Blessed are you, Simon son of Jonah, for this was not revealed to you by man, but by my Father in Heaven." (Matthew 16:15-17)

Peter got a vision of a spiritual reality that's hidden from the eyes of most people in this world. He saw that Jesus is something more than this world; he can't be explained in terms of this world. One has to drop back to *revelation* if one is to understand the spiritual God – God himself must tell us who he is through the Spirit, because there are no words or concepts in our experience that are adequate to describe him. The natural man – the man of this world – cannot understand the things of God, because they are spiritually discerned. (1 Corinthians 2:14)

God is holy. "Holy, holy, holy is the LORD Almighty; the whole earth is full of his glory." (Isaiah 6:3) Whatever God does, it is upright, true, righteous, faithful, and pure. There is nothing there that anybody can find fault with. It's in exact conformity to the Law of God.

Actually this is a bit confusing, because the Law is nothing other than a description of God's nature. He doesn't do things in order to conform to the Law, as if the Law is higher than he is. Rather, what he does can be described by the Law – it's by looking at what God does that we know what righteousness and holiness is.

Adam and Eve first discovered the holiness of God. After they disobeyed him and ate the fruit of the Tree of the Knowledge of Good and Evil, God came "walking in the garden" and they hid from him in the trees. Why did they hide from him? It was because of his holiness, his purity and uprightness, his abhorrence of anything evil and unclean. They felt so naked and dirty in his presence.

The Lord displayed his holiness when he destroyed Sodom and Gomorrah. He simply would not allow these people's sins to continue. "Your eyes are too pure to look on evil; you cannot tolerate wrong." (Habakkuk 1:13) He prefers the clean air of his own pure nature; the foul air of rebellion and sin offends him. One way or another he is going to get rid of the source of the odor of sin, the stench of death.

The Israelites learned the hard way that God was holy. They faithfully performed the Temple ceremonies and called on his Name, but evidently they underestimated God's holiness somewhere along the line.

> These people come near to me with their mouth and honor me with their lips, but their hearts are far from me. Their worship of me is made up only of rules taught by men. (Isaiah 29:13)

They thought that they could worship God and still keep their sins. But the Lord vowed that this would change – "they will acknowledge the

Holy One of Jacob, and will stand in awe of the God of Israel" (Isaiah 29:23) – and off they went in exile to Babylon! He is too holy to tolerate hypocrisy.

His holiness also forces everything around him to conform to his standards. Like a furnace that burns the impurities out of ore, God's extreme holiness burns the sin and immorality from everyone who comes near. Isaiah himself experienced this when he came before God's throne.

> "Woe to me!" I cried. "I am ruined! For I am a man of unclean lips, and I live among a people of unclean lips, and my eyes have seen the King, the Lord Almighty." Then one of the seraphs flew to me with a live coal in his hand, which he had taken with tongs from the altar. With it he touched my mouth and said, "See, this has touched your lips; your guilt is taken away and your sin atoned for." (Isaiah 6:5-7)

In a touching and characteristically gentle way, Jesus also purified those around him. He was holy, and he was determined to make his surroundings holy – including his disciples. When they went to the upper room for the Passover meal, he started to wash their feet, and Peter objected to this action:

> "No," said Peter, "you shall never wash my feet." Jesus answered,

> "Unless I wash you, you have no part with me." (John 13:8)

These are the words of a holy God, intent on making his surroundings holy.

God is good. "'Why do you call me good?' Jesus answered. 'No one is good – except God alone.'" (Luke 18:19) One of Jesus' more perplexing statements, he is actually teaching us a fundamental truth about God: he is the *only* source of good in the universe. Anything and anybody else that's good can only claim to borrow that goodness from God. Even Jesus, the Son of God, claimed that he did "only what he sees his Father doing" (John 5:19) – which means that all the good that Jesus did came directly from God.

"Good" is a much used word and it means a multitude of things. In respect to God, though, "good" means he's going to take care of us. David appealed to the goodness of God when he asked him,

> Remember not the sins of my youth and my rebellious ways; according to your love remember me, for you are good, O LORD. Good and upright is the LORD; therefore he instructs sinners in his ways. (Psalm 25:7)

In the first place, he asked that God would be good to him and refrain from punishing him for his past sins. That's good because punishment would have meant death! In the second place, not being satisfied with simply forgiving sin, God will train David in how not to sin – how to live righteously and please God with his life. That's good too – and it reveals an ulterior motive on God's part. A righteous life is to God's liking, and it preserves David in the future from the risk of punishment.

So, in keeping with the doctrine from Hebrews 12:10 ("God disciplines us for our good, that we may share in his holiness"), God did David an immense amount of good when he killed the son of adultery of David and Bathsheba. (2 Samuel 12:14) In cases like these, "good" is what is good for the soul in the long run; God is making sure that we will end up safe and blessed in him. Of course we often can't tell that what he's doing is good for us; usually we only feel the pain and we don't understand. But since God does what is *really good*, we should always distrust our own opinions and believe in his love.

The Lord did an inestimable amount of good for Jacob and his family when he took Joseph to Egypt. Look at *those* circumstances! First the treachery of his brothers, then selling him as a slave, then the heartache of Jacob over his apparently dead son. Then a series of rises and setbacks for Joseph in Egypt, in which he could have easily lost hope and sunk to the bottom of the social ladder for the rest of his life. But he kept his faith alive in his God; as far as he was concerned, God only does good to his people. He told his brothers this later when they discovered that he was alive after all:

> You intended to harm me, but God intended it for good to accomplish what is now being done, the saving of many lives. (Genesis 50:20)

Jesus, it was said, "went around doing good." (Acts 10:38). Usually his good works went unappreciated. But there were times when we are given a glance at the spiritual depth of the well of the goodness of God. In one instance (Mark 2:1-12 – the story of the paralytic) he did a man the most good that he knew to do – he saved him from his sins. When someone challenged his authority to dispense such precious remedies, he followed it up with physical good – a lesser good, he tells us, than the spiritual healing that he administered first.

God is powerful. "You are in error because you do not know the Scriptures or the power of God." (Matthew 22:29) Nobody would dispute that God is all powerful. Even unbelievers who don't think that there is a God will agree that, if God did in fact exist, he certainly would have infinite strength. That seems to go along with the idea of God in everyone's mind. Maybe that's because we love to see a hero, a "superman", who can do anything he wishes. Limitations don't fit well with the hero image.

And certainly we have examples from the Bible of God's tremendous power over creation. Well, creation itself is an example. With a mere Word he created the Heavens and the earth. And he later brought on a world-wide flood that completely devastated the surface of the globe. Another time he split the Red Sea in two, allowing his people to cross over safely, and then brought the two towering walls of water crashing down on the Egyptians. The examples of God's power are simply too numerous to mention: there was the earth splitting apart to swallow Korah and his followers, the fire that dropped down out of Heaven and destroyed Sodom and Gomorrah, the unseen force that collapsed Jericho's walls, the power that killed 185,000 Assyrian troops overnight outside Jerusalem's walls while they slept, the power that calmed the stormy Sea of Galilee, the power that split the Temple veil in two when Jesus died on the cross.

But still I contend that we underestimate God's power. He can do anything, we say, but when *certain kinds* of problems come up then we start doubting that he can actually help. For example, can God do anything for me when my heart is hardened in sin, and prayer and the Word don't move me? Don't think that this is a small problem! If mountains are in the way, God simply moves them out of the way; they are just inanimate masses of rock. Man can do that too with a bulldozer! But a hardened sinner is a spoiled flower, a beautiful creation gone bad, sweet milk gone sour. How does one reverse the effects of death and bring life back – not to speak of a life that will never again die?

But – and here faith "hopes against all hope" – God can even do that. Abraham knew that even if the Lord did kill his only son Isaac, God "had power to do what he had promised" and give him back his son. (Hebrews 11:17-19) In fact Abraham put his finger on the deepest aspect of the power of God; it was the same resurrection power that he gives to us ...

> ... his incomparably great power for us who believe. That power is like the working of his mighty strength, which he exerted in Christ when he raised him from the dead and seated him at his right hand in the Heavenly realms, far above all rule and authority, power and dominion, and every title that can be given, not only in the present age but also in the one to come. (Ephesians 1:19-21)

It's this power that raised Christ from the grave that God used to crack Paul's hard heart. He poured out this power on the disciples so that they had the ability to go "to every tribe and nation," doing miracles in Christ's name and declaring the Gospel without fear. This is the power that had the Jews running in fear before the young Church. This is the same power – seemingly powerless, mind you, in the world's eyes – that in time brought Rome herself down to the dust. Paul understood the tremendous power of the Gospel when he called it "the power of God for the salvation of everyone who believes." (Romans 1:16)

God is wise. "His wisdom is profound." (Job 9:4) We think we know what wisdom is; but when we watch God at work it isn't long till we are embarrassed at our amateur ways of doing things.

Wisdom is not only having the facts, and being skillful in one's work, but it's also in knowing what's the *best* thing to do and *how* one must go about getting there. There are many people who have the facts! The trouble is that they don't know how to handle the facts. A fool draws wrong conclusions, does stupid things, falls over his own feet trying to get somewhere – he does everything wrong and expends a lot of energy doing it. A wise man, on the other hand, can with just a little effort pull off a resounding success. "A wise man has great power, and a man of knowledge increases strength." (Proverbs 24:5)

The Lord shows profound wisdom in everything he does. Creation is where we must start, of course, because it's the most awesome visible display of his infinite knowledge. "But God made the earth by his power; he founded the world by his wisdom and stretched out the Heavens by his understanding." (Jeremiah 10:12) Everything fits together like a tight jigsaw puzzle; take one small part away and the whole thing would fail. The vast scales of the expanding universe of galaxies and clusters of galaxies is equally matched by the almost infinite micro-scale of the atomic world. We seem to be suspended in between the two extremes, and we depend on the perfection of both realms for our lives. Science can tell us amazing stories about the infinite complexity and superb suitability of the world around us.

But creation was only the beginning of God's works of wisdom. He planned out a way to save man's soul from the very beginning of time –

he knew everything that it would take, long before it happened – and started it rolling just as soon as Adam and Eve fell into sin. What was the plan? Over the centuries men got little glimpses here and there, but they couldn't see the whole thing. He made a promise to Abraham about the coming Seed – but who was God talking about? He made mention to Moses that there was a Heavenly pattern for the Tabernacle that the Israelites were to build – what did it look like? He said that David's son would rule over God's people "forever" – did people think that Solomon was that son? He told the Israelites that he would "give you a new heart and put a new Spirit in you" (Ezekiel 36:26) – when was he planning to do that, and what would it look like?

It wasn't until Christ came that the whole plan started making sense. Paul explains it like this:

> Although I am less than the least of all God's people, this grace was given me: to preach to the Gentiles the unsearchable riches of Christ, and to make plain to everyone the administration of this mystery, which for ages past was kept hidden in God, who created all things. His intent was that now, through the church, the manifold wisdom of God should be made known to the rulers and authorities in the Heavenly realms, according to his eternal purpose which he accomplished in

> Christ Jesus our Lord. (Ephesians 3:8-11)

In Christ all the past actions of God become plain. The Temple economy – now we understand why two goats were used, and why one was sent out into the wilderness. Now we know why they had to use a lamb without blemish for the Passover meal. Now we see the reason for the veil in front of the mercy seat. At the time, it may have appeared to the Jews to be a lot of capricious rules that didn't make any sense; but we see now in Christ that it all reflected his spiritual ministry and *it had to be* – it was a complex, multi-faceted system in which every piece played its part, from Abraham down to the last Temple in Jerusalem.

And the Lord continues to use wisdom as he works in the world. Was it wisdom or foolishness that made Jesus go to the cross? His enemies thought that they had him at last – weak and helpless, dying and friendless, he couldn't do anything to upset their world any more. Little did they know! That very act of helpless death became the foundation for an eternal kingdom, and their act of crucifying the Lord of Glory was like opening Pandora's Box. He defeated sin and death, set the prisoners free, overcame the world, rose to reign at God's right hand – all the promises of God came true in that one act.

> We preach Christ crucified: a stumbling block to Jews and foolishness to Gentiles, but to those whom God has called, both Jews and Greeks, Christ the power of God and

> the wisdom of God. For the foolishness of God is wiser than man's wisdom, and the weakness of God is stronger than man's strength. (1 Corinthians 1:23-25)

He fooled them all with his superior wisdom. In fact, he continues to work like this through his people. It still looks like he's giving the field over to the enemy by resorting to weak and half-way measures; whenever the Church gets half a chance to succeed at something, something else comes along – persecution, fighting inside the ranks, apathy – and knocks her down in the dust again. The world despises this weak, helpless, ignorant Church. But they shouldn't – they should know by now that God works according to profound wisdom to bring about his will, and it will never fail.

> Brothers, think of what you were when you were called. Not many of you were wise by human standards; not many were influential; not many were of noble birth. But God chose the foolish things of the world to shame the wise; God chose the weak things of the world to shame the strong. He chose the lowly things of this world and the despised things– and the things that are not – to nullify the things that are, so that no one may boast before him. It is because of him that you are in Christ Jesus, who has become for us wisdom from God – that is, our

righteousness, holiness and redemption. Therefore, as it is written: "Let him who boasts boast in the Lord." (1 Corinthians 1:26-31)

These insignificant little people of today's Church are overturning strongholds. They are winning other converts to Christianity with their quiet testimonies, and they are training their children in the ways of the Lord, and they are "salting" their environment with holiness. If it weren't for the Church our civilization would have self-destructed long ago! If it weren't for the "insignificant" Bible and the little people who teach it and believe it, our society would have been founded on corrupt principles and fallen apart long before now.

God is unchanging. "I the LORD do not change. So you, O descendents of Jacob, are not consumed." (Malachi 3:6) This is more than just a doctrine about God; it's both a terrifying and a wonderful piece of news about him – depending on who examines his works, that is. It's terrifying to realize that the same God who threw man out of the Garden of Eden is still around now, denying sinners any access to eternal life. The same God who destroyed the world with a flood and burned Sodom and Gomorrah to the ground is still upset with modern men's wickedness; and he has new plans for *their* elimination as well, this time melting the very elements of the universe and remaking Heaven and earth. The same God who judged Israel for not obeying the Law and sent his own people into Exile for their unfaithfulness is still judging his people by the Law, and he won't hesitate to "start with his own household" and clear out the dead wood – the hypocrites, the liars, the gossips, the lazy gluttons, the creators of dissention – out of the ranks of his precious Church.

It seems that each generation has its party of "wise" men who tell us that the Old Testament is not the book for modern Christians. They have many people fooled about this; the result is that many Christians think that the God of the New Testament is different from the God of the Old Testament. They believe that the Old Testament is like a dirty lens through which people got a mistaken idea of who God really is, and Jesus is the clean lens who focuses on a tender God of Love who has good intentions toward all.

But this is one of those false doctrines that the New Testament writers warn us about. The God and Father of the Lord Jesus Christ is the same yesterday, today, and forever just as much as his Son is the same! Do we know now through Christ that God is a God of love? The Israelites knew that too! The Lord drew the Israelites out of Egypt, "out of bondage," and gave them a land filled with houses and fields and vineyards and plowed fields. He sent Jonah to Nineveh – a Gentile city, mind you – to preach to them first before he sent judgment, with the hope that they would hear and repent of their sins and he would spare them. Jonah himself was more bloodthirsty for their destruction than God was! God was reluctant to punish his people, and after *several hundred years* of sending prophets to them and watching the rebels killing his servants one by one, and turning their backs on his pleadings, and listening to insults and jeers when he "wooed" his people like a wounded husband, he finally did what he had to do. Even then it wasn't to destroy his people, but to remedy their hearts; he fully intended to preserve a remnant out of the Exile who would become faithful to him. There's just too much in the Old Testament that shows that God the Father is more like Christ than modern critics give him credit for. The family resemblance is undeniable.

And it works the other way too. Does the Old Testament teach that God is very particular about his Law and he punishes sinners when they break it? We see that clearly in the ministry of Christ himself. He warned us that the least infraction of the Law – even *thinking* evil thoughts, which is a more severe interpretation of the original Ten Commandments than we like to hear – deserves death. He said that anybody who teaches someone to treat God's Law lightly or of no consequence ought to be dropped into the middle of the ocean with a heavy millstone around his neck! Our gentle Shepherd!

The Apostles too depended on the fact that God hadn't changed over these thousands of years; you can tell by the way they kept quoting from the Old Testament to support their arguments. One example: Paul remembers that Elijah once went to God in despair, thinking that he was the only one left in Israel who was faithful to God. But Elijah found out that God doesn't let a situation get that bad; "I have reserved for myself seven thousand who have not bowed the knee to Baal." Paul draws a lesson from this and concludes, "So too, at the present time there is a remnant chosen by grace." (Romans 11:2-5) God chose a select group of believers to rally around the cause *then*, and he works that way *now* too.

God is just. "Far be it from you to do such a thing – to kill the righteous with the wicked, treating the righteous and the wicked alike. Far be it from you! Will not the Judge of all the earth do right?" (Genesis 18:25) Abraham knew his God. He knew that if there were righteous people in a city – even if that city were Sodom! – God would have mercy on the place just for the sake of those few righteous people. And he was right. There weren't enough righteous there to spare Sodom, but the Lord did get Lot and his family out of there before destroying the city.

The Lord is just in everything he does, which means he judges fairly – neither punishing nor rewarding more than the situation requires. He sizes up the circumstances and decides exactly what's to be done. For instance, it was particularly appropriate that devious Jacob got a taste of his own medicine; after tricking his brother Esau out of his birthright, and deceiving his father Isaac into blessing him instead of his older brother, he ran right into a master deceiver in his uncle Laban! The old codger used his daughters to trick Jacob into working for him for fourteen years!

Job thought that God was terribly unjust in sending death and plague and destruction into his life; surely there must be some mistake. He thought that if he could just come before God's throne he could change God's mind about the terrible treatment he was receiving. But when God spoke out of the whirlwind and laid out to Job the full picture of himself – the Creator of all, the one who knows all things, the one who does all things well, the one who rules his kingdom in fairness even if nobody else thinks he does – Job changed *his* mind instead.

> You asked, 'Who is this that obscures my counsel without knowledge?' Surely I spoke of things I did not understand, things too wonderful for me to know. (Job 42:3)

He realized that whatever God does *has* to be right; if it doesn't seem right to us, it's simply because we don't see things from God's perspective. And as a matter of fact, God's reason for putting Job through all that trouble is at the beginning of the book: there's nothing unjust about making Job a deeper believer in God and putting to rest the false accusations of Satan also!

Probably the most striking and moving of all the works of God in this area of justice is the story about Jesus and the adulterous woman, and the Pharisees who brought her to him for condemnation. We've looked at this already; with the wisdom and the capacity that only God has, Jesus easily did justice to both parties. The Pharisees got more than they bargained for, but no more than they deserved; the woman got less than she expected – or more, depending on how you look at it. She got no punishment, only a warning to sin no more. But she was forgiven of her sin which was much more than she could have dreamed for. Was this unjust of Jesus, to let her off so easily? Not when you consider that he had the *right* to forgive her: he himself would soon pay the exact penalty of her adultery, thus doing justice by the Law; therefore he had the right to forgive her of that debt.

God is loving. "The Lord is righteous in all his ways, and loving toward all he has made." (Psalm 145:17) David was struck with this characteristic of God when he looked at both creation and the people of God. It's easy to see that when you look at creation, because the Lord provides all our necessities no matter what kind of creature we might be.

> The eyes of all look to you, and you give them their food at the proper time. You open your hand and satisfy the desires of every living thing. (Psalm 145:15-16)

We have air to breathe, water to drink, food to eat, warmth and comfort, shelter from the elements, family and friends, work to do, a beautiful creation all around us to enjoy – sometimes we forget that we live in a world of sin and death, and we praise God for the good life that we have. And of course he has taken pains to provide us with protections and blessings that we aren't even aware of. It has only been in this century, for example, that we've discovered how much of a protected environment we actually live in; the intricacies of our atmosphere and the magnetic envelope of the earth protect us from all sorts of harmful materials that the Sun throws at us.

Do we deserve all this? None of us deserve it, and some less than others. Still God faithfully provides all his creatures with what they need to live and be satisfied. Is his love any the less when some creatures can't get food, or they get sick, or they get attacked and wounded, or they die? No, because sin and death can't be laid at his doorstep like that. It wasn't his fault that his beautiful world got ruined! Someday he intends to fix that too.

> The wolf and the lamb will feed together, and the lion will eat straw like the ox, but dust will be the serpent's food. They will neither harm nor destroy in all my holy mountain, says the LORD. (Isaiah 65:25)

We can easily see that the Lord has been especially loving toward his people. Actually he reserves a special love for his people, a love that he doesn't show toward others. It's the love of a father toward his children, the love of a husband for his wife. Outsiders can't expect him to share *that* kind of love with them! This is a private love, a tender love, a privileged love that his people can count on. For example, to whom did he give his Law? Only to Israel!

> He has revealed his Word to Jacob,
> his laws and decrees to Israel. He

has done this for no other nation; they do not know his laws. (Psalm 147:19-20)

Giving his Law to Israel was an act of love; they of all the nations could know God as he truly is, and they could live to please him; whereas other peoples sinned against what little light they had, and had absolutely no way of finding forgiveness for their sin.

Look at a passage from Psalms, and you will see a love that perhaps you didn't realize was so startlingly real. When David was in trouble – "the cords of death entangled me," he puts it – and he cried to God to come help him, we find the reaction in Heaven to be this:

> The earth trembled and quaked, and the foundations of the mountains shook; they trembled because he was angry. Smoke rose from his nostrils; consuming fire came from his mouth, burning coals blazed out of it ... The LORD thundered from Heaven; the voice of the Most High resounded. He shot his arrows and scattered the enemies, great bolts of lightning and routed them ... He reached down from on high and took hold of me; he drew me out of deep waters. He rescued me from my powerful enemy ... He rescued me because he delighted in me. (Psalm 18:4-19)

You ought to read the entire passage just to get the feel of the thing. Can you see the picture of an almighty God rising to his feet, face full of wrath, creatures fleeing in all directions from in front of him for fear of their lives? What has made God so angry? That someone dared to touch one of his precious ones! Here is a love that stirs the heart of the most despondent Christian; here is a Father who will move Heaven and earth to rescue his child from danger.

I believe that we don't give God enough credit for loving us. He loves us so deeply that eternity won't be enough time to tell of it. If you are more sensitive to his loving heart as you read the Scriptures, you will start seeing that love working all over the place, in both the Old and New Testaments. His love, after all, is the motivating force behind the entire plan of salvation from the beginning of time to the end of time.

I hope you realize that these are just a few examples that teach us what God is like. You can find many more passages that prove, by God's actions, that he is what he claims to be. You *ought* to find them. The more that you learn about God by his works, the better you will know him, and the more you will benefit from the knowledge.

HIS WORKS REVEAL HIS WAYS

You might not have thought about the fact that the Lord has "ways." Actually the Bible talks about the "ways of the Lord" quite a bit. In fact, we find several passages where we not only can learn what his ways are, but *we'd better be finding out his ways or else!* Take this passage, for instance:

> That is why I was angry with that generation, and I said, "Their hearts are always going astray, and they have not known my ways." So I declared on oath in my anger, "They shall never enter my rest." (Hebrews 3:10-11)

The idea of "ways" can be described like this: *first*, the road that one takes; *second*, peculiar characteristics of personality. When one wants to get from point A to point B he has to choose the way to take; there may be many ways or there may be only one way to get there. And in respect to the second idea, everyone has ways about them; we all do things in certain ways that make us different from other people. It may be that I like to part my hair in a certain place; others might think it looks silly, but I like it that way. That's just my way of doing things.

Well, God has ways in both these senses. He moves along certain paths to get to his goals and he uses those particular paths for good reason. He wants us to follow in those same paths! "He instructs sinners in his ways." (Psalm 25:8) "The way of the LORD is a refuge for the righteous." (Proverbs 10:29) And the Lord also has characteristics about him that make him different from everyone else. He does things in certain ways, and when we get to know him (as is the only way to learn someone's peculiarities, since it takes time and familiarity to learn their ways) we begin to learn how he prefers to do things.

Studying the works of the Lord is an excellent way to learn the ways of the Lord. It's like carefully scrutinizing the work of a master furniture maker. Each craftsman has his own way of working, and the trained eye will see the characteristic marks of the worker. It isn't any trouble to identify someone's work if we've seen that kind of work before. And it isn't any trouble to identify the work of the Lord if we've trained ourselves to spot his characteristic ways of doing things.

It's no offence to him to examine his work like this. He *wants* us to know his ways! His ways, it turns out, are the best possible ways of doing things. We will be in awe of him, and we will praise him, when we know more about how he does things. We will learn that God is far more skilled at saving men and dealing with the enemy than we could ever be, mainly because of the way he handles the situation.

It was said of Stonewall Jackson that he would stand by quietly and listen to the junior officers hash out the possibilities for the battle plan, and then close the argument and go out to the field without disclosing his mind in the matter. Then he would arrange his units in such a way that they thought he was out of his mind! It wasn't long, however, until everyone saw the marks of a genius at work; his ways, always strange and unexpected, worked every time. In the same way, the Lord doesn't necessarily tell anybody why he does things the way he does; but time and circumstance prove that it is, in fact, the only way such a thing will work. His ways are perfect.

Actually we've been dealing with some of the ways of the Lord already in what we've studied so far. So we will only deal here with a few examples of the ways of the Lord; you will find these and many more when you study his works.

> ***He uses small things.*** "The kingdom of Heaven is like a mustard seed, which a man took and planted in his field. Though it is the smallest of all your seeds, yet when it grows, it is the largest of garden plants and becomes a tree, so that the birds of the air come and perch in its branches." (Matthew

13:31-32) Perk up your ears whenever Jesus says "The kingdom of Heaven is like ..." – this means that he's going to tell you a fundamental characteristic of the way God does things.

The Lord doesn't share our opinions about what's big and important, and what's small and insignificant. We overlook little details because we think that they don't contribute anything important to our lives. We like to major on the big things: like money, and comfort, and esteem, and accomplishments, and, on the negative side, dangers. Little things get in our way or don't even get noticed at all.

God, however, thinks that our "big" things are really pretty unimportant. Is money a big issue to him? Jesus told us to put our attention on treasures in Heaven *instead of* treasures on earth! Is esteem and respect important? The Lord told us to expect abuse and ridicule from others when we follow in his ways. Are our accomplishments important? Not to God – he's going to reject people even when they've prophesied and driven out demons and performed miracles in his Name! (Matthew 7:21-23) Is our comfort important to him? Evidently not, because his servants have been tortured, exiled, beheaded, stoned, and mistreated in a myriad of ways.

What is a big issue to God? He considers things like these to be important:

His kingdom. Whether we share his interest or not, he is consumed with this issue of building his kingdom. He's bringing all his efforts to bear on this most important of projects, because he wants a finished product at the end of time. He wants to have complete dominion over all creatures, including man; and he wants the kingdom to be a place of perfect peace and righteousness.

The enemy defeated. The enemy is anything and anyone that stands against him and his kingdom. He won't tolerate this state of affairs for long. He's going to pry the fingers of the world, the flesh, and the devil off his precious lambs and hurl the rebellious lot into eternal fire. There's so much to do to defeat the enemy because the devil has inroads into every area of our lives, and he uses clever tools and techniques to make his hold all the stronger. For now the Lord allows the wheat and the weeds to grow together, for the sake of his wheat; but the day will come when he will separate the weeds out and burn them.

Sinners saved. After all, this is the meaning of all the work that God has been about since the beginning of time. Jesus' name means "the LORD saves;" he came for the express purpose of "saving his people from their sins." God intends to save us from the power and the presence of sin, so completely that there won't be any traces of rebellion in our hearts, and the only way we *can* act is in perfect holiness and purity.

All the glory. Since God is engineering this whole thing, he ought to get the credit for it.

In fact he ought to get the credit for everything that has ever happened since the beginning of time; because he is, in fact, the Creator, the Provider, the source of all good, the Truth itself, the source of all light, the Savior, the Redeemer, the Judge – he's everything to this world of ours! But he doesn't get credit for much of it, unfortunately. That has to change; it's going to be a big job, but one day everyone will realize that God alone deserves all glory.

This is what God considers important. And since these are issues that are most important to God, you would think that he's going to get out the big guns and get his way – right? Wrong! He surprises everyone by going about it in small ways, little insignificant ways that nobody would ever dream could achieve the goals he has in mind.

For example, how does he begin his righteous kingdom on earth? He calls a nobody (his name has never shown up in secular history sources) out of the city of Ur and sends him west to claim a land that isn't his. Abraham went not knowing what to expect, and when he got to Canaan he found the peoples there firmly entrenched on the land and having no intentions of moving away just because of the revelation that Abraham received. Yet out of these unpromising conditions the Lord raised up a nation of millions, and they did in fact settle in that very land after killing all the inhabitants.

How did God start the process of saving sinners? He sends a Son who was born to a poor carpenter, hounded by the authorities, grew up a despised Nazarene, who had no formal education, who challenged the Jewish system and lost his life because of it. From this small and seemingly ineffective beginning the Lord has built a spiritual Temple where anyone – *anyone* – who comes there will be completely and forever saved from sin and death.

There are many small things in our lives that God is working through – things that we consider of small worth and importance, but things that he is using to build a great kingdom. The Word that you hear, either in sermon or Bible study or by reading on your own, is a small thing in many people's eyes. What is this book anyway? An ancient document that doesn't have much relevance to me. Who is that preacher or teacher who presumes to tell me how to think and live? But what we don't realize is that this book holds the secrets of eternal life; in it is recorded the mind of God. Our whole future rests on what we learn from it. And the mortal who stands to teach the Word is the vessel through which God speaks to his people – "How can they hear without someone preaching to them? ... How beautiful are the feet of those who bring good news!" (Romans 10:14-15)

> And we also thank God continually because, when you received the Word of God, which you heard from us, you accepted it not as the word of men, but as it actually is, the Word of God, which is at work in you who believe. (1 Thessalonians 2:13)

He uses a "cup of cold water" in the hands of his saints to bless people; for that little act they will receive the crown of life. He uses a couple of loaves of bread to feed thousands. He uses a widow to feed a prophet when the whole nation was against him. He uses the Jordan River, a little thing in the eyes of a great general, to heal him of his leprosy. He uses a few hundred faithful soldiers, and Gideon who was the runt of his tribe, to rout the entire army of Midianites.

It's so characteristic of God to pick up the little things around him when he has work to do that we ought to train ourselves to watch for that. Like David, all he needs to bring down the giant problems in our lives is a couple of smooth pebbles. He works the same way in your life, too.

He glorifies himself. "But I will gain glory for myself through Pharaoh and all his army, and the Egyptians will know that I am the LORD." (Exodus 14:4) The Lord used Pharaoh. We might think that this was a harsh thing to do, but the Lord is determined to show the world how great he is, and he will use even the stubborn resistance of his enemies to prove it. In fact he relishes a showdown like this. The proud nation of Egypt thought that Israel was an insignificant people and their God the Lord was a poor comparison to their own gods – and the Lord decided it was about time the Egyptians were taught a good lesson. They got the point.

We may not understand this relentless drive on God's part to get glory, but then there are a lot of God's ways that we don't necessarily understand. He's just that way. Everything he does is right, though, and he has perfectly good reasons for what he does. It isn't long before we see that *he deserves glory* – he really is as great as the Scriptures say he is.

There are reasons that we need to see his glory. For one thing, we find out who the real God is. A king might be mistaken for a peasant if he travels through his kingdom in rags; but there's no mistaking him when he's dressed in the royal robes and sitting on the throne. We might just as easily mistake the myriad of false gods to be real if that's all we could see around us; but when the real God shows up, we *know* who is God. When Elijah challenged the prophets of Baal to a showdown, they should have known better than to accept his challenge – but then they had never met the real God! They called on their god to send fire down to burn the sacrifice and nothing happened; so much for Baal. Then Elijah poured water over everything and then called on God to show his glory – and the fire fell from the sky and burned the whole thing up, water and all. The people were immediately convinced as to who was the real God in Israel. (1 Kings 18:16-40)

Another reason that it's important that we see God's glory is that it teaches us to rely on God for what we want, not on ourselves or in others. If God really is the source of all good things, as it says in James 1, then why don't we live as if it's true? Abraham learned that lesson himself when he started thinking about this matter of a son. He knew the Lord promised him a son through his wife Sarah, but after all they were both getting *very* old and it was much too late for them to be thinking of having children together. So he took matters in his own hands and had a son through Sarah's handmaid Hagar – and he thought he solved his problem as well as God's. He was wrong. God still intended to give a son to Abraham but *not through Hagar*; Sarah was going to have that son, believe it or not. And when Isaac was born to Sarah they were all amazed at what God was able to do – and Abraham's faith was strengthened in the God who works miracles to give us what we need. (Genesis 17:15-19)

The Lord will always make sure that, in whatever he's doing, everyone will be sure to see his glory in it. For example, when Jesus heard about his friend Lazarus being sick he told his disciples that "This sickness will not end in death. No, it is for God's glory so that God's Son may be glorified through it." (John 11:4) When he finally arrived at the tomb where Lazarus was buried, seemingly too late to do anything about it, a crowd gathered around Jesus and the two mourning sisters of the dead man. Then Jesus prayed,

> Father, I thank you that you have heard me. I knew that you always hear me, but I said this for the benefit of the people standing here, that they may believe that you sent me. (John 11:41-42)

So, with everyone watching, the glory of God shone forth. Jesus showed them clearly, in the open and plain to see, who it is that gives life –

God the Father – and how he does it – by sending his Son to call us from the dead with the word of life. It was a showcase of the process of salvation from sin and death.

When you study the works of God you ought to be sensitive to the fact that God is drawing your attention to something about himself that you need to know. He always glorifies himself in his works.

He uses faith to do the big jobs. "I tell you the truth, if you have faith as small as a mustard seed, you can say to this mountain, 'Move from here to there' and it will move. Nothing will be impossible for you." (Matthew 17:20) This is a fundamental key to working in the kingdom of God – this faith – but unfortunately we don't realize how much power there is in it.

Life is full of problems, and the Lord made us in such a way that we want to jump right in and solve problems. We've been solving problems since we were born. But in order to solve a problem you need material and skill – and where do you find that? That's the big question. So we've developed our own little toolkits for problem solving, which we pull out and use when the need arises. We each have our own ways of solving problems: children cry until Mommy comes running; a wife nags until her husband finally does what she wants; a husband hides behind the paper until his wife gives up (a no-win situation!) or he spends the evening away with his buddies; a businessman borrows more money; a factory worker quits under the pressure; a high school student turns to drugs.

The trouble is that we can't achieve any of our goals this way. It doesn't matter what the problem is – physical or spiritual – and it doesn't matter what tools we use to try to solve it; nothing really gets solved. The housewife's sink is going to start leaking again and the businessman is going to need more money. The nature of this world dictates that there will always be problems, more and more problems that keep coming and will never go away until we finally lay down to die, which in itself is the final unsolvable problem.

The Lord's way of solving problems, however, is completely failsafe, works every time, and solves them for good. Faith sees the miracle-working God. Now you have to understand that the Bible doesn't mean that faith in itself can do anything; the point is that *true faith sees that God will do the job for you.* Of course there's nothing in ourselves that can move a mountain; but the Bible talks all the time about God being able to do such things. Abraham learned the steps of true faith; you have to learn what he learned if you want to use this tool to the best advantage. Basically the steps are these:

> ***Hear God's promise.*** This is the all-important first step of faith. If you don't start here then you're going to make some serious errors. Only what God promises to do is what needs to be done; anything else doesn't rate as something important enough to do. You might otherwise call something a

problem that really isn't one! And where are you going to find out what he promised to do? His Word! So study it! If you're a child of God then you really want only what he wants for you; it's his will for your life that should be important to you.

Look at the problem squarely. The all-important second step, and the step that even dedicated Christians often fail to take. You have to see clearly for yourself the full extent of the problem, to the degree that you can plainly see it's *beyond your capabilities to solve*. If you're not convinced of this then go back and study it some more. After all, if there is any way you could help the situation then why do you need God? You've got to see the impossibility of the thing before you're ready to trust God completely for it.

Don't try it yourself. Very important. Keep your hands off the problem. We often break down at this point and try *something*, just so we don't look as if we're irresponsibly ignoring the problem. The thing is, if we try to bring about God's will ourselves, we will inevitably fail. What we will end up with is a second rate solution that's typical of the world – and doomed to go the way of the world, too; it will be destroyed at the end of time because it's not a work of God.

Turn to God for the answer. This is where your knowledge of God comes in. You should know that God does the impossible, that he has done this very thing in the past for others, that he promised to do it and he therefore fully intends to do it again for you. Go to him, then and ask him to fulfill his promise to you. He who asks, receives; and he who seeks, finds. You honor him when you go to him to solve your problems.

Wait. The last step, and the step where people usually give up too soon. The Lord almost never solves problems as soon as they come up; he almost always takes time to do it. And this, by the way, is a very wise thing on his part, because when he does take his time then we show our real colors. If we really believe in his promise, and we fully understand that it's impossible for us to do it ourselves, and if we really do want him to do it, then time is no concern to us; we are committed to waiting on him. If we aren't convinced that he knows what he's doing then the waiting just kills us and we jump ship looking for an alternative solution. In this way the Lord finds out who is really serious about this Christianity business.

This is the way the Lord works in our lives – through this process of faith. Now we'll look at just a couple of examples of people who conformed to the way that the Lord works through faith to solve problems.

First we'll look at **Abraham** because Paul calls him "the father of all who believe" (Romans 4:11) – his story exactly conforms to the way God uses faith to accomplish his will in our lives. *First,* Abraham received God's promise of a son who would one day be a great nation – in fact, the Lord promised to bless all nations through this "Seed" (which we now know was Christ himself). This was more than Abraham had originally intended, but it's important that we focus on what God wants for all of us. *Second*, Abraham looked at the situation squarely and saw how hopeless it was. "Without weakening in his faith, he faced the fact that his body was as good as dead – since he was about a hundred years old – and that Sarah's womb was also dead." (Romans 4:19) Now he's ready to turn to God to do it for him. *Third*, don't try it yourself – but here he slipped up. He did try, out of desperation, to get a son in another way; but the Lord convinced him that Ishmael just wouldn't do as the father of the Messianic line. He had to learn to keep his hands off the problem and not try to solve it himself. *Fourth*, he turned completely to God as being the answer – "Yet he did not waver through unbelief regarding the promise of God, but was strengthened in his faith and gave glory to God, being fully persuaded that God had power to do what he had promised." (Romans 4:20-21) The Lord likes that; he counted that faith as righteousness to Abraham. *Fifth*, Abraham waited. In characteristic fashion the Lord took his time – 25 years! – until the thought of having a son was a joke in the world's eyes and then he did the impossible. Abraham finally received the answer that he wanted.

One more example. When the disciples took their boat across the Sea of Galilee one time, Jesus followed them later by walking on the water out to them. (Matthew 14:22-33) They, of course, were startled when they saw him walking up!

Peter wanted to try it for himself. He got the command to come – the Lord called him to come – and over the side he went. At first it seemed to work fine; but then he began to sink into the water and he didn't know what to do. There was his first mistake. He suddenly realized that he was standing on water, an impossibility for him, but he failed to see that Jesus was able to keep him on top. He thought the problem was bigger than Jesus. He failed in several of the steps of the process of faith. When Jesus rescued him and took him back to the boat, he rebuked Peter for his lack of faith; Peter should have known better than to think that Jesus was incapable of helping him; after all, Jesus did call him out, and that was an implicit promise to support him. Instead Peter thought that *with a little help from Jesus* he could do it on his own willpower. That's not true faith.

BEING ABLE TO SEE HIM IN HIS WORKS

God is revealed in his works, but that doesn't mean that people can see him. There are many reasons for this, but first we have to make the point that one isn't necessarily able to see God. Some people think that the knowledge of God is easy to get! Especially Christians tend to think that. It's not true. It *is* true that learning about God is a long, difficult study that we have to work hard at. Some people don't think that it's worth the trouble and so they don't start, and others start but then give up when it costs them too much effort. Only a few will meditate on the works of God, and pray without ceasing, and take the trouble to become "wiser than their teachers."

Because of the fact that sin clouds our vision and we can't see beyond the things of this world, there is only one way that we can see the spiritual realities of God and his world: by the Spirit himself. It was the Spirit who first gave us spiritual life (Romans 8:11); it's by the Spirit that we pray (Ephesians 6:18), and it's the Spirit who shows us the things of God. (1 Corinthians 2:9-15) It's also the Spirit who explains what we are looking at when we study God's kingdom; Jesus said that he would send the Spirit to us to teach us "all things." (John 14:26)

The Spirit of God has to open our eyes so that we can see God revealed in his works. It would take an entire book to find out how the Spirit teaches us, and what we can do to be open to the Spirit's teaching; but we can hit on a few of the highlights here:

He uses Scripture. "And I will ask the Father, and he will give you another Counselor to be with you forever – the Spirit of Truth." (John 14:16-17) "Sanctify them by the truth; your Word is Truth." (John 17:17)

There is only one true, infallible guide to the works of God and that's the Bible. Indeed, the definition of the Bible is this: God himself revealing to us what he wants us to know about him. The history of the Bible is the record of what God did, and the doctrine of the Bible is a description of what our God is like. There isn't any other reliable source material on the subject of God, simply because no other source material is the work of God himself. Whatever man claims to know about God apart from the Bible may be his humble opinion but it can't be trusted to be a true description of spiritual realities, because of his innate sinfulness and the obscurity that hides the subject from his physical eyes.

"The Spirit searches all things, even the deep things of God." (1 Corinthians 2:10) It's the Spirit who brings us news of what's going on in God's kingdom. But even that news would be totally confusing to us if we didn't have the Spirit to interpret it for us. You've probably had the experience of reading something from the Bible and it just doesn't click; you don't understand it or it just doesn't impress you yet. That's because we can have the raw data about God and yet not be able to see the real meaning and usefulness of it. Left to ourselves, we will inevitably miss the point or even come up with the wrong interpretation. History is facts *plus* interpretation; and rather than let us interpret the meaning for ourselves and get it all wrong, the Spirit prefers to give us the correct interpretation when we study the Bible. This is why there are so many interpretations of the Bible! There are everyone else's interpretations, and then there is the Spirit's interpretation. Only one is right.

Some people think that they get direct revelations from the Spirit and they don't get it by way of the Bible; or at least they think that what they receive must be Biblical because they got it (they thought!) from the Spirit. For one thing, they are mistaken if they think that they have a hot line to God apart from the Word of God. The Spirit, Jesus said, takes *his words* and reminds us of them. (John 14:26) You won't get anything new from Heaven as far as data; it's all been said already in the Bible and the Spirit works through the Bible to teach us. He uses the testimony of the Law, the prophets, the words of Christ, and the foundation of the Apostles to build God's Church – any other foundation that can be laid is not the work of God but of man.

Secondly, you're a fool if you take any spiritual "experience" on its face value and don't check it against God's self-revelation. God tells us in the Bible that "*this* is what I am, *this* is how I work" – why should you run the risk of being wrong about God when the information is so accessible and clear for you? There are many spirits in this world; there are many religions and false doctrines; there are many false gods that will be happy to deceive you. In fact, most of the people in the world *are* deceived about the real God; they don't have the benefit of the Word of God and the Spirit who opens one's eyes to see the true God. And if you care to check back in history you will find that many, too many people in the Church itself have fallen prey to false doctrines and heretical views because they went against the simple statements of the revelation of God. The purpose of the Bible is to check the validity of all other claims of truth to see if they really are the truth. Any other contenders for the title of the Truth of God are either liars or just borrowers from the Biblical system of truth. "The Spirit clearly says that in later times some will abandon the faith and follow deceiving spirits and things taught by demons." (1 Timothy 4:1) We, however, would do well to stick to the Spirit's own Word.

He uses the testimony of others. "If you have any encouragement from being united with Christ, if any comfort from his love, if any fellowship with the Spirit, if any tenderness and compassion, then make my joy complete by being like-minded, having the same love, being one in spirit and in purpose." (Philippians 2:1-2)

This is perhaps the keystone of the Church. The sign that the Church of God is real, that people really are the Children of God and this isn't all just a made-up story, is that the Spirit of God is making something out of us that couldn't possibly happen otherwise. People just don't naturally get along together! And even if they do get along for a while, they don't agree on everything. But the Spirit builds God's people into *one* Temple – they *are* going to get along! – and he teaches us *one* Truth – we *are* going to agree on it!

I know that people pride themselves on having the right to interpret Scripture as they see fit. And I know that none of us know God's mind perfectly, being spiritually short-sighted as we are. But remember that *truth is what God says it is*, not what we say it is. Just because we have a dozen interpretations of a particular passage doesn't mean that there *are* a dozen true interpretations for it! The Lord has his own understanding on the passage (which often isn't what our dozen interpretations say about it) and the Spirit's task is to teach us the mind of God on it. "We have not received the spirit of the world but the Spirit who is from God, that we may understand what God has freely given us." (1 Corinthians 2:12)

One of the sure signs that you are understanding the truth from God's perspective when you study his Word – and his works – is that your results match what other reliable Christians have found in their study. Doctrinally we call this the "testimony of the historic Church." There will always be, of course, other people in our churches who don't agree with us. But there may be some that do, and if you extend your search outside of the walls of your own church you will find Christians of other denominations and Christians back through history that agree with what you are finding in the Word. The reason this is true is because all of God's children have the same Spirit and therefore have the same source of truth; God isn't going to tell his mind to one group of Christians and then tell another group something contrary or different.

Still, you should be careful with this procedure. There are some far-out groups of people who have found their peculiar brand of errors in the history of the Church and claimed that they, therefore, have the truth that has always been held by the Church. Well, there have always been errors in the Church too! Same devil, same false doctrines. The *first* foundation of our authority has to be the Bible itself; the second is testimony of reliable Christians. Who is a reliable Christian? Whoever testifies to the truth of the Bible! I know that sounds circular, but everything has to come back to God in some way. "For from him and through him and to him are all things." (Romans 11:36)

He uses faith. "It is written: 'I believed; therefore I have spoken.' With that same Spirit of faith we also believe and therefore speak." (2 Corinthians 4:13)

Paul is referring to the fact that the works of God – in this case, raising Christ from the dead – become the means of building faith in us through the Spirit working on our hearts. He says a little later that God "has given us the Spirit as a deposit, guaranteeing what is to come." (2 Corinthians 5:5); how then do we live when the Spirit is in us? "We live by faith, not by sight." (2 Corinthians 5:7) So when we study God's works in his Word, and the Spirit opens our eyes to see God in them, and we understand spiritually what it all means, there should be one result in us: faith in that same God to work the same way in our lives.

If you study the Bible and you don't grow in faith, there is something missing somewhere. The Spirit always builds faith in God's people; he doesn't just throw the facts at them and leave them alone to work it all out. The reason that God wants you to study this material in the first place is so that you will claim it too! *This is how God works.* He wants you to get that into your head and heart, and start using the principles that you find in the Bible. "As the body without the spirit is dead, so faith without deeds is dead." (James 2:26) And if a person studies the Bible without the Spirit, he studies with a dead heart that can never see God in it, and he will never be able to do what the text says to do.

> Do not merely listen to the Word, and so deceive yourselves. Do what it says. Anyone who listens to the Word but does not do what it says is like a man who looks at his face in a mirror and, after looking at himself, goes away and immediately forgets what he looks like. But the man who looks intently into the perfect law that gives freedom, and continues to do this, not forgetting what he has heard, but doing it – he will be blessed in what he does. (James 1:22-25)

The key to following up on what you've learned is the Spirit working it out in your life. The Lord looks for fruit from you, the "fruit of the Spirit," as proof that you are a worthwhile tree that he has planted. If you have a few things wrong then he will prune you, but if you aren't bearing fruit at all – if you can read the Bible and "worship" on Sundays and talk religiously but you aren't changing at all in faith and speech and life and love and purity – then he's going to dig you up and throw you away. (Luke 13:6-9)

One more point. By now you should realize that there is a vast difference between the physical world and the spiritual world. When God works in this physical world we may see the spiritual realities behind it and then again we may not; if we don't, then we are simply what the Bible calls "blind." Naturally, we are dead to God, completely insensitive to his presence, unable to see beyond the physical veil, and therefore we can't even taste the good things of Heaven. There were many Jews who suffered from this blindness when Jesus came into the world; they couldn't see that he was the Son of God. All they could see was a righteous man, a strange yet powerful man, a teacher who challenged the authorities, a miracle worker, a criminal on a cross.

But there were some people who could see the spiritual reality in Jesus. They knew that he was the Son of God. Some of these people liked what they saw, but then some of them didn't like it. Judas, for instance: he was one of the twelve who lived and worked with Jesus for three years and "saw his glory." There were certainly others who could see who he really was. And later, in the age of the Church, Paul and some of the other Apostles talked about certain people who saw the glory of Christ and turned their backs on him in the end. This kind of person is different than the regular, run-of-the-mill sinner in that they have been given the special sight to look into Heavenly realities – and they rejected what they saw.

I believe that this is what Jesus referred to as the "unforgivable sin." There's been a lot of discussion over the following passage:

> He who is not with me is against me, and he who does not gather with me scatters. And so I tell you, every sin and blasphemy will be forgiven men, but the blasphemy against the Spirit will not be forgiven. Anyone who speaks a word against the Son of Man will be forgiven, but anyone who speaks against the Holy Spirit will not be forgiven, either in this age or in the age to come. (Matthew 12:30-32)

This passage makes sense when you know what it is that the Spirit of God does. People will continually look at Jesus and not understand who he really is; that's to be expected, because he put aside his glory and came in humility and in the form of a servant. Since we don't naturally have eyes that are sensitive to the light of Heaven, we will invariably miss the significance of Christ. This is why people can despise the Son of God. They've heard his testimony and they hear others talk about him so excitedly, but they themselves don't see the glory in him. They are afraid of him; they hate what they hear him say and they don't want to get close to him for fear that everything that they value in life will come apart. So they heap insults on him out of their ignorance.

But when someone *sees* Christ's glory, the story becomes entirely different. The only way a person could ever see Jesus' glory is if the Spirit opens their eyes to the truth. Now they *know* he's the Savior; they can see that. They *know* that God sent him; there isn't any doubt about that now. They can see that he's the Lord of Heaven and earth. They can see that his blood is the only thing that saves sinners from their sin; they know the value that God places in that sacrifice and they've seen the ceremony in the spiritual Temple that took sin away. All this is the work of the Spirit who carried that person into the spiritual realm of God to learn the truth.

Now when someone turns away from what he knows is the truth, which is different from someone who never knew the truth and simply despises what he doesn't understand, that's a different kind of sin. "You Samaritans worship what you do not know; we worship what we do know, for salvation is from the Jews." (John 4:22) "From everyone who has been given much, much will be demanded; and from the one who has been entrusted with much, much more will be asked." (Luke 12:48)

> It is impossible for those who have been once enlightened, who have tasted of the Heavenly gift, who have shared in the Holy Spirit, who have tasted the goodness of the Word of God and the powers of the coming age, if they fall away, to be

brought back to repentance, because to their loss they are crucifying the Son of God all over again and subjecting him to public disgrace. (Hebrews 6:4-6)

How much more severely do you think a man deserves to be punished who has trampled the Son of God underfoot, who has treated as an unholy thing the blood of the covenant that sanctified him, and who has insulted the Spirit of grace? (Hebrews 10:29)

All this is to say that you need to heed this warning of Christ when you study God's works. If indeed the Spirit opens your eyes to the truth of God there, and you see God working, and you learn something about the nature of God and his ways, then you are now responsible for what you've seen. The Spirit of God has committed you to action; you *must* act on it now.

The Lord's Works accomplish his will

If Christianity were a matter of doing whatever we liked then there would be a lot more converts than there are. But its primary characteristic is that we are living under the authority of God now, and we aren't living to please ourselves anymore. Unbelievers sense this in us right away; it's this loss of their personal freedom that scares them off from becoming a Christian.

But though we know that we owe everything to the Lord, and that we belong to him now so that he has rights over every part of our lives, it seems to be a difficult thing to let go of our personal freedom. What I mean is this: people have known for the entire age of the Church that Christ is the Lord, yet Christians continue to struggle with various feelings of rebellion and self-will. There has even been some confusion about the Lord himself and our relationship toward him; people talk about becoming a Christian, and then they talk about the second step – taken later on – of "making Jesus Lord of our lives." One can very easily be a believer, they say, and yet not be submissive to Christ's Lordship.

While it's true that everyone struggles with submitting to the Lord's authority, it's not true that the Lord has been sitting around waiting for us to do that. We don't "make him Lord" over us – he *is* Lord, and he always deals with us as the supreme authority. He is Lord because he does the works of a king, not because we happen to tip our hats to his office. He is Lord whether we like it or not.

And we will find that whatever he wants to do, he does. We can learn at least two things about the Lord by studying his works: *first*, we learn what he wants to get done, and *second*, we learn that whatever he wants to do, he does! There's a great deal of difference between us and God in this respect. We want things, but we often are unable to bring them about; God wants things, and they *will* happen because he wants them to happen. There's no doubt about whether God will get what he wants.

There's another aspect of God's will: we are completely unable to do it. We might want the same things that God wants – in fact, God may plainly tell us to do it. But when it comes time for us to try to do God's works, we fail completely. Only God *can* do what he wants done.

What we want to look at now is that, through his works, God does what he wants. His works accomplish his will.

HE IS THE LORD

We use this phrase a lot but I don't believe it has really hit us yet. The fact that God is the Lord – that Jesus Christ is the Lord – is a profound reality. Like spokes around the hub of a wheel, the whole universe revolves around this central King who rules and controls all things according to his own liking.

We needn't be offended that God holds such complete authority over everything. Kings of old used to mistreat their subjects and use their powers for their own ends; in fact, our own country started in rebellion against that very kind of tyranny. We've grown accustomed, over the last two hundred years, to many kinds of freedoms that we don't want to give up now. But God is the King of a kingdom, like it or not. And, yes, he rules with an iron fist, but he is completely fair to all. Nobody can take him to task about how he runs his kingdom. Sinners are punished according to the strict requirements of the Law, saints are rewarded with the crown of their faithfulness, food and clothing are there when we need them, the next world waits in the wings while this world heads for its doom – surely God does all things well, and with an eye to meeting the needs of every creature.

But though he is fair and just, he is also a tough God. He has particular views on things and he expects us to believe the way he does. He has goals in mind that he doesn't want anybody to mess up. He likes his surroundings to be a certain way: he loves holiness, he hates wickedness and rebellion, he loves faith, he hates pride. God has a lot of expectations that he doesn't intend to give up.

Here is the definition of the title "Lord" – that everything has to conform to his standards and not ours. *We* have to change, not God. In fact, his will extends to the smallest details of our lives – to the smallest details of the entire universe. He has an opinion on every little thing and he won't be satisfied until everything comes under his authority and control.

How important is the will of God? It's at the head of God's list! Everyone has priorities in their lives, and God has his priorities too. Unfortunately we don't always agree with God on what's really important. Prayer is a good indicator of what we consider important; you can tell what you live *for* by what you pray *about*. Jesus taught us what the priorities of a Christian should be when he taught us what to pray about, and behold, the will of God is the first item on the agenda:

> This is how you should pray: Our Father in Heaven, hallowed be your Name, your kingdom

come, *your will be done* on earth as it is in Heaven. (Matthew 6:9-10)

You have probably known someone who seems to attract everyone around them. They are always the center of attention; everyone tries to please them, and when they don't like something then they make their feelings known immediately and something has to change. Well, God is that way to the extreme; he "draws all men to himself" (John 12:32) and demands that we change our lives to suit him. He made every one of us to serve him, and we will either do what he tells us or he will find somewhere to stick us out of his way. The more we study the Lord, the more we realize that we aren't living in this world to do what we want but what he wants. We are all his servants, his slaves, whether we are aware of it or not.

HE DOES WHAT HE WANTS

If he's the absolute Lord of the entire universe, the Master of angel and devil and saint and sinner, we can expect to see him bending everything to his will. His will is the important thing, as is true with any king. He not only wants something but he intends to get it; and since he's the Creator and the Provider and the Savior and the Father, then his will *is* going to happen.

Here we enter into strange territory. We know what it means to want something, but what we want doesn't always happen. In fact, much of what we want remains only a wish – a longing for a reality that can't happen, no matter how hard we try.

God doesn't know anything about that. When he wants something, it just happens. When he wanted a universe he simply spoke and it came into existence. When he wanted a nation of his own, he drew them out of the clutches of Pharaoh and led them through the desert to the Promised Land. When he wanted more wine to set at ease his mother's worries, Jesus simply spoke and the thing was done. You see, creation seems to jump at his merest wish and conform to his will. His Word has a creative force to it, so that when he speaks his will then the Word goes out ...

> It will not return to me empty, but will accomplish what I desire and achieve the purpose for which I sent it. (Isaiah 55:11)

He doesn't think it strange at all that mountains leap out of his way when he comes close to the earth, or that the seas roll back from his feet. Everything bends to his divine will, and he expects it.

He will not tolerate any rebellion; he gets extremely upset when he doesn't get his way. There are good reasons that his will should be done – for one thing, because he knows, in any situation, all the circumstances and people involved to a degree that we can't possibly hope to know; only someone with an infinite and wise understanding can come up with the course of action that is needed and good. We may be offended at the way God demands his will, but an expert needs to be respected, not scorned; our well-being hangs in the balance.

He will go to great measures to force us to conform to his will. If laying down the Law won't suffice, he will bring the sentence of death down upon our heads – which is what he did after Adam and Eve's rebellion against his will. (Genesis 3) When the Lord demanded obedience from Saul, and Saul thought he had a better idea, the Lord tore the kingdom away from Saul and gave it to another. (1 Samuel 13:1-15) When he commanded Jonah to go to Nineveh and preach, and Jonah headed the opposite direction in rebellion, the Lord brought a great fish to swallow the prophet and gave him three days to think about it again! There are many other examples throughout the Bible of the Lord getting his own way and things turning out better because of it.

GOD'S WILL OVERRIDES OUR SIN

Of course we naturally raise the question, what about man's sin? God may want holiness and obedience, but it's clear that he isn't getting it from us. From the animals, maybe, and from the rest of creation, but not from us, to our eternal shame. How can we say that God does his will when we sin against his will and mess things up?

Traditional Christian doctrine has always distinguished between what God *himself* intends to do – no matter what man might want to do to the contrary – and what he expects of *us*. We may not know much about what he intends to do, but that doesn't matter; he's going to do it anyway. He has fully published in the Bible, however, what he expects of us and it's this aspect of his will that we have sinned against. We refuse to do his *expressed will*. He laid down certain requirements when he made man; he wanted us to obey him in everything, to represent him on earth, to rule over all the creatures in his Name, to bear his image as a testimony to the world. Of course we have turned away from all of these expectations and devised a lifestyle of our own choosing, according to our own wills.

Does this put a crimp on God's eternal plans? We mustn't underestimate the damage that sin has done; we may consider God to be the unshakable, the Eternal One, the Almighty, but the fact remains that we ruined our own natures and brought the creation of God down with us. Sin is damaging to the works of God. We are the one loose nut in God's beautiful world. Whereas everything else fulfills its function according to God's will (indeed, everything has no choice but to conform to God's will – how can a tree be anything else than what he made it to be?) we alone have thrown off our duty. He made us, of all the creatures, *able* to resist his will when he made us *free* to do his will. We have turned our freedom into license and traded God's will for our own wills. Our distinctive trait became our downfall.

So what does God do in light of our willfulness? Here is where we enter the Hall of Mysteries, where we will see things that we can't understand but they are true nonetheless. *God overrides our willfulness and does his will anyway.* Remember, he can't tolerate any will other than his own; he never has and he never will. He alone is God, the Lord! There is no other god before him – and especially we are not God. So he is going to get what he wants from us even when we are doing what he doesn't want us to do.

How does he do that? Nobody knows. Nobody can explain how Pharaoh can resist the Lord and still be playing right into the Lord's hand. Nobody knows how Samson can be so stupid and fleshly and still the Lord accomplishes his will through him against the Philistines. Nobody knows how Jesus worked with Judas, gave him abilities that the other disciples had, sent him out to preach with the others and yet knew full well the deed that this man would soon commit against him. What is even more amazing is that this act of sin, this crime against the Son of Man, resulted in the salvation of people all through the world and through all time. God planned for it! How does God take the sins of men and use them to do his will?

We don't understand such things because we can't do the impossible as he can. In order to do good deeds we need good men. In order to accomplish our goals we need the right materials. If people fight us then we can't get anywhere; enemies make it difficult if not impossible to get things done.

When we need to build a house, we need materials that are good for building houses.

But God works *through* our sinfulness and rebellion, not around it. He doesn't need our cooperation in order to do what he wants. (He expects it, but he doesn't need it.) When a sinner thinks that he has finally beaten God, he finds out that he played right into God's hands. Gold sinks men *deeper* into Hell; living without God ends up to be an eternity without God; a trap set for the children of God turns out to be a trap that the wicked themselves fall into. Whatever man does against God boomerangs back on his own head. God is smarter than any of us!

> Do not be deceived: God cannot be mocked. A man reaps what he sows. The one who sows to please his sinful nature, from that nature will reap destruction; the one who sows to please the Spirit, from the Spirit will reap eternal life. (Galatians 6:7-8)

So, even though we seem to successfully sin against him, we end up hurting ourselves, not him. He ends up the conqueror.

Now beyond this point we can't go; we can't presume to understand how God even allows sin in his universe. There are some mysteries that the Bible doesn't explain to us, and we aren't called to dream up theories to explain them. A lot of people have lost sleep worrying about how God can do all of his will and yet allow sin – does he actually *will* the sin? Such questions will only lead us to say heretical and disrespectful things about God. Nobody knows how these two realities – sin and God – exist in the same universe; but they do, and it's best to let God handle that problem. Our job is to get rid of this sin and conform to his will; we aren't called to be philosophers about this but to be saved from our sin.

WHAT IS HIS WILL?

That's the question, isn't it? Everyone is wondering what God's will is. When we first become Christians and are awake (the Bible calls it "alive") to the reality of God, we are sensitive to the fact that God is there with his will. We want to know what it is and start doing it for a change. After all, we've spent all our lives living according to our own wills – we are ready to start doing things his way now!

But soon problems set in and complications arise. Often we don't get very good teaching at the beginning, mainly because the Christians around us haven't gotten good teaching themselves, and we start falling back on our own resources again to get through life. It's not that we want to rebel against God – it's just that we still don't know what God's will is for our lives.

You've probably heard many Christians longing to know what God's will is. That's because they don't know where to look for it, though it's right under their noses. For one thing, if they would study the works of the Lord they would know his will – he did what he *wants* done! He conformed men and women to his image, and we can read how he did it and what he was after. He defeated the enemy his way, and we can learn how he wants to defeat the enemy in our day. Our problem is that we need to sit down and study his works for a while if we want to know what his will is.

Let's go back through some of the material in the Bible and try to find out what God's will is:

He wants to reveal himself. "No longer will a man teach his neighbor, or a man his brother, saying, 'Know the Lord,' because they will all know me, from the least of them to the greatest." (Hebrews 8:11) This is the ultimate experience for man – to know God. He has the mind and heart that are capable of seeing and knowing who God is, and he's capable of glorifying him. Man alone, of all creatures, can draw close to the Divine being; he was made to live in two worlds at the same time – the physical and the spiritual.

Yet because of sin we have all been plunged into a darkness that none of us can see out of. Sin has robbed us of the eyes to see God's world; now we can only see this world. Sin has killed the spiritual life in our hearts so that we only feel the need for physical comforts. God's world is so far from our minds now that, if he didn't forcibly come and get our attention, we would be content to spend our entire lives in total ignorance of who he really is, which is what actually happens with most of mankind. We live only for this world and what we can see and touch, and we know virtually nothing about God.

The Lord, however, for reasons known only to himself, chose not to leave us in such abysmal ignorance. He wanted to restore man to the position of citizen of two kingdoms; he wanted to reveal himself to man so that man could know who God really is. In order to do this, God must put life into man's heart where there has only been spiritual death – he has to wake us up to the spiritual world so that we *can* see and know spiritual realities. He doesn't do this with everyone! But here and there he comes close to someone and raises them out of death into the world of light and life, and they see God.

> Wake up, O sleeper,
> rise from the dead,
> and Christ will shine on you.
> (Ephesians 5:14)

The first item of business for someone who has just woken up from the dead is to learn who God is. This is especially important to God, though we will often miss the point ourselves. Our very survival in the spiritual kingdom of Christ depends on how well we know God, as we will see shortly. So we immediately learn such things about God as these: that he's our Father, that Jesus is the Shepherd who called us back to the fold of God's people, that the Father will provide for all of our daily needs, and so on. We learn the importance of prayer, that through it we find strength and help in time of need. We learn that we must start living according to the wishes of the Father; we must die to self and follow Christ where he leads us.

The Israelites went through this kind of experience when God brought them out of Egypt. They had been over four centuries in that pagan land with little formal learning in the ways of God. They knew hardly anything about him! So after they got out, the first thing that God started doing with them is teaching them all about himself. He brought them to Mt. Sinai and there showed himself to them on the mountain; he gave them his Law and taught them that it represented his own holy nature, that they must conform to its standards if they wanted him to live among them. He told them what they had to do to worship him. He showed them what he was capable of in order to protect them from their enemies and provide them with food and water. They learned all sorts of things about their God that was going to come in handy in the future, things that a people need to know about God. This was their learning time.

After the initial learning phase, God's people are supposed to be able to live according to that knowledge. They are supposed to walk before the Lord in holiness and fear, trusting in him for all their needs, coming close to worship him as is his due. But what often happens is that we drop out of learning mode and think that we can do well enough on what little we know. Soon we begin to run into problems that we've never encountered before, like a world that opposes the things of God. The enemy finds clever ways to trip us up into sin and unbelief. We start wandering in confusion, wondering where God went and why he isn't helping us anymore. We feel alone again, like the times before our conversion. Here again, the antidote is the knowledge of God. The way we begin to resist the devil and start living for God again is to get back into learning mode and find out more about who God is:

> For this reason, since the day we heard about you, we have not stopped praying for you and asking God to fill you with the knowledge of his will through all spiritual wisdom and understanding. And we pray this in

order that you may live a life worthy of the Lord and may please him in every way: bearing fruit in every good work, growing in the knowledge of God, being strengthened with all power according to his glorious might so that you may have great endurance and patience, and joyfully giving thanks to the Father, who has qualified you to share in the inheritance of the saints in the kingdom of light. (Colossians 1:9-12)

We begin finding out (hopefully, that is – too many Christians seem not to reach this stage; they seem content to wander in confusion as long as the problems don't get too bad) that there's more to learn about God, more things about our spiritual inheritance that we need to know about.

Job discovered this when he was going through his troubles. He thought he knew his God! He was certainly a righteous man; it says that he "was blameless and upright; he feared God and shunned evil." (Job 1:1) He sacrificed on behalf of his children, thinking "perhaps my children have sinned and cursed God in their hearts." (Job 1:5) Who can claim to have a better life than Job? But the time came when Job lost everything he had, possessions as well as children; he was thrown on hard times that would try the faith of the best saints. As his world crumbled around him, and friends and wife encouraged him to give up, Job held on to the belief that there was more here than met the eye. Little did he know that what he needed was a deeper understanding of the ways of God! The Lord was forcing Job to see his own spiritual blindness, his lack of faith in the God who does what he wills, his self-pride in the face of the Holy One. The Lord took Job through deep waters in order to make him see more of God:

> My ears had heard of you, but now my eyes have seen you. Therefore I despise myself and repent in dust and ashes. (Job 42:5-6)

Some people simply don't come to this realization, however. Going ever deeper into their sins, being pushed around by the world, immersing themselves in the physical pleasures of life and then coming out bankrupt and having nothing to show for themselves on Judgment Day, they seem to be oblivious to the fact that their only hope is to get back to God.

> My people are destroyed from lack of knowledge. Because you have rejected knowledge, I also reject you as my priests; because you have ignored the Law of your God, I also will ignore your children. (Hosea 4:6)

Although this was spoken about the Israelites who experienced suffering because of ignorance of God's ways (the destruction of Jerusalem and the Exile to Babylon), I can't think of a more tragic example of spiritual ignorance than the case of the Jews in Jesus' time. Of all things to miss – their own Messiah! They knew all about the Word of God, but they couldn't see the spiritual reality of it:

> You diligently study the Scriptures because you think that by them you possess eternal life. These are the Scriptures that testify about me, yet you refuse to come to me to have life. (John 5:39-40)

Even though Jesus spoke and taught among them, they couldn't hear the voice of God or see the Son of God working:

> If I am telling the truth, why don't you believe me? He who belongs to God hears what God says. The reason you do not hear is that you do not belong to God. (John 8:46-47)

After doing all his miracles and teaching the very words of his Father, Jesus later stood over Jerusalem and shook his head, weeping:

> O Jerusalem, Jerusalem, you who kill the prophets and stone those sent to you, how often I have longed to gather your children together, as a hen gathers her chicks under her wings, but you were not willing! Look, your house is left to you desolate. I tell you, you will not see me again until you say, "Blessed is he who comes in the name of the Lord." (Luke 13:34-35)

I think that this is all true of modern Christians as well. Rather than admit our weakness and ignorance, we are all too willing to make what we can out of life with the little we know about God, not realizing that the little we know isn't nearly as sufficient as we hope. We will inevitably suffer until we humbly return to our God and sit at his feet and learn. Some call it "living the victorious Christian life" – we would all like to, but try as we might we just can't seem to get the old fire back again. Some people, of course, don't want that old fire back – they want the name and privilege of Christian but not the spiritual realities of it! But some really do hurt when God seems far away, and they want the Lord to "restore to me the joy of your salvation." (Psalm 51:12)

One of the reasons that we are doing this study on the Works of God is so that our knowledge of him will increase and we will be better able to trust him in the trials and problems of life. We can't afford *not* to learn more of him! If we adopt the self-righteous, smug attitude that the Pharisees had in Jesus' day, the "day of grace" will pass us by without our even knowing it and we will not be able to stand solidly on God our Foundation when trouble hits us.

There's another reason that God wants to reveal himself, and that's so that he can get glory for himself. We've already looked at this idea before, but we need to realize more than we do the importance of God's glory. One example will be sufficient. When Balaam was hired by the

Moabites to curse the Israelites on their way to the Promised Land, he saddled up his donkey and headed for Moab. On the way he experienced quite a bit of difficulty from his donkey! The animal at times simply refused to cooperate, until finally she resisted going any further. All the while Balaam thought that he just had a particularly stubborn mule on his hands; but God wasn't done yet. First he made the donkey talk back to Balaam, and then he sent an angel to confront the man. Balaam suddenly found out the reason for his donkey's reluctance to go further! He found out that God was responsible for his troubles – that the Israelites' God was near, doing whatever was necessary to protect his people from the curses of the enemy. Balaam learned that he had a greater enemy than man to contend with if he was going to go through with this cursing. (Numbers 22:21-35)

Like Balaam, we are often too prone to put the wrong construction on things simply because we don't know enough about God and his ways. The Lord won't be satisfied with that, however; one way or another he's going to do something that will clearly reveal to us his presence and his purposes. He wants the glory, the credit, the attention; he won't share it with anybody else and he won't run the risk of our misunderstanding the situation and taking glory for ourselves. The proud will be humbled, the humble will be lifted up, the wicked will perish, the righteous will inherit the land, the widow and the orphan will be cared for – and when all of this happens, it will be obvious who is responsible for it.

He wants to judge. "Will not the Judge of all the earth do right?" (Genesis 18:25) There is no lack of examples for this truth in the Bible. Over and over again we see the Lord straightening out a situation to make it conform to his standards, either by punishment or by teaching or by reward.

The problem with this world is that it doesn't reflect the spiritual world very well. Nor should it, really; this world has peculiarities about it that suit our living here, but it can do nothing for the state of our souls. It's man who is supposed to cross between the two worlds; he's supposed to introduce the realities of God's kingdom into this world and conform the physical to the standards of the spiritual. Take his own body, for instance. Left to itself it will dominate a man with its lusts and desires because it has no built-in controls except self-destruction. If a man wants to keep his body in line then he needs to apply a spiritual control to it, a standard from another world, that will force his body to conform to God's limits for the body.

> For if you live according to the sinful nature, you will die; but if by the Spirit you put to death the misdeeds of the body, you will live. (Romans 8:13)

But man has no intention of willingly living by spiritual principles, unfortunately; by falling into sin and the life of sin, he threw away his mandate to rule this world in God's Name and now he's intent on conforming himself to the demands of the physical. Now the situation has become serious – the honor and glory of God the

Creator is at stake. To look at how people are living all over the world you would think that there are no such things as morals or righteousness or Heaven and hell. Everyone and everything is in a state of confusion; nobody knows what we are here for, or why we should even take the trouble to be scrupulous about anything. People murder and steal and cheat and lie and hate and hurt, all the while thinking that God isn't watching and nobody cares (except the victim, of course, and who cares about him?). "When the sentence for a crime is not quickly carried out, the hearts of the people are filled with schemes to do wrong." (Ecclesiastes 8:11)

This, of course, is unacceptable to God. To him it's very important that right is called right and wrong is called wrong. The wicked have to get their due, and the righteous their reward. The hurt has to be healed, the damage undone, the works of sinners torn down and the works of God put in their place. Death must be reversed and the graves emptied. The flesh must be made to conform to the laws of Heaven; the will of God must once again rule the earth as it does in Heaven.

It's this great desire of God to rectify every wrong that drives his actions in the Bible. We can see his judgment everywhere in the book, but we perhaps don't realize how important it is to him to judge the earth. Our misconceptions are distorting our knowledge of him. For one thing, because judgment doesn't come immediately and in every circumstance, we gather from this that judgment is a "sometimes" thing with him and he can easily dispense with it. Not so –

> For if God did not spare angels when they sinned, but sent them to hell, putting them into gloomy dungeons to be held for judgment; if he did not spare the ancient world when he brought the flood on its ungodly people ... if he condemned the cities of Sodom and Gomorrah by burning them to ashes, and made them an example of what is going to happen to the ungodly ... then the Lord knows how to rescue godly men from trials and to hold the unrighteous for the day of judgment, while continuing their punishment. (2 Peter 2:4-6,9)

We don't know the heart of God very well if we think he's content to watch the world go its own way. For example, a leper came to Jesus wanting healing. He knew that Jesus *could* heal him; what he wasn't sure about was whether Jesus *wanted* to heal him. He didn't know what God's will was for his life! He found out that this is one of the things that God is most willing to do; it's his will to heal disease in his people:

> A man with leprosy came and knelt before him and said, "Lord, if you are willing, you can make me clean." Jesus reached out his hand and touched the man. "I am willing," he said. "Be clean!" Immediately he

was cured of his leprosy. (Matthew 8:2-3)

When God judges, he takes something that shouldn't be and makes it what it should be. This is very important to him. When Samuel went looking for a king for the nation Israel, the Lord directed him to Jesse's house and there he saw Jesse's seven strong, outstanding sons who seemed eligible enough for the office. But he made a wrong judgment; the things he considered important for a king weren't what God considered important, and the Lord wasn't going to let Samuel pick the wrong man. He spoke his will directly to Samuel:

> The LORD said to Samuel, "Do not consider his appearance or his height, for I have rejected him. The LORD does not look at the things man looks at. Man looks at the outward appearance, but the LORD looks at the heart." (1 Samuel 16:7)

The Lord then judged the situation correctly and had Samuel anoint David, the runt of the lot – who turned out to be a man "after God's own heart." History proved how well the choice was made.

You will find in the Bible that God always judges the actions of men. He has strong opinions on everything we do! He isn't sitting up there in Heaven busying himself with other matters, only thinking about our problems when we bother him with them. The Lord works constantly on the problems of sin and death, bringing all his powers to bear on the problems. One of the most useful tools at his disposal is his Law, which he uses to check the value or worth of men and nations. He never fails to refer to it or use it to judge us. The Law is, after all, his description of a perfect world; so we shouldn't be surprised that his will is in strict conformity to the standards of that Law. His will has always been that the world obey him as the Law specifies, and he judges all of our actions by how well we have performed the requirements of the Law.

It isn't long before we are introduced to the Law of God – it comes up in detail in the second book of the Bible. Four out of the first five books of the Bible deal specifically with spelling out the details of God's Law. We get the impression that the Lord wants us to know this! The Jews got the idea very well; they called the first five books the "Torah," which is Hebrew for "Law." They considered the rest of the Bible – the "Prophets" and the "Writings" – as just a commentary and expansion on this Torah. The Law was the heart and foundation of the entire Scriptures.

> Take to heart all the words I have solemnly declared to you this day, so that you may command your children to obey carefully all the words of this Law. They are not just idle words for you – they are your life. By them you will live long in the land you are crossing the Jordan to possess. (Deuteronomy 32:46-47)

This great desire of God that his Law be obeyed explains many of his actions of judgment that we read in the Bible. To take one example, we read how the kingdom of Israel was split into two pieces – north and south – when Jeroboam rebelled against Rehoboam, the son of Solomon and the heir to all his father's kingdom. The rebellion was the story from man's point of view; what happened from God's point of view was that the fault lay with Solomon himself:

> [*speaking to Jeroboam*] See, I am going to tear the kingdom out of Solomon's hand and give you ten tribes … I will do this because they have forsaken me and worshiped Ashtoreth … and have not walked in my ways, nor done what is right in my eyes, nor kept my statutes and laws as David, Solomon's father, did. (1 Kings 11:31,33)

It was a drastic move, and this division proved to be a constant source of trouble to both sides. One would think that the Lord would have done things to preserve the peace instead of deliberately setting up for trouble! But he was incensed that Solomon and the Israelites had broken his clear commands about worship; he was much more interested in obedience to the Law than he was in peace.

We Christians haven't escaped from the demands of the Law! Even though Christ has fulfilled the Law for us, God isn't satisfied with letting us live a life that is contrary to the Law.

Christ *saved us from sin* – which being defined means, saved us from breaking the Law of God. "Sin is lawlessness," (1 John 3:4) we are told. When Christ bought our pardon he also bought the righteousness that the Law demands and is now applying that Law righteousness on our sinful natures. By sending Christ, God – again as the judge …

> … condemned sin in sinful man, in order that the righteous requirements of the Law might be fully met in us, who do not live according to the sinful nature but according to the Spirit. (Romans 8:4)

The Lord fully intends to rectify this problem of sin in us. Jesus told us that you will know a tree by its fruit – you can tell if someone is being saved from sin because you will see the Law's righteousness in their lives. This is a theme that Paul picks up on too:

> But the fruit of the Spirit is love, joy, peace, patience, kindness, goodness, faithfulness, gentleness and self-control. Against such things there is no Law. (Galatians 5:22-23)

But we can't judge things ourselves very well. Even though the Law is the standard of righteousness, it isn't safe for us to play the judge – we usually won't use the tool wisely and someone is going to get hurt if not misled. Jesus showed quite skillfully how well he could judge men's hearts with the Law; he also showed how carelessly those men handled the Law themselves. When the Pharisees brought a woman caught in adultery to him, he didn't excuse what the woman had done; but he also didn't excuse those men from their sins either. The Law that they so callously burdened her with was turned back on their own heads in condemnation! This is why Jesus counseled us about judging others:

> Do not judge, or you too will be judged. For in the same way you judge others, you will be judged, and with the same measure you use, it will be measured to you. (Matthew 7:1-2)

On the other hand, not only is the Lord able to judge us, he's most definitely going to judge us. He intends to separate the sheep from the goats and he's going to do a good job at it too.

One more point under this heading. Part of the idea of judging is to make plain what's really going on. Since we have a problem seeing spiritual realities, and since we are often misled by the things in this world, we have great need for God to show us the truth. But does he *want* to show us the truth? What is his will?

> It is for your good that I am going away. Unless I go away, the Counselor will not come to you; but if I go, I will send him to you. When he comes, he will convict the world of guilt in regard to sin and righteousness and judgment ... I

> have much more to say to you, more than you can now bear. But when he, the Spirit of truth, comes, he will guide you into all truth. (John 16:7-8,12-13)

When Jesus was about to leave his disciples for good, and they were going to face overwhelming difficulties, he told them that he intended to send the Spirit who would make plain to them the truth about Christ and the Kingdom. Not only would the Spirit show them the realities of Heaven, he would also make it plain to the sinners of the world that they are guilty when they touch one of God's elect. It's so important to God that we all know what's really going on! Otherwise the wicked would take heart from never hearing about judgment, and we would lose heart from the apparent victories of the world. God won't allow that to happen.

He wants to save. "He is patient with you, not wanting anyone to perish, but everyone to come to repentance." (2 Peter 3:9) We have a lot of our own priorities for our lives, and it seems that we don't mind telling God about them. Examine your prayers once and you will see what I mean. Make a list of the things that you pray for, of the things that you think are important and that you want God to address. Then look at the Bible and see what's at the top of God's list.

> You are to give him the name Jesus, because he will *save his people from their sins*. (Matthew 1:21)

... the Lord Jesus Christ, who gave himself for our sins *to rescue us from the present evil age*, according to the will of our God and Father. (Galatians 1:3-4)

You need to persevere so that when you have *done the will of God*, you will receive what he has promised ... But we are not of those who shrink back and are destroyed, but of those who *believe and are saved.* (Hebrews 10:36,39)

Therefore, since Christ suffered in his body, arm yourselves also with the same attitude, because he who has suffered in his body is done with sin. As a result, he does not live the rest of his earthly life for evil human desires, but rather *for the will of God.* (1 Peter 4:1-2)

These passages point out one truth that every Christian ought to get into his head: sin is our fundamental problem, and God is primarily interested in saving us from it. There are other things he wants to do as well, but saving us from sin is the first priority item.

God hates sin. We just don't realize how much it bothers him. We read the stories of the Old Testament where he punished people because of their sin and we think, why did he bring such a violent punishment down on their heads for doing such a little act of sin? Why is sin so deserving of the wrath of God? But we wouldn't need to ask this question if we once got a glimpse of God in his Heavenly Temple:

> I saw the LORD seated on a throne, high and exalted, and the train of his robe filled the temple ... Holy, holy, holy is the LORD Almighty; the whole earth is full of his glory ... "Woe is me!" I cried. "I am ruined! For I am a man of unclean lips, and I live among a people of unclean lips, and my eyes have seen the King, the LORD Almighty." (Isaiah 6:1,3,5)

Like a child who knows when he's in trouble, man knows deep within that he has angered God. We fear to come to him for that reason. We try to justify ourselves and we have all sorts of excuses as to why we live the way we do; but they all die on our lips when we see God face to face. There are no excuses for us. The soul that sins must die; the man who lives in rebellion against God and his commands must die. It's this fear that hangs over us when we think about God – this fear of a haunting conscience that accuses us, of an angry God who waits for us on his throne of judgment, of the awful and unthinkable punishment "prepared for the devil and his angels." (Matthew 25:41)

Sin ruins things. God has every reason to be angry about sin. For one thing, take a walk through the hospitals and special homes for the handicapped and the elderly, the mentally insane, the crippled and people born with debilitating defects. These people are safely tucked away from the public eye so we aren't much aware of them. But their families are aware of them, and they are always agonizing over the question "why?" – why did this happen? At the root of it all is sin; not sin by the handicapped, per se, but sin in the human race that has twisted what was beautiful into something that's ugly and useless.

For another example, read the newspaper for accounts of man against man. It takes all kinds of forms – wars all around the world, businesses putting each other out of business, gangsters dumping victims in the river, local street gangs fighting and killing and looting, the rapists stalking the community at night, racial anger and race wars, strikes – why does all this happen? The Bible makes it clear that it's sin at the bottom of it all. Man is against man because of his selfishness and self-centeredness. (James 4:1-3)

These are just two examples of the fact that sin dominates our world. God never meant this world to be dominated by sin; he made it to be a place of peace and joy and love and wholeness and health – as men and women submit to him. He made man to bend the knee to God in all things, to trust him for all things, to follow God's will in all things – not just tip his hat toward God in a quick ceremony.

An earthly king demands to be obeyed. Someone can quickly lose their head, literally, if they don't pay attention and do all that the king commands. Hopefully the king doesn't rule by caprice – by whims that last a day or two and then change completely. A good king has excellent reasons (reasons of state, for the good of the kingdom) for issuing the particular edicts that he does.

So does God, in every respect. It isn't necessary that we always understand why God forbids certain things or commands other things. But if we don't obey them we are guilty of two sins: *first*, for not obeying the Lord, which in itself is a punishable act; and *second*, for introducing a damaging complication in the scheme of things. This second sin is even more fit for punishment because we include not only ourselves in the resulting damage but the honor of God and the well-being (perhaps spiritual!) of others as well. So we can be assured that the Lord's expressed will for our lives is going to be a blessing to ourselves, others, and a witness to the honor and glory of God – if we will just do it.

There's the problem. We rarely if ever do his will, either negatively or positively. It's in our bones, so to speak, to sin against the will of God:

> So I find this law at work: When I want to do good, evil is right there with me. For in my inner being I delight in God's Law; but I see another law at work in the members of my body, waging war against the law of my mind and making me a prisoner of the law of sin at work within my members. What a wretched man I am! Who will

rescue me from this body of death?
(Romans 7:21-24)

But the Lord isn't going to sit around waiting for our obedience. He determined long ago to take care of this problem of sin once and for all, and he started making plans for saving us from it "before the world began." Since the creation of the world he has been busy forming his salvation plan into a system that works. It started out small, in little doses of grace here and there, through shadows and types and earthly models that had no ability in themselves to save from sin. But eventually all the pieces came together, and he unveiled the great masterpiece of salvation for all the world to see and come to.

It was sin that offended God so much against Adam and Eve. He actually threw them out of the garden that he had specially made for them! He cursed the entire human race through the first human pair, doomed to live in sorrow and die like animals. Let's get the immensity of the tragedy in full view. If God would not do some amazing thing to counteract the devastating power of sin on the human soul, then this creature man who was destined to be the companion of God would exist forever *without* God in unspeakable misery, all because of his sin against God.

Someone once said that it's the Fall of man, not the love of God, that's hard to understand. The Lord at once began the process of rescuing sinners out of the furnace of death that we had plunged ourselves into. Everywhere you turn in the Bible you will find this theme of rescuing, saving, "plucking from the fire," that is so all-important to God.

Take for instance the Sermon on the Mount. At first glance it seems as though Jesus is simply telling us how hard it is to be a Christian. You thought this stuff is easy, he is saying; well let me tell you that "unless your righteousness surpasses that of the Pharisees and the teachers of the Law, you will certainly not enter the kingdom of Heaven." (Matthew 5:20) Sounds tough!

But take a closer look. With your mind's eye, imagine that you are standing there listening to Jesus. Please understand that this is no ordinary teacher instructing you; this is the Lord of glory, the King of Heaven, the one whom you must please if you hope to enter into his kingdom. Here he is standing in front of the door to his kingdom – telling you what you must be like if you want to come in! He *knows* what it's like in there – the consuming fire, the fearful judgment, the blood of the sacrifice for sin, the angels who worship day and night, the Father who must be obeyed at all costs. What if Jesus would let you in without telling you what you must do in preparation? You would certainly die! So this Sermon is a mercy, the first stage of salvation, the instruction that must come before the reality. This is what the Lord intends to do to *your* heart to prepare you for your entrance to the throne of God.

Not content with merely telling us what we must be like to be acceptable to God, Jesus started doing it to his disciples. He instructed them in the ways of God; they should have felt privileged because of the mysteries they were learning! Kings longed to look into the things that Jesus was quietly teaching his disciples. He forgave them their sins, a necessary prerequisite for living with God and getting anything further from him. He gave them power from on high to preach the Gospel and raise the dead and heal the sick. He banded them together with love and the Holy Spirit, to make one spiritual unit out of them – the Church – that the "gates of Hell" couldn't prevail against. He did all these things to save his disciples from their sin.

God is determined to save his people in spite of the sin that's in them. The Old Testament is a record of the frustrating experiences between God and his people – they were supposed to be totally committed to him and following all his commandments. Unfortunately they rarely did. In Ezekiel we get a glimpse of God's plans to end this charade once and for all:

> I will sprinkle clean water on you, and you will be clean; I will cleanse you from all your impurities and from all your idols. I will give you a new heart and put a new spirit in you. I will remove from you your heart of stone and give you a heart of flesh. And I will put my Spirit in you and move you to follow my decrees and be careful to keep my laws. (Ezekiel 36:25-27)

And he did!

> Live by the Spirit, and you will not gratify the desires of your sinful nature ... the fruit of the Spirit is love, joy, peace, patience, kindness, goodness, faithfulness, gentleness and self-control. Against such things there is no law. Those who belong to Christ Jesus have crucified the sinful nature with its passions and desires. Since we live by the Spirit, let us keep in step with the Spirit. (Galatians 5:16,22-25)

We have a power living in us now that can and does crucify the power of sin, so that we are free to serve God without the things that held us back before. Once we were enemies of God, but now we are his sons and we love to serve him. The difference is the amazing work of God on our hearts, conforming us to the image of his Son and making us useful in his kingdom.

> For we are God's workmanship, created in Christ Jesus to do good works, which God prepared in advance for us to do. (Ephesians 2:10)

There are many examples of God working his will to save. He saved his people Israel from Egypt; he continually saved the Israelites from the Philistines and the Moabites and other enemy nations; he saved Hezekiah and Jerusalem from Sennacherib's massive army of Assyria; he saved Nehemiah and the fledgling group of Jews, who were working to restore Jerusalem, from the hateful attacks of their envious neighbors. These are all examples of physical salvation from physical evils, but the foundation is laid there for understanding God's overall salvation process in the spiritual realm.

The Lord saved his disciples from their sins of denial and cowardice and made them strong defenders of the Faith in the face of fearful odds. He saved Paul from the raging sin in his heart against the Christians and made him the foremost Apostle of the Gospel. He saved a few here, a few there, in cities all over the civilized world, and they came together to form the foundation stones of the eternal Church of God. He saved Christians down through history – including us – from their lives of no purpose and selfishness and pride and corruption, making them fit vessels for the Holy Spirit. Ask any of these witnesses, if you are curious to know how God works, if it was God's doing or their own that made them free of their sin. You will find without exception that God was at work in them all, delivering them from their sins, without consulting them on the matter, just doing what he wanted and not taking "no" for an answer.

We don't clearly see the results of salvation right now, but we will later. Right now the mists and fog of this world hide what God is doing; weeds are growing in with the wheat (Matthew 13:24-30) and we don't know if we *are* being saved from sin – there's still so much of it! We no sooner overcome a particular sin than ten more settle in, like devils, in its place. And you don't read of the Lord's victories in the newspaper, either, because man is much more interested in his own works than in the things that the Lord is doing. Nevertheless, God is doing his quiet work among his people, which will one day be uncovered for all the world to see. He will force them to look at it; his work was the most important work all along, and only his work will last into eternity. The works of man will fade away like dead weeds, and the works of God will "shine like stars in the universe" forever. (Philippians 2:15)

He wants to put all in submission to him. "For he must reign until he has put all his enemies under his feet. The last enemy to be destroyed is death." (1 Corinthians 15:25-26) Again, we have to center on the meaning of the title "Lord" if we want to understand what God is doing in our world. He will not be satisfied until everything is going *his* way, until everyone and everything is doing what he wants them to do. As long as there are pockets of self-will here and there, he won't quit chasing down the rebels and forcing them to conform to his will.

Originally this world was made with this principle in mind. God *is* the Lord, and you can see how the physical creation obeys him across the great expanses of the universe as well as the microscopic size of the atomic world. It's really amazing how well everything is fulfilling every wish of his. For this is the only interpretation that the Bible allows us to have about our world; the mountains and seas and stars literally obey the will of their Maker by doing what they were made to do.

> His lightning lights up the world,
>   the earth sees and trembles.
> The mountains melt like wax before the LORD,
>   before the LORD of all the earth.
> The Heavens proclaim his righteousness,
>   and all the peoples see his glory.
>
> (Psalm 97:4-6)

Does this sound incredible? What would happen if the elements suddenly decided to follow their own will – what the scientists call self-determination, evolution, entropy, the "laws of nature" – just an impersonal world of cause and effect, the conservation of matter and energy? We would have chaos on our hands! Matter can't direct itself, nor can it hold itself in existence or keep its form, despite what the scientists say. For "in him all things hold together" (Colossians 1:17); without God's will the universe would cease to exist because its purpose for existing would be gone. Everything exists to fulfill some special purpose of his; everything looks to him for what it needs to keep going. (Psalm 145:15-16)

The only hitch in the scheme is the rebellion of man. Here is where everything came apart. Made to obey God and to glorify him on the earth, man instead chose a life of self-will; he intentionally turned away from God's Law and made his own set of rules to live by. He's been doing it ever since.

The result is all around us. Don't think that a little sin never hurt anybody! That little sin in the Garden of Eden, for example, brought the knowledge of death to man – a gruesome reality that he wasn't made to experience; there's nothing natural about death. That little sin plunged every human being into a state of determined and total rebellion against the person and the works and the ways of God; all men everywhere in the world share the characteristic of sinfulness and an amazing apathy toward the God of the Bible. This spiritual disease is everywhere, and we can easily see what it has done to us and our world. People everywhere ...

> ... have become filled with every kind of wickedness, evil, greed and depravity. They are full of envy, murder, strife, deceit and malice. They are gossips, slanderers, God-haters, insolent, arrogant and boastful; they invent ways of doing evil; they disobey their parents, they are senseless, faithless, heartless, ruthless. Although they know God's righteous decree that those who do such things deserve death, they not only continue to do these very things but also approve of those who practice them. (Romans 1:29-32)

An ugly picture of the world, isn't it? Yet Paul hasn't begun to describe the situation in its massive scope. *We are all infected with the lawless nature of our first parents,* to the degree that in some form or another we either willfully disobey God or do so out of ignorance. Either way, there's much of our lives that God hates.

The Lord isn't going to let this rebellion go by the board; not at all. He must be in full control of everybody's lives or his name doesn't mean what it says. He is the Lord! Every detail in this world *must* conform to his will; there mustn't be a single thing in existence outside of the divine plan. This renegade man must be dealt with.

So we find the Lord bending the works of man – yes, even the sins of man – to conform to his own will. Even though God doesn't claim credit for man's sin and the ruin that man has brought on the world, he will force his own results out of the situation.

For example, we can't begin to realize the damage that we've done to our world. Ecologists and biologists are still putting together a list of the atrocities that we've committed on our environment and on the plant and animal species all over the world. We've unleashed the forbidden power of the sun on the surface of our tender planet – atomic fission – and we don't seem to care that this deadly poison doesn't belong here, especially in the form of bombs. We are poisoning the atmosphere with the by-products of our manufacturing, poisoning fresh and salt waters, and poisoning the ground with waste that will threaten life for generations. Our capacity to destroy the earth has been growing exponentially in recent decades, and we're having no mercy on our planet – our greed is driving us. Even a non-environmentalist must take stock of the alarming situation. More than ever, then, this passage means a great deal:

> The creation waits in eager expectation for the sons of God to be revealed. For the creation was subjected to frustration, not by its own choice, but by the will of the one who subjected it, in hope that the creation itself will be liberated from its bondage to decay and brought into the glorious freedom of the children of God. We know that the whole creation has been groaning as in the pains of childbirth right up to the present time. (Romans 8:19-22)

Whatever has been done to the world, God is going to undo it. No longer will creation suffer under the sin of man. Because once again it will enjoy the will of its Creator and be what God always intended it to be – a perfect world, perfectly reflecting the glory of its Maker.

But this is only the beginning of pulling the reins short on this wild horse of sin. Already we can see that God has been busy forcing man's ways to achieve his own purposes. Joseph's brothers thought they were getting rid of their pesky brother; God twisted their sin around to result in the salvation of Jacob and his family during the great famine. The Canaanites thought they had a strong hold on their land of Palestine; little did they know that the Lord had other plans – soon they were all put to death to make room for the Israelites. The Israelites wanted a king, so the Lord gave them Saul. The whole affair wasn't much to God's liking in the first place ("But you have now rejected your God, who saves you out of all your calamities and distresses. And you have said, 'No, set a king over us.'"), but he turned a poor situation into a model of the kingship of Christ when he chose David to be king over Israel. Out of David's sin of adultery came the wisest king who ever ruled Israel. On and on the list goes. Man sins, he is determined to have things his own way, but God inevitably steps in and forces the situation to conform to his own will instead. He makes everyone submit to his authority and he makes the results of all our labors ultimately acceptable to him.

He doesn't always leave things as they stand, however. Sometimes he brings terror or destruction in order to do away with what he doesn't like. "The Lord works out everything for his own ends – even the wicked for a day of disaster." (Proverbs 16:4) This serves his purposes too, because it lets others know just how serious the Lord is about conforming everything to his will. Rather than let wickedness and rebellion clutter up his universe, he gets rid of it. Can anybody blame him?

> What if God, choosing to show his wrath and make his power known, bore with great patience the objects of his wrath – prepared for destruction? What if he did this to make the riches of his glory known to the objects of his mercy, whom he prepared in advance for glory? (Romans 9:22-23)

This is a fearful thought, that there will be men and women eternally destroyed under the wrath of God Almighty; but such a judgment will serve the eternal purposes of God in a way that no other course of action can satisfy. That's why we are counseled that nobody can win against God; in the end there will be a day of reckoning when even the wicked will submit to his will.

The church is perhaps the clearest example of God bending a situation to conform to his will. There is an excellent reason for this: this is his house that he's building; he intends to live in it forever. (Hebrews 3:1-6; 1 Peter 2:5) And as is natural with any homeowner, he prefers to build his house his own way. You will see, then, certain things going on in the Church that please the Lord – whether or not they please men. Things like getting rid of sin, putting love in its place, bringing about peace, instilling an atmosphere of fear and hope and faith in God. The Lord Jesus is the master of his own house, and we should expect to see him getting his own way there. Though we often don't see his will, that doesn't mean that it isn't going on; he taught us in the kingdom parables that what God does behind the scenes, in little ways, doesn't depend at all on what man does and will one day overturn the works of man. His work in the Church is sure and certain, though largely unrecognized and unaided by us.

One last example. When Jesus started his public ministry he identified himself with the prophecy from Isaiah (Isaiah 61:1-2) that foretold the special work that the Messiah would do when he came:

> The Spirit of the Lord is upon me, because he has anointed me to preach good news to the poor. He has sent me to proclaim freedom for the prisoners and recovery of sight for the blind, to release the oppressed, to proclaim the year of the Lord's favor. (Luke 4:18-19)

In order to impress his hearers with his resolve to do every detail in this list, he added, "Today this Scripture is fulfilled in your hearing." (Luke 4:21) For the next three years he worked to bring all these things about. What happened was that wrongs were made right, God's people were pulled out of darkness into light, people were forgiven of their sin and set on the path of righteousness, the downcast were encouraged to follow him, the sick were healed, demons were driven out of people's hearts, the enemies of God were defeated and driven back, the Jewish leaders were confused and the Romans mystified while the disciples rejoiced – he changed his country and his countrymen in a permanent way.

There was never such a stir in Israel as when this remarkable man showed up on the scene. Trees withered at his command, he settled the storms down to calm the seas, he raised the dead, he drove moneychangers from the Temple – everything he did caused a lot of discussion and change. It seemed that not only was he *able* to change the nation and the people, he was *intent* on doing so. For those who had eyes to see, it was nothing short of the hand of God forcing his will upon the people. The Messiah came to set up a new kingdom where God alone would rule; those are the unmistakable signs when we read the record. He came to impose his will on men's lives. He lowered the mountains and raised up the valleys to make way for his coming on the earth. Did he succeed? If we look at the thing from man's point of view, we would have to say that he only succeeded partially; but when we get a glimpse into God's world we see that Christ has been, and is becoming, Master over everything since he first arrived on earth.

> I have installed my King on Zion, my holy hill ... Ask of me, and I will make the nations your inheritance, the ends of the earth your possession. You will rule them with an iron scepter; you will dash them to pieces like pottery. (Psalm 2:6,8-9)

He's bending everything into conformity to his will, from the beginning of time to the end of time, all nations and all men, all the world. He's doing this in order to restore God's rightful place as Lord over all the earth, a very necessary procedure as the kingdom of God is set up in Heaven and on earth.

ONLY HIS WORKS CAN ACCOMPLISH HIS WILL

Now we ask the question, what does all this have to do with me? So God is doing his will; how does that affect my life? Won't he just go on doing his will regardless of what I do or want?

But there's the problem. Assuming that you are a Christian, you should want what God wants. You should want his will for your life; you should want to glorify him, to testify of him to the world. You should want the good things that he has in store for you – that's why you put little or no worth on the beads and baubles of this world. But if you are a typical Christian then you are probably trying to bring these things about in your life by yourself, not realizing that only God can do them.

God works his will in our lives; we can't. For one thing, we don't know what his will really is! In any particular circumstance, only he knows fully what he wants and what's necessary. For another, we couldn't do it if we tried. Living by the works of the Law is the same thing as trying to do God's will for him; you can't do it – Jews and Gentiles both have tried for millennia and they haven't succeeded yet.

Only God's works accomplish his will, not our works. Our works are poor imitations of the Father's eternal work. A child may imitate his father at work, but the father's customer won't hesitate to reject a child's efforts – it just doesn't fit the bill. In the same way, we can try to do the works of God for him, and we can try to bring about God's righteous kingdom for him, and we can try to fulfill the righteous requirements of the Law in our hearts; but we will always fail in our childish ignorance and weakness. *We will never grow out of the need for God's works in our lives.* They are the foundation of a Christian's daily experience; he has to have the Lord work his will in his heart on a regular basis or he will surely die spiritually.

Look back over the four things that God wants to do. This is his perfect will for your life as well as for the rest of the world. Do you think that you stand a chance of doing any of it on your own? Imagine the perfection that God requires of the whole thing, and the fact that whatever is done has to last forever. Is any of this really something that man can hope to do? Surely this is the time for God to work!

Here is a corollary to this truth: if your heart is dry of the things of God, it isn't because you haven't been trying your best to get back the old fire that you once knew. Your spiritual dryness and ineffectiveness is due solely to the fact that God isn't working in your heart. You may be full of good intentions; you may be faithfully performing your duty as God proscribed in the Word. But it takes more than your efforts to make you a Christian. If your prayers aren't answered, if you don't feel much interest in the Bible, if your love for the brothers and sisters has grown cold to the point that you aren't actively involved with ministering the grace of God to them, then the problem is that God is far away from you right now. He isn't working in you.

We have an understandable reaction to all this alarming news. When things are beginning to drag spiritually, we apply more pressure. We find more things to do; we "get involved" more; we study more; we pray more; we force our lives to conform to God's standards better. Do, do, do – as if any of this physical activity will bring about a spiritual change.

> You foolish Galatians! Who has bewitched you? Before your very eyes Jesus Christ was clearly portrayed as crucified. I would like to learn just one thing from you: Did you receive the Spirit by observing the Law, or by believing what you heard? Are you so foolish? After beginning with the Spirit, are you now trying to attain your goal by human effort? Have you suffered so much for nothing – if it really was for nothing? Does God give you his Spirit and work miracles among you

> because you observe the Law, or because you believe what you have heard? (Galatians 3:1-5)

This is a real danger for every Christian. We were taught from the very beginning the real order of things: first the spiritual reality, then the physical result. We are made righteous; *then* we do righteous acts. We are made children of God; *then* we come to our Father.

This truth has to guide our every step throughout our lives. If we once forget that God reserves his work to himself, that we can't do his work for him, then we will get into trouble. The arm of flesh has never been and will never be able to bring about God's righteous kingdom. All we can do, if we try it, is mess things up. At the very least we are going to waste our time trying; at the worst we will end up misleading people with lies and inflicting heavy burdens upon them that God never called them to carry.

> Since you died with Christ to the basic principles of this world, why, as though you still belonged to it, do you submit to its rules: "Do not handle! Do not taste! Do not touch!"? These are all destined to perish with use, because they are based on human commands and teachings. Such regulations indeed have an appearance of wisdom, with their self-imposed worship, their false humility and their harsh treatment of the body, but they lack any value for restraining sensual indulgence. (Colossians 2:20-23)

If we run the risk of messing things up, you can perhaps see the importance now of *knowing what God's works are!* The more you know about them, the clearer they will be in your mind, and the better able you will be to trust God for them instead of trying it yourself.

And you run the risk of missing out on God's works when you don't know what they are and aren't trusting him for them. If we decide we want to do things ourselves, our own way, the Lord just may step back and let us try. We won't succeed, of course, but the lesson will be good for us. Like a father who lets his son fail in order to impress him, God lets us fail miserably – and hurt from it – in order to bring our trust back to him. Do you enjoy living without God? Are you satisfied with a life without the evidence of God's works? If you don't, then it's about time you returned to him and pleaded his forgiveness for your mistrust of him.

The spiritual kingdom of God will never come about from human effort. We can work, and we do work, but –

Unless the LORD builds the house, its builders labor in vain. (Psalm 127:1)

There are just some things that only God can do. He made the world, and only he can restore it from its present decay. He made man upright, and only he can save man from his sin. There's a lot that God wants, but man is helpless and unable to do any of it; it's impossible for him. "Who then can be saved?" (Mark 10:26) It's time for God to come and do his will.

This is not to say that we must quit working. There are some works that are strictly reserved for the Lord, and then there are other things that he specifically instructed us to do. Again, the importance of knowing God's works! By knowing them well, we will understand what it is that he wants *us* to do.

Without going into a lot of detail on his commands, will find that he expects certain duties of us even here. ***First***, understand what his works are. (I keep saying it over and over, don't I? But this is the foundation of being a faithful Christian; fail here, and you will fail everywhere!) ***Second***, pray. Knowing what his works are isn't good enough; you have to ask for them. God's will must be your will. When you start praying for his will – his works – then your spirit is lining up with his will and he will answer your prayers. If you are unwilling to ask for the things that God does, then certainly you can't expect to benefit from simply knowing what those things are. ***Third***, wait. After you've asked for God's works, wait on him to do them. For one thing, the longer you wait and refrain from resorting to your own solutions, the greater the proof that you really do believe that only God can do it right. For another thing, and this is the point of this lesson, it will show that you believe that God *is* going to do it, whether it takes him a long time or not. God will inevitably do his will; his people are waiting to see his works.

The Lord's Works support his people

One of the most important things on God's mind is to take care of his people. It's a good thing, because nobody else wants to! We have been made into a different breed of man, set apart from the rest of the world with different ways of living and different goals that we are striving for. We like what the world hates and we hate what the world likes. There isn't anybody on our side anymore. We've burned our bridges with all the support systems that unbelievers depend on. We are stranded in an unfriendly world – we are armed soldiers in the middle of enemy territory, surrounded by hostile forces and unfriendly people. We need all the help that God can give us!

We are also in a peculiar position because of our faith – the things that used to be so useful to us are now useless to us. The way that the world goes about things leaves a bad taste in our mouths. We have to find new ways of solving problems because our consciences won't let us do it the old way anymore. We can see through a lot of the world's lies and deceits, and now we need something more substantial to live for and to love.

Of course the Lord has always done his works in dependable, useful, profitable ways, but nobody was really paying attention then. Nobody appreciated what God had been doing in the world, either through creation or providence or salvation. But now Christians have been wakened to the reality of God, and they can see God's world. They are able to appreciate God's works. So we should expect to see these people growing in the knowledge of God and his works.

And because God is their Father, he starts bringing all these works of his to bear on the lives of his children. Now that they are in the family, they are going to start benefiting from the works that they formerly heard about. Now the Father has a vested interest in these people! He woke them up, he gave them life, he introduced them to the realities of Heaven – and he intends to keep them moving toward more light and life. He is going to work *for them* – for their benefit, for their life and growth and joy and learning. In a special way, God's works support his people.

TREMENDOUS NEEDS

As was mentioned above, Christians immediately find themselves in a predicament. The old world, the old way of living, suddenly is totally inappropriate for living the Christian life. We find ourselves faced with tremendous and overwhelming needs of a spiritual nature that our old physical life-styles are unable to satisfy or support.

For one thing, a new Christian finds that he has a voracious spiritual appetite. He just can't get enough of God's Word or the things of God! He wants to talk about this new life with everyone; he wants to learn how to dig into the Bible; he wants to go to church and soak in as much as he can. No wonder – for years he has gone without spiritual food and subsisted on the husks and chaff that this world feeds its own. It's time to drink deeply from the well of life and be satisfied for once.

We have spent our years without God sitting at the feet of Satan, learning his ways and valuing what he values. We've got so much to unlearn! Once Jesus could say of us,

> Why is my language not clear to you? Because you are unable to hear what I say. You belong to your father, the devil, and you want to carry out your father's desire. (John 8:43-44)

For years we belonged to him, even though we didn't know it, and the grip of sin and death relentlessly drove us on toward destruction:

> As for you, you were dead in your transgressions and sins, in which you used to live when you followed the ways of this world and of the ruler of the kingdom of the air, the spirit who is now at work in those who are disobedient. All of us also lived among them at one time, gratifying the cravings of our sinful nature and following its desires and thoughts. (Ephesians 2:1-3)

But now that we've been brought out of bondage to the devil, and brought into the kingdom of light where God rules, we are like new-born babes with a lot to learn. We need to …

> … rid yourselves of all malice and all deceit, hypocrisy, envy, and slander of every kind. Like newborn babies, crave pure spiritual milk, so that by it you may grow up in your salvation, now that you have tasted that the Lord is good. (1 Peter 2:1-3)

We will also find, in this new life of ours, that the world suddenly hates us. Once we loved the world; now there is enmity between us. We won't always understand why that's true, but it comes up in the most surprising circumstances and we are often caught off guard by it. When we are working alongside unbelievers they will (for no apparent reason) start cursing and ridiculing religion. They immerse themselves in their daily ritual of sin, and ...

> ... they think it strange that you do not plunge with them into the same flood of dissipation, and they heap abuse on you. (1 Peter 4:4)

But their ways are the ways of death; you have no business fraternizing with them anymore.

> Do not be yoked together with unbelievers. For what do righteousness and wickedness have in common? Or what fellowship can light have with darkness? What harmony is there between Christ and Belial? What does a believer have in common with an unbeliever? What agreement is there between the temple of God and idols? For we are the temple of the living God. As God said, "I will live with them and walk among them, and I will be their God, and they will be my people." "Therefore come out from them and be separate," says the Lord. (2 Corinthians 6:14-17)

Of course the world will misinterpret this attitude as pride and arrogance – they will accuse us of thinking ourselves too good for them. Let's hope we *are* getting better, or we will never see God! But the fact remains that we are "aliens and strangers on earth." (Hebrews 11:13)

> Do not love the world or anything in the world. If anyone loves the world, the love of the Father is not in him. For everything in the world – the cravings of sinful man, the lust of his eyes and the boasting of what he has and does – comes not

from the Father but from the world. The world and its desires pass away, but the man who does the will of God lives forever. (1 John 2:15-17)

So, we find ourselves cut off from what we used to love and depend on.

We will also find that we are awake to the enemy now. Our enemy, the devil, is an awesome foe. We dare not trifle with him. Unbelievers make him out to be a joke – all the better for what he wants to do. If he can keep people in the dark about what he's doing to them, then he will achieve his goals and their condemnation.

But a Christian, to some extent, is aware of him now. We aren't completely ignorant of him. For one thing, we've been delivered from his bondage and deceit and now we are under the direct guidance of the Lord Jesus. The change is bound to feel better! For another thing, we have spiritual eyes to see realities that we were ignorant of before. We can see that the devil does parade around like an angel of light, and that his temptations and accusations are hollow lies and deceits. Just being able to name him – as the demons were forced to name themselves before Jesus – goes a long way to counteracting his deadly work.

Nevertheless we shouldn't underestimate his power of destruction.

Be self-controlled and alert. Your enemy the devil prowls around like a roaring lion looking for someone to devour. (1 Peter 5:8)

Paul counseled us to beware of giving the devil a foothold. (Ephesians 4:27) In other words, there are things to avoid doing, and things to begin doing, to counteract the works of the devil. Do you know what they are? Do you know your enemy very well? Do you know what will protect you from his attacks and spiritual weapons? (Ephesians 6:10-18) Do you know your old weaknesses that the devil helped develop in you in past years? These are naturally going to be his first targets!

In light of all these new realities in our lives, we need God's works. We certainly are like new-born babies! Weak and helpless, faced with vicious and experienced enemies, surrounded by an unfriendly world, new to the spiritual things of God – we are prime material for the works of God. It's a powerful blessing, this promise that the works of God especially support his needy people.

WHY OTHER SUPPORTS WON'T DO

We used to depend solely on what this world has to give. We were as much a part of the world as everyone else is. But things have changed; we are aliens to the world now; we have taken our stand with Christ Jesus and now the world hates us as much as it hates him. We may not understand this, or we may not appreciate it – like Lot's wife we sometimes cast a longing glance back to the life we once knew, wishing that things were the same again or at least that we didn't have such a rough time being a Christian. But Jesus sternly calls us on:

> No one who puts his hand to the plow and looks
> back is fit for service in the kingdom of God.
> (Luke 9:62)

Jesus isn't being arbitrarily mean to us. He knows far better than we do that the world can't keep its promises to us. He can see that the life we once loved won't sit well with our new spiritual appetites. He sees and mourns those who still have their houses built on sand, doomed to self-destruct when hard times come. It's for our good that he drives us on past the things of this world; we have a more glorious inheritance waiting for us in Heaven.

The comforts and securities of this world are designed to satisfy the flesh. In some respects that isn't necessarily bad; food is good to the hungry, sleep is good for the weary, family is good for the lonely. There are many things in this world that are called "blessings" because they are good things for the physical side of us. But to live solely for physical comfort and security is not only unsatisfying to a Christian, it can be downright dangerous! It's unsatisfying because it doesn't do a thing for our souls; we can eat like a king and enjoy vacations and fill our houses with good things, and still be starving for the work of the Holy Spirit in us. Our hearts can easily be dry of all signs of the Spirit, unfruitful and very displeasing to our Father. As one man found out, the good things of this world do absolutely nothing for getting us ready for the next world:

> Then he said, "This is what I'll do. I will tear down my barns and build bigger ones, and there I will store all my grain and my goods. And I'll say to myself, 'You have plenty of good things laid up for many years. Take life easy; eat, drink and be merry.'" But God said to him, "You fool! This very night your life will be demanded from you. Then who will get what you have prepared for yourself?" This is how it will be with anyone who stores up things for himself but is not rich toward God. (Luke 12:18-21)

It's also dangerous to live solely for the things of this world because we can easily be misled into thinking that "all is well with our souls" when in fact we are in desperate need of God's grace.

> You say, "I am rich; I have acquired wealth and do not need a thing." But you do not realize that you are wretched, pitiful, poor, blind and naked. I counsel you to buy from me gold refined in the fire, so you can become rich; and white clothes to wear, so you can cover your shameful nakedness; and salve to put on your eyes, so you can see. (Revelation 3:17-18)

There's another problem about depending on the things of this world to support us – the fact that they are designed to bring about results that we are no longer interested in. For example, as sons of God we aren't called to beat people over the heads to accept the good news of the Gospel. When the disciples saw people rejecting Christ they thought that it was time for action!

> When the disciples James and John saw this, they asked, "Lord, do you want us to call fire down from Heaven to destroy them?" But Jesus turned and rebuked them. (Luke 9:54-55)

What the world uses to solve problems aren't good enough for us now. Fire from Heaven doesn't change men's hearts! We are often tempted to use the world's weapons against sinners – like anger – but a Christian learns that ...

> Man's anger does not bring about the righteous life that God desires. (James 1: 20)

The old ways of doing things don't suffice for building a spiritual kingdom. Money is a powerful tool in the hands of the unbeliever, but it's pretty useless to a Christian trying to build up the kingdom of God. Hobnobbing with the important people of the community may get you into the community's important affairs, but it won't get you anywhere in God's works – you have to hobnob with nobodies to do that. Worldly learning gets people pretty far in positions of influence and power; but not in God's world. Far from being an asset it's often a liability; "ignorant" people often know much more of the truth and ways of God than the highly educated know. This new way of living can be very frustrating for a new Christian as he finds how useless are his old lifestyle and the things he once valued.

HOW GOD'S WORKS SUPPORT US

Given our predicament in this world, it's understandable how important it is to God that he support us in every way. There's too much at stake – he can't leave us on our own. We would fail on all levels: we would collapse under the strain of the demands of an eternal world; the physical world would tempt us and pull at us to return to our old ways of living; the Name and honor of God would suffer as we show the world how incapable God's people are of making good on their claims; we would get discouraged and perhaps give up when we see that things just aren't going to work as he promised. But this just won't do – the Lord is going to step in and hold up the sagging superstructure that we are trying to support. In fact, he's going to take over the entire building project and manage it himself. All we will have to do is stand back and watch him do it.

It's important to know *how* God supports us. It's possible to be ignorant about this, and miss out on a great deal of blessing. Paul kept using that phrase in his letters: "Now I do not want you to be ignorant, brothers, about ..." – and he would bring up something that God did that they need to know about. God works for the support of his people, but they can just as easily sin against his work and not take advantage of its saving and strengthening nature. He can be working right in their midst and they may be totally unaware of it! It's like putting money in front of a blind man, or giving a power tool to an aborigine. They either don't see it or they don't understand what it's for.

What benefit can there be when Christians don't know what God is doing on their behalf? They will be saved, but like babies saved from a burning building; they will never be able to understand God's works or build their lives intelligently on his works.

So, let's look at how God supports his people through his works.

He creates a spiritual environment. "Since, then, you have been raised with Christ, set your hearts on things above, where Christ is seated at the right hand of God. Set your minds on things above, not on earthly things. For you died, and your life is now hidden with Christ in God." (Colossians 3:1-3)

Just as a newborn babe needs food, shelter, warmth, clothing, loving parents and protection, a newborn Christian needs an environment that will both protect and nurture him spiritually. The Lord has done that already for each one of us, whether we are aware of it or not. Usually we aren't aware of it, for the same reason that a baby is unaware of all the work that his parents have invested in his well-being: he doesn't have the skill to see many of the works of God yet, nor would he understand them if he did see them. So God often goes without praise for his most profound works on behalf of his children – which he doesn't mind as long as they are still babies. When they grow up, however, he expects them to be able to know and appreciate his work for them.

The spiritual "shell" that God builds around us is an interesting thing. Naturally speaking, we are the same people that we were before we became Christians; there isn't any difference in our work or studies or food or shelter that anybody can see (aside from cleaning up the immorality). This is the really misleading thing about us when the world tries to figure out what we are up to. It doesn't appear that we are any different, physically speaking, than anybody else. We have the same physical needs that they do. So where is the change? What has happened to us that makes us different? Aside from the fact that we are different in our hearts (which we will see in a minute) there is a new, unseen reality around us now that supports us. It's a world that this physical world knows nothing about. We are actually living in two worlds at once – this physical world to support our bodies, and God's spiritual world to support our souls.

One thing that we need in order to live on a spiritual level is light. The Lord has provided an abundance of light so that we can see the things of God.

> Light has come into the world... whoever lives by the truth comes into the light, so that it may be seen plainly that what he has done has been done through God. (John 3:19,21)

If God had remained shrouded in mystery then none of us would have learned anything useful about him. Where would we be if we didn't know the ways of God, or the grace in Christ for forgiveness, or how the Holy Spirit comforts and leads us? But God has brought all this truth about him to light so that his children can learn any and all of it easily. It used to be that men tried to find out things about God, but they were largely unsuccessful in their attempt.

> Concerning this salvation, the prophets, who spoke of the grace that was to come to you, searched intently and with the greatest care, trying to find out the time and circumstances to which the Spirit of Christ in them was pointing when he predicted the sufferings of Christ and the glories that would follow. (1 Peter 1:10-11)

Now that knowledge is in our hands, easily seen and learned.

> No longer will a man teach his neighbor, or a man his brother, saying, "Know the Lord," because they will all know me, from the least of them to the greatest. (Hebrews 8:11)

> This grace was given me: to preach to the Gentiles the unsearchable riches of Christ, and to make plain to everyone the administration of this mystery, which for ages past was kept hidden in God, who created all things. His intent was that now, through the church, the manifold wisdom of God should be made

known to the rulers and authorities in the Heavenly realms … (Ephesians 3:8-10)

We often take for granted that the light of God – the "seeableness" of the things of God and his kingdom – is available to us now. We have this ability to see and hear God in his Word. Our consciences have been awakened and honed to a sharp edge, so that when we sin we know about it immediately. We can see that someone is our brother or sister in the Lord because they show characteristic signs of God's work in their lives; this is why Christ told us that we can judge a tree by its fruit – we have the ability to discern that fruit now. We know when the enemy is near, because he casts a dark shadow in this world that we can see, but others can't see and therefore stumble in. As our eyes adjust to the new perspective that God has given us, we learn and grow and work as Christians ought. Of course the light is still dim, compared to what it will be at the end of time (1 Corinthians 13:12), but what a blessing that we have this much of it now! Look at the people who have to do without – look at the mess their lives are in, with no hope of ever seeing the truth.

Another reality that God has brought into our lives for our support is the Holy Spirit. The Spirit isn't something additional to God, but is God himself; he wasn't new with the coming of Christ or the New Testament times. He has always been around – "In the beginning" the Spirit hovered over the waters of the deep and brought the elements of the world together. The Spirit has always been, and will always continue to be, because he is God.

There's much that the Holy Spirit does for God's people, and it isn't within our scope here to explore it all. But we do want to look at how he supports God's people. He's called the Comforter, because he comes close so that he can live inside us and encourage us with the hope of our salvation. Jesus made it a point to send us the Spirit when he left this world:

> Unless I go away, the Counselor will not come to you; but if I go, I will send him to you. (John 16:7)

The Spirit seals us with the sign of salvation; which simply means that he marks us with the characteristics of God's workings on a soul – salvation from sin, holiness, faith, hope, the fruits of the Spirit, etc. The Spirit will "guide you into all truth" (John 16:13) – he stands ready to both teach us what the truth is and take us by the arm and lead our steps in it. He also helps us when we don't know what to pray; when we search for the will of God …

> … the Spirit himself intercedes for us with groans that words cannot express. And he who searches our hearts knows the mind of the Spirit, because the Spirit intercedes for the saints in accordance with God's will. (Romans 8:26-27)

Without the help of the Spirit we would have to do without the presence of God, the wisdom of God, the encouragement from God, the strength of God, the intercession of God, the life-giving fruitfulness of God – we would literally die on the vine! Again we don't often appreciate this amazing and necessary power in our lives, because the Spirit is hard to detect (John 3:8) and we are so slow to understand the realities of God's world. But God provides the Spirit for us anyway, whether we know what he's doing or not, and we live spiritually because of the Holy Spirit's constant oversight and providence.

Another support that God has given us is the brotherhood. The Church of God is the cradle of Christianity in this world. Here are all the necessary items for spiritual life to blossom and grow and bear fruit. The Church is a garden plot in a world of weeds. If we had to get along the best we could in the dark and dangerous world we live in from day to day, we would soon die. But in the Church we are protected and nourished and pruned of harmful growths so that we will be "mature, attaining to the whole measure of the fullness of Christ." (Ephesians 4:13)

Everyone knows that there's strength in numbers, and that's no less true in the Church – but not for the same reason. Men rely on their combined strengths and wisdom in order to do great things, even to building a tower that reaches to the Heavens and building a name for themselves that will last forever. But in God's spiritual world there is only one Name worth remembering, and there is only one strength and one wisdom that will ever bring about the will of God. The Church is a gathering of God's people who have come under the umbrella of God's strength and wisdom, who have taken on his Name and therefore his fortunes upon themselves. We come together not to pool our resources but to immerse ourselves in his pool of resources.

It's in the Church that God does his work of salvation and spiritual growth. In the first place, here is where the Spirit comes when he blesses his people:

> How good and pleasant it is when brothers live together in unity! It is like precious oil poured on the head … It is as if the dew of Hermon were falling on Mount Zion. For there the LORD bestows his blessing, even life forevermore. (Psalm 133:1-3)

That unity, we find out from Paul, comes because the Spirit binds us together into one body.

> There is one body and one Spirit – just as you were called to one hope when you were called – one Lord, one faith, one baptism; one God and Father of all, who is over all and through all and in all. (Ephesians 4:4-6)

He goes on to tell us how that benefits us: through the workings of the Spirit, each is enabled to do spiritual work for the building up of the Church until "we all reach unity in the faith … and become mature." (Ephesians 4:13) In the Church we experience the gifts of God through brothers and sisters working under the guidance of the Spirit.

We need this desperately. There's a saying that "No man is an island," and Christians need each other to survive. We can teach each other, admonish each other, pray with each other, encourage each other, lead each other, hold each other up and share the burden – which can be very much appreciated in our hour of need. Without this support system we will either grow cold spiritually from lack of interest, or we will run unchecked in our sin, or we will go astray from the truth, or we will stumble under the burden of troubles, or we will lose interest in helping others. On and on our problems will go when we leave our support system of the Church. This doesn't mean, of course, that if the works of the Spirit aren't happening in your local church then *you* are necessarily in spiritual trouble. Like I said, God has already faithfully provided you with this support, whether it is in your local church or it is through Christian friends at work or school or in your neighborhood. He always does; look for it anywhere.

He makes us grow spiritually. "… So that the body of Christ may be built up until we all reach unity in the faith and in the knowledge of the Son of God and become mature, attaining to the whole measure of the fullness of Christ." (Ephesians 4:12-13)

This is God's ultimate aim for us, though it often isn't our ultimate aim. We would prefer to take things easy; a life of comfort and security sound pretty good to us. But the Lord isn't so concerned with our comfort and security. As a matter of fact, he will often take us through periods of great discomfort and instability to make us grow spiritually.

The basic element of life is food. Without food we would all shortly die. Spiritually we have the same situation, because our souls were made to constantly feast on the realities of God just as our bodies were made to constantly restore themselves through food. The Lord is always busy providing us spiritual food to eat because he wants us to grow in the knowledge of God, to be able to take on the work that God has for us, to be responsible sons and daughters who glorify the Lord in all that we do and say. The food, as you may have guessed, is the bread that comes down from Heaven:

> For the bread of God is he who
> comes down from Heaven and gives
> life to the world. (John 6:33)

Jesus is called the bread of life because he puts the life of God into everyone who trusts in him. Christ (through his Spirit) has come to us now, and he brings the truth of God into our hearts. We are able to hear God's truth and we are able to conform our lives to the truth because Christ brings it into us and makes it part of us. We get holiness the same way – it's Christ's holiness that people see in us; we "ate" the righteousness of Christ, through faith in him, and now it has become part of us.

A spiritual feast lies all around us. We can get good out of what unbelievers choke over! The humility of Christ and his apparent weakness and failure is our strength – it's through personal weakness that God works his miracles – but to an unbeliever it's the very reason *not* to believe in Christ.

> A stone that causes men to stumble and a rock that makes them fall. (1 Peter 2:8)

When unbelievers have to live through hardship, they complain about a hard life and get no good out of it. But when a Christian lives through troubles and problems, it's spiritual food for him and very necessary for his spiritual growth:

> Endure hardship as discipline; God is treating you as sons ... No discipline seems pleasant at the time, but painful. Later on, however, it produces a harvest of righteousness and peace for those who have been trained by it. (Hebrews 12:7,11)

That's why Christ counseled you to "take up your cross and follow me" (Matthew 16:24) – he knows that it will be food to your soul and cause you to grow into his image.

"My food," said Jesus, "is to do the will of him who sent me and to finish his work." (John 4:34)

Another item that God has provided for our benefit is his strength. What would Christians do without it! When we are the most weak and helpless, when the world and the devil all attack us and make us despair of ever getting out of our problems, the strength of God comes through like an electric shock and we suddenly rise up above all the problems.

It's humanly unexplainable, this thing about God's strength. For those who have experienced it, it's clearly something from outside themselves and very real. Paul tells us how it changed his life:

> To keep me from becoming conceited because of these surpassingly great revelations, there was given me a thorn in my flesh, a messenger of Satan, to torment me. Three times I pleaded with the Lord to take it away from me. But he said to me, "My grace is sufficient for you, for my power is made perfect in weakness." Therefore I will boast all the more gladly about my weaknesses, so that Christ's power may rest on me. That is why, for Christ's sake, I delight in weaknesses, in insults, in hardships, in persecutions, in difficulties. For when I am weak, then I am strong. (2 Corinthians 12:7-10)

This is a most eloquent testimony of a man who found God's strength to be all that he needed. He also found that this strength is close at hand – the Lord's response to him leads us to believe that all Paul had to do was quit fighting and wait on the Lord to come through. It's at the *moment* of weakness that God's strength appears; it's just when we fail that God steps in and succeeds in us. When the unbeliever becomes weak he gives up, or when he fails he tries again. The Christian, however, turns to God who is never far away. That dreaded moment of humiliation or failure or heartache that would send an unbeliever scrambling for a way out will drive us instead to the arms of our Heavenly Father, who will always receive us and hold us in his powerful arms. His promise is to strengthen us, to hold us up, to support us in our weakness – and we will find out that this is true.

That strength of God will become part of our lives as we grow older spiritually. Instead of building our lives through our own efforts and muscle, we become accustomed to relying more and more on the Lord's strength. One day we will discover that we are on a "solid foundation, whose builder and maker is God." The strength of God will be in everything we do. Everything we work on will last. "I can do everything through him who gives me strength." (Philippians 4:13)

God will also make sure that we grow spiritually. Growth is perceptible progress; we measure the growth of a child by checking his height against a measuring stick. If he stops growing before he's supposed to, then something is wrong. Christians also grow, and that growth is no less perceptible. There are measuring sticks that we can use to measure our spiritual growth, which we won't go into right now. The point is that God makes us grow since we are spiritually alive.

Paul realized that man can't make himself or others grow. A Christian is a living thing, spiritually as well as physically, and ministers of the Word do their part to doling out the food that makes Christians grow. But only God can make it work:

> I planted the seed, Apollos watered it, but God made it grow. So neither he who plants nor he who waters is anything, but only God, who makes things grow. (1 Corinthians 3:6-7)

And the Lord makes sure that his children grow. He won't have a bunch of babies on his hands forever! He wants mature Christians, Christians who understand what God's will is, who can do the work that the Father has for them to do, who don't have to be bottle-fed and spoon-fed all their lives. He wants the Church to be filled with people who are doing their responsible share to extend the kingdom of God. Count on it, growth will happen if God has anything to do with your spiritual life.

The children of God can grow in strange soils. Unbelievers require the hot, torpid environment of sin and moral corruption, of physical comfort and physical security. Christians can grow in much harsher conditions – and often require those conditions for spiritual growth. This doesn't mean that the perfect life for God's children is that of a hermit or monk; we leave the manner of growth to God to work out – we don't decide how we will grow. But don't be surprised when he puts us in soil that would kill someone else; he evidently feels that the conditions are just right for getting you to know him and his ways better, or to better shape your ways.

At the end of his efforts at making you grow, you will find a spiritual discernment for the things of God that wasn't there before. You will find a quiet faith that isn't easily shaken by upsetting events. You will find that you are more patient and enduring with others, knowing that God will in time make them grow too without you beating them over the head. You will appreciate what God has done in Christ for you – spiritual growth gives us a much bigger picture of the Lord Jesus and what he did. All this is the maturity that God is aiming at when he works in your life.

One more thing that God starts doing in us – he makes us bear fruit. He isn't interested in unfruitful Christians – let's get that straight from the beginning. It's very important to him that we bear spiritual fruit that pleases him. We get an idea about how important it is to him from the following passage:

> I will sing to the one I love a song about his vineyard: My loved one had a vineyard on a fertile hillside. He dug it up and cleared it of stones

> and planted it with the choicest vines. He built a watchtower in it and cut out a winepress as well. Then he looked for a crop of good grapes, but it yielded only bad fruit. (Isaiah 5:1-2)

This is intolerable to God. He must have fruit! He must have Christians that show unmistakable signs of the presence and work of the Spirit in them. There's no such thing as "saved" Christians who don't live holy lives. We may fail, but there must be *some* sign in us that we are alive to the things of God or he will consider us still dead and cut us down. (Luke 13:6-9)

The Lord has ways of making sure that we bear fruit.

> He cuts off every branch in me that bears no fruit, while every branch that does bear fruit he trims clean so that it will be even more fruitful. (John 15:2)

The Lord prunes his people through circumstances – rough times that would break a man who isn't resilient with spiritual life. Like a dead branch, an unbeliever will break under the strain of problems and hard times; but a believer has life in him, life from above, the life that overcomes this world no matter what it throws at him. So God takes advantage of that fact and uses the hard times to trim off the worldly ways we still have – the ugly spots that remained from our lives of sin and unbelief – so that good, solid branches of obedience strengthen us into action.

> For we are God's workmanship, created in Christ Jesus to do good works, which God prepared in advance for us to do. (Ephesians 2:10)

He makes our works work. "I worked harder than all of them – yet not I, but the grace of God that was with me." (1 Corinthians 15:10)

This world being what it is, it isn't hard to work one's whole life away and not have anything to show for it at the end.

> To the man who pleases him, God gives wisdom, knowledge and happiness, but to the sinner he gives the task of gathering and storing up wealth to hand it over to the one who pleases God. This too is meaningless, a chasing after the wind. (Ecclesiastes 2:26)

Man has to work – it's built into his makeup – but nobody said he would accomplish anything lasting from his work. He can accumulate a little bit of possessions in a few years, but a few years after he's gone it will all float away to others who will accumulate it. He can pile up some money, but his children (or the government!) will get all of that when he's gone. He can bring about some changes in his community, but his community will tear them down when he's gone and put something else in its place. In a few generations (sometimes not even that long!) there will be little or no trace that he was even here, aside from a grave marker. So much for the works of man.

But when a person becomes a Christian he enters the realm of eternity. Here things last forever. Work at this level is destined to last for ages and ages without end. It's a great privilege to work in God's kingdom, because the whole world will one day look in awe at what was done in history through God's power. We will be known as "God's fellow workers." (1 Corinthians 3:9)

But let's get some things straight first. We have never been called upon to do God's work for him. His work, as we have already seen, is special to him and only he can do it. Our first job is to find out those things that only God can do and simply trust him to do them. Once that's cleared up then we must next find out what it is that we should do – what *is* our work? What has he called us to? As a matter of fact, that may be a puzzler at first: what could we possibly do that would last forever? How can we presume to work on something spiritual when we are still burdened with this physical life – and especially with our sin?

This takes great discernment and skill, which comes from years of experience in the ways of God. At first we are like children who play at working, which is cute but not very profitable. Over the years, however, as our parents kept feeding us and training us and giving us a few chores to do which got more complex as time went on, we got accustomed to real work. The same thing happens to Christians. At first, they are wonderfully excited about the reality of the spiritual world and they want to go out and win the whole world to Christ! But it doesn't take long before they realize (hopefully – not everyone sees this) that this is going to take some skill and wisdom to do. Paul called himself an "expert builder" who was *able* to lay a good foundation; many people wouldn't know what a good foundation is. The writer of Hebrews assumes that being a Christian necessarily leads into a spiritual skill of ministering to others' needs:

> We have much to say about this, but it is hard to explain because you are slow to learn. In fact, though by this time you ought to be teachers, you need someone to teach you the elementary truths of God's Word all over again. You need milk, not solid food! (Hebrews 5:11-12)

What all this amounts to is that there is much "work" that goes on in God's Name that may simply be wasted effort, for lack of good training and spiritual wisdom. Can such a thing really be said of what you and I do? Dare we doubt the worth of what we claim to do for God? Yes, we dare! We must doubt it! A good engineer would never trust the lives of thousands of people to a bridge that he refused to submit to some simple testing; pride mustn't get in the way here. A Christian has every right to test everything that claims to be of God, especially when that work has the spiritual benefit of others as a goal. The only work that we mustn't doubt is God's work; all other work must be tested for its ultimate worth or we are foolish to depend on it:

> His work ... will be revealed with fire, and the fire will test the quality of each man's work. If what he has built survives, he will receive his reward. If it is burned up, he will suffer loss; he himself will be saved, but only as one escaping through the flames. (1 Corinthians 3:13-15)

The question is, *can* we do something for God that is worth something? We've already seen that God prepares his people for working, and he prepared those projects for us ahead of time. He made the Church so that we are trained "for works of service." (Ephesians 4:12) Evidently he thinks that it's not only possible for us to work in the spiritual kingdom, it's necessary for us to do so. How does this happen?

What we've come to is this idea that God makes the necessary changes in our lives that make the impossible possible. What we could never hope to do before, we *can* do now, thanks to God's special setup for us. The disciples discovered that they suddenly gained a new power, an ability that they didn't used to possess – and not through their own efforts, either!

> "He who listens to you listens to me; he who rejects you rejects me; but he who rejects me rejects him who

sent me." The seventy-two returned with joy and said, "Lord, even the demons submit to us in your Name." (Luke 10:16-17)

Jesus went on to counsel them about their new-found powers: they got them because God is with them, not because of any new abilities on their own.

Paul knew that his work wasn't in vain, because he worked in the power of God. He could boldly tell the Thessalonians that ...

... when you received the Word of God, which you heard from us, you accepted it not as the word of men, but as it actually is, the Word of God, which is at work in you who believe. (1 Thessalonians 2:13)

This kind of work, Paul knew, will last through all the difficult times in life. A spiritual seed was planted in their hearts that would grow into eternity and never die.

Though we can assume such things about our work in God's kingdom, however, we should ask the question, "What does that work look like?" What is it that God requires of us as fellow workers? The whole thing boils down to what Paul referred to in 1 Corinthians 2 as laying the foundation: *our work, if it is to be worth anything, is to use and depend on the works of God.* His works are readily available, easily understood, and easily used in one's life. Our job is to use those spiritual realities in our own life and in the lives of others. Here is the key to successful Christian living: build your life on the works of God; use his works like stones in your wall of life.

It's possible, and unfortunately too prevalent, for even Christians to use the worthless things of this world to build up their lives. But we aren't called to work this way, and we will end up with a lot of wasted time and effort to account for on Judgment Day. What we *are* called to do, however, is to start finding and picking up the works of God to build with.

When you start using God's works as building materials for your own life, you will discover that the Lord knew what he was doing all along. He made sure that his works would do you good, that his works would get you to the goal of your Christian life, that his works would fill your life with meaning and purpose. He laid his works around us like building materials on the construction site; we shouldn't be so surprised that they are admirably fitted to the job of life. This is why I say that the Lord supports us in our works – he makes our work fruitful and lasting by supplying us with materials that fulfill the requirements of the job.

He protects us. "I am the good shepherd. The good shepherd lays down his life for the sheep." (John 10:11)

Here is something that the Lord does for us that we don't understand much about. Children don't understand the tremendous efforts of their parents for their safety and well-being; at least they don't really appreciate what their parents did until they grow up and have children of their own. In the same way, Christians don't have much understanding about how God protects them and puts them in a spiritually secure environment. But unless the Lord does this for us, we would soon be overwhelmed with our enemies and the harsh realities of life.

The battle for our souls is the fiercest battle known to man. No earthly battle matches it for the awesome firepower that our enemies array against us. The strategies used on both sides would overwhelm and confuse the most capable generals. Man has very little idea of the forces involved or the movements of armies or the subtle gains made or the devastating losses sustained in this spiritual war. Wars between men waste material and human lives, and can change the course of history. But the spiritual battle going on over our heads involves billions of souls: their eternal fate hangs in the balance as forces of evil struggle against the power and Word of God. The results aren't temporary losses or temporary wins – they are no less than Heaven or Hell.

Paul was awed with the reality of the struggle. He shrugs off our fears of men and nations, telling us that ...

> Our struggle is not against flesh and blood, but against the rulers, against the authorities, against the powers of this dark world and against the

spiritual forces of evil in the Heavenly realms. (Ephesians 6:12)

This has tremendous implications for the Christian. The unbeliever, of course, is totally unaware of all this and he happily sins his life away, a tool of the devil and doing the devil's will. But a Christian serves the Captain of the Lord's army, the Lord of Hosts. When *he* sins, he gives ground to the enemy, putting the work of the Church in great jeopardy. That's why the Lord deals more severely with insurrection in his own ranks than he does among unbelievers; whoever sins against the light that he has will be all the more responsible for that sin. (James 3:1)

Having painted this bleak picture of our spiritual surroundings, I hasten to add that the Lord protects us faithfully from all of this danger. Some Christians live their entire lives without knowing anything about the spiritual dangers that were close by on their right and left. Though it would be better to know something about it (so we don't run off in the direction of danger!) it isn't always necessary for us to know; God protects us anyway. Like a lonely shepherd keeping watch at night, he doesn't always feel the need to tell us in the morning what dangers he had to face for our sake.

The coming of Christ was like clearing a space out of enemy territory for Christians to camp in. He faced the enemy, and the enemy backed down. Now, behind his back and fully protected from any enemy advances, we are busy building our lives according to the will of our commander.

He wants to see us busy – fortifications, preparations for battle, unpacking weapons and training for war – while he holds the front line intact against the enemy. We may not even be called to face the enemy directly on the front line; they also serve who only stand and wait, as the saying goes. But even those who fight desperate spiritual battles little realize how much the Lord does in their behalf to defeat the enemy.

We will find that the Lord directs our paths so that we will be assured of protection and spiritual growth. He sets the prisoner free; he sets a table of food before the hungry; he sets the lonely in families; he sets our feet on a solid rock; he gives sight to the blind so that they can see; he gives us wisdom and insight into the ways of God. In many ways he makes sure that we are surrounded with the necessities of spiritual life.

He also provides us with the armor that we will need when we do have to face the enemy. This in itself is a tremendous blessing; if left to ourselves we would never know how to defeat Satan, and we would surely die against his subtle temptations or his concentrated efforts to undo us. The normal problems of life are bad enough without having a skilled enemy screwing them into our hearts to kill us! But God gives us a special protection against such onslaughts on our souls:

> Finally, be strong in the Lord and in his mighty power. Put on the full armor of God so that you can take your stand against the devil's schemes. (Ephesians 6:10-11)

We will find that the things that God gives us to protect us are amazingly effective. Problems that would literally bring an unbeliever to ruin and despair have a strengthening effect on us, because such things drive us to a God who works miracles. When others around us fail in hard times, we find renewed strength to keep going:

> Surely he will save you from the fowler's snare and from the deadly pestilence. He will cover you with his feathers, and under his wings you will find refuge; his faithfulness will be your shield and rampart. You will not fear the terror of night, nor the arrow that flies by day, nor the pestilence that stalks in the darkness, nor the plague that destroys at midday. A thousand may fall at your side, ten thousand at your right hand, but it will not come near you. You will only observe with your eyes and see the punishment of the wicked. (Psalm 91:3-8)

One enemy that we need protection from is sin itself. Such a deadly and deceitful enemy – it lurks in our hearts already! We are prone to sin "as the sparks fly upward." (Job 5:7) But the Lord helps us even here; he often steers us around the temptations that would cause us to stumble otherwise. Without our knowing about it, he saves us from our sin and makes us avoid confrontation with sin. There is good reason behind Jesus' counsel to pray for this kind of protection:

And lead us not into temptation, but deliver us from the evil one. (Matthew 6:13)

These are all, remember, the works and efforts of God on our behalf. They protect us in necessary ways in all circumstances; they help us where we can't help ourselves.

He increases our faith. "These have come so that your faith – of greater worth than gold, which perishes even though refined by fire – may be proved genuine and may result in praise, glory and honor when Jesus Christ is revealed." (1 Peter 1:7)

Something needs to be said about a most important work that God does on our behalf: he builds up our faith. This isn't so much a supporting work as it is a strengthening work. The support comes in when our faith, strengthened to turn to God, finds in him the support that we need.

God does his work even though people may be totally unaware of it. He builds superstructures, lays building materials out around the job site, and gives us the strength and skill to do our work well. But we can, nevertheless, miss the entire point of what he's doing. Without faith we will miss out on the works of God and live spiritually poor lives.

Faith is a gift of God. It's the ability to see past the deceitful appearances of this world into God's world. It's the ability to turn away from one's own works for salvation, for what only God can do, and the ability to rest entirely on God for his grace. For natural man this is impossible; the urge to play God and do things his own way is just too strong to overcome. But for a Christian it is the only way to get along in the kingdom:

The righteous shall live by faith. (Romans 1:17)

Without faith it is impossible to please God. (Hebrews 11:6)

If faith is so important to the Christian, you can be sure that God is working to get it solidly into us. He has his ways of doing this – we are often misled by circumstances and we think that God is ill-treating us – but his work is sure and certain, and the faith that he first planted in our hearts to believe on his Son will come to full fruit in the last day. That which he started, he will finish.

We already looked at two passages that show us how God works faith into us. (Hebrews 12:4-13; 1 Peter 1:6-9) This thing of faith is not a small matter. There are just too many instances in everyday life in which we stand at a spiritual crossroads – we could very well go down the road of disobedience, wasted time and energy, hurting others as well as ourselves, and dishonoring God simply by "looking only on the surface of things." (2 Corinthians 10:7) We have to "live by faith, not by sight." (2 Corinthians 5:7) At first the Lord gives us enough faith to simply survive spiritually, by causing us to pray and read his Word and seek the company of the saints. As time goes on, however, more faith is needed – our responsibilities increase and the work to be done is much more involved. But most Christians are still living on the little faith they had when they first met Christ! They don't realize that their personal failures and the failure they inflict on the Church is due to their lack of mature faith:

> After Jesus had gone indoors, his disciples asked him privately, "Why couldn't we drive it out?" He replied, "This kind can come out only by prayer." (Mark 9:28-29)

The prayer, that is, that comes from deep faith in the power of God. The constant problem of the disciples was their "little faith." If you just had the faith of a mustard seed, Jesus often complained of them, then you could do all the work that God expects of you.

So, because the spiritual needs are so great, the Father will take whatever measures are necessary to build faith into our hearts. We have got to start getting hold of the realities of the kingdom of God; we have to believe that he exists and that he rewards those who seek him. (Hebrews 11:6) So he sends a few problems our way, and corners us until we have no choice but to turn to him, and lo! – we find that he is sufficient for our every need. Hence our faith in him is strengthened for the next time.

We will see below that God's works of support often go unheeded and therefore are not enjoyed as they ought to be. But that has nothing to do with the fact that the Lord will support his people, to some degree at least, whether or not they appreciate it. Parents know how to take care of their children, and often their thankless task causes them some problems – but not enough to make them quit taking care of their children! They might have to back up and use some discipline, and it might get pretty grim around the house, but they will always care for their own children in necessary ways. God takes care of his ungrateful children much more than we give him credit for; "while they are still sinners" God cares for them. His love for them is amazing; it is undying.

WHAT ABOUT THINGS NEEDED BUT NOT HAPPENING?

Now we have a sensitive question on our hands: if God really does support his people, why aren't we seeing more of it? If his works are profoundly effective, and he's determined to do his people good, why do we so often wallow in our sins and failures as if God were far away from us? How can we account for the discrepancy between what the Word says God *will do* and what little, in fact, actually happens to us?

Perhaps the whole thing can be summed up in the following passage:

> And he did not do many miracles there because of their lack of faith. (Matthew 13:58)

The people in Christ's home town took offence at him. They thought, why should we come to this man for what we need? All unbelievers feel the same way about the humble Son of God. They don't want to rely on his counsel or to be saved by him; they feel that they have better goals for their lives than he has, and they can reach those goals without his interference.

Unfortunately Christians do the same thing. They take little thought of what God can do, what God wants to do for them. They don't "consider his works" or "meditate on his works" to see how fitting it is that he does such things for them. They hardly know anything about what he does – so how can they turn to him when they need his works? They don't know what to pray for! They end up asking him for what he most definitely *won't* do! They expect him to support *their* works.

Such ignorance and stubbornness about his works is intolerable to God. Remember one thing about him: he *will* get glory. He obligated himself to care for our basic spiritual needs – he will do a "few" miracles on our behalf simply to keep us spiritually alive – but he refuses to encourage us in our ignorance. He won't risk our misunderstanding him; when we don't know anything about him, he certainly won't encourage us to believe what's wrong about him.

For example, there's a fascinating passage in the Old Testament that may surprise you. The context is the story about King Jehoiakim's reign and how he continued in the sins of his fathers and so brought destruction down on his own head as well as the country he ruled:

> Surely these things happened to Judah according to the LORD's command, in order to remove them from his presence because of the sins of Manasseh and all he had done, including the shedding of innocent blood. For he had filled Jerusalem with innocent blood, *and the Lord was not willing to forgive.* (2 Kings 24:3-4)

We can assume that the Temple was still in Jerusalem and that the priests continued to worship God there in accordance with the Law. We can also assume that the Israelites expected God's blessing on them and success in arms. They got neither! Did they think that one of God's works is to forgive sin and help people succeed simply because they bear his Name? They misunderstood him terribly if they thought that. They overlooked some of his other works – like the Law and its spiritual requirements, and sending the prophets, and punishment for sin, and protection so that they could grow in the knowledge of God without aggravations from pagan nations, and so on and so on. If they would have considered the things that he did for them in the past, they might have realized that forgiveness only comes when one repents and looks to God in fear and trust. They had models to follow for this kind of thing. People in past times experienced God's forgiveness in God's way, who could have told them how to take advantage of God's works.

The idea is really very simple. *When we know what it is that God does and how he does it, then we ask for it.* This is all he wants from us. When we turn to him for these things, then he knows that we are convinced they are works of God and not things that we can do ourselves. This is what God's glory means – men and women understand that only God can save, only God can build a spiritual kingdom, only God can judge this world aright. If we don't get a good hold on this idea, the Lord will do very little for us over and above what it takes to keep us alive. He can't – we might think that these wonderful things are happening because we ourselves are clever or holy or industrious. If we want the Lord to work his spiritual works in us, we must turn to him and ask him to do them. This is why it's so important to study God's works and to live by them.

Remember the Works of the Lord

There are about seventy places in the Bible, throughout the Old Testament and the New, where we are counseled to *remember* what God has done. We have a pretty good idea of what it means to live a holy life, and the commands that we have to obey. But remembering – do we realize how important an activity this is for every Christian? Faith, love, and hope – we know that these things are cornerstones for our Christian walk. But do we realize that we are in danger of not reaching our goal if we fail to remember God? If you consider some of the passages that deal with remembering, you will be impressed with its unique importance.

This step of remembering is the logical conclusion of the study of the works of the Lord. If you go back over the chapters you will see a progression.

- First we **identify** what his works are (since the Bible told us that this is something we should know).

- Next, we find out that these works **reveal** God – we learn what he is like, and how he prefers to do things.

- Next we discover that these things happen because God **wills** them to happen; he does what he wants.

This makes his works an important study for discovering his will.

- Then we see that the Lord **supports** his people through his works. This makes it personal for us, bringing us close to the one who works these great things for our benefit.

- Finally, what we will see in this lesson, we find that this isn't just an academic study. **Remembering** his works is a key sent from Heaven that opens the treasure house of God's power and wisdom. As we remember what he has done in the past, those things will happen in our day as well.

As important as God's works are, we won't get any benefit from them at all if we don't remember them. There's an art to remembering his works – or should I say, it's a gift from God; not many do it well, and too many don't do it at all. This may be the most important reason that so many Christians suffer from extreme spiritual poverty in our day.

WHY REMEMBER?

A human being spends a lot of his time remembering things. It's such an instinctive activity that we don't really think about what we are doing – we just do it. But though we are very good at it, we may have to look at what it means to "remember" in order to use it to good effect when it comes to the works of the Lord.

To remember something is to replay certain events over in our minds, like running a film through a second time. The mind has hundreds of thousands, if not millions, of pieces of data stored away from the past, most of which is available upon demand. Like rummaging through a filing cabinet, a person runs through his mental data-bank of historical events until he finds the one he wants to look at again – in a split second, of course. Then with the data in hand, so to speak, he reviews it by running some or all the details by in sequence.

The process of remembering something is an extremely valuable asset for a person. Important events usually only happen once – which is a pity, because it may have been exciting or deeply moving, and it may have changed the person forever, and it would be great to experience it again. But through the process of memory we can re-live those moments as often as we like, and so the pity of not experiencing that moment again is softened a bit. Our lives are full of devices to help us form and recover those memories, like photographs and tape recordings and class reunions and history books and diaries. The aggravating thing is when we can't remember something that we want to remember; when that happens then we've lost the ability to bring the event back to mind and enjoy it again. A piece of ourselves from the past is forever lost.

There's a practical side of memory too. The business of everyday life depends on being able to remember things – from simple things like tying one's shoes to passing school tests to performing one's job well. If it weren't for our memories we wouldn't be able to do anything a second time without looking it up in a book or having someone tell us what to do! Memory is an indispensable tool that helps us perform our duties reliably.

One can have any of an unlimited number of reasons for remembering something. We may want to experience the emotion again that we had when the memory was first formed. We may need to remember something in order to pass a test, or perform a job well, or win a game. We may need motivation during times of loneliness and depression, and certain memories tend to cheer us up and get us going. Desire feeds off memories – things we've seen in the past or lived through will motivate us to reach out for those pleasures again. Memories can also be unpleasant; though we have ways of suppressing bad memories, they also serve their purpose of keeping us out of the painful situation that we were in then. Finally, memory is a storehouse of data from which to draw valuable facts when we are trying to figure out what to do. Though we may not have had any direct experience like the one we are now in, there have been times in the past that can provide clues or helps for getting us through this present time.

REMEMBER GOD'S WORKS

All that we have said so far about memory, about remembering things, is also very true when it comes to remembering the works of the Lord. Motivation, emotion, data for decisions, comfort, fear, doing one's job – these are all part of remembering God's works.

There's just one difference, and it's an important one. The storehouse of data from which we draw our memories of the works of God is much more than our own minds; it's the entire Bible – the collective record of the people of God who saw what God did. Basically it's the same type of data that each one of us carries in our own heads, with which we form memories and remember. But many people have seen the acts of God and have stored away their memories in the Scriptures (inspired, guided, and interpreted by the Holy Spirit so that they would be dependable memories!) so that it can be available to all of God's people.

This gets around an otherwise serious limitation that we all have: we ourselves were not present when God did any of those works. If all we had to go by, when considering the works of God, is what we have seen with our own eyes, it might not fill a single sheet of paper! Having a collected record like the Bible is a tremendous asset to the Church. We can draw on events and realities that we ourselves haven't seen, but we can accept as real because of the testimony of our brothers and sisters in the past. This is why the Scriptures make such a big deal out of the witness of the prophets and Apostles:

> ... built on the foundation of the Apostles and prophets, with Christ Jesus himself as the chief cornerstone. (Ephesians 2:20)

> This is the disciple who testifies to these things and who wrote them down. We know that his testimony is true. (John 21:24)

> Though you have not seen him, you love him; and even though you do not see him now, you believe in him and are filled with an inexpressible and glorious joy, for you are receiving the goal of your faith, the salvation of your souls. (1 Peter 1:8-9)

> I want you to recall the words spoken in the past by the holy prophets and the command given by our Lord and Savior through your Apostles. (2 Peter 3:2)

We need this reliable record of what God did in order to base our own spiritual growth on God's works. For one thing, we are servants of the Lord and he expects us to find out what is the acceptable way of serving him. Not just anything will do!

> Remember these things, O Jacob, for you are my servant, O Israel. I have made you, you are my servant; O Israel, I will not forget you. (Isaiah 44:21)

A servant who doesn't know or understand his master's business is a pretty useless servant. He can't be depended on to do the things that will best serve his master's business. In fact, he will be more than useless; he is using up his master's food and shelter and not giving anything back in the way of profit. The Lord feels the same way about us – we had better show a profit before he returns to earth the second time or we are going to be dealt with very harshly. (Luke 19:27) It's time we learned what it is that the Lord wants to do in this world, and do our little bit to help it along.

Another reason that we need to remember God's works is because of the excitement and life-changing atmosphere that they caused when he first did them. We want more of this sort of thing:

> LORD, I have heard of your fame; I stand in awe of your deeds, O LORD. Renew them in our day, in our time make them known; in wrath remember mercy. (Habakkuk 3:2)

If we really love the Lord, and if we really want his kingdom here on earth where men and women need him badly, then we want what God did in the past. We want the old victories, the comforting news of God coming close to earth and moving mountains to save his people. Unbelievers don't want God to come close like he did in the past; but for God's people it would be the best news in the world!

There's another point to keep in mind about remembering God's works, and we've seen this over and over again in our study. We have to go back through the material in the Bible to find out what it is, exactly, that God does – we want to be clear on what his works really are. There are too many religious movements that claim God's involvement when he actually isn't at all interested in what they are doing. It's too easy to stick God's Name on something when it doesn't belong there; God seems far away, the situation demands a stamp of authority, and who better than God to claim as your patron when you want people to respect what you are doing? So people are all the time using God's Name to give an air of authority and importance to their works; the need has never been greater than now for a little bit of discernment. If we didn't study God's works for any other reason than this, it would be a worthwhile study. "Test everything. Hold on to the good. Avoid every kind of evil." (1 Thessalonians 5:21-22)

> Dear friends, do not believe every spirit, but test the spirits to see whether they are from God, because many false prophets have gone out into the world. (1 John 4:1)

And you should study God's works because they will explain why things are the way they are now, and why you and your faith are what they are. School children are required to study the history of the nation because it makes them informed citizens; when they know the history of the country then they are better able to help direct the future course of the country. In the same way, we can better appreciate the present day Church when we learn its history. We can work along with God instead of against him when we understand what he has been doing all these ages past. We can get a better grasp on the really important issues of Christianity when we look at the broad sweep of God's works in the past instead of at the piddly little issues of today that divide brother from brother.

Finally, you should study God's works because it's about time you did. You keep sinning against God without really understanding why it's so serious; you fret and worry about your problems even in the light of God's promises; you are reluctant to extend your hand to help others even though you are able to help others; you say that you worship God but you haven't really checked to see if he's satisfied with your worship; you say that you know God, but you act as if you are ignorant of what he wants from you. You are a typical Christian, like all of us, and you have a lot of work to do to straighten out your Christian witness before God is pleased with your performance. The study of the works of God will go a long way to reforming your thinking and setting your priorities straight again; in the hands of the Spirit they will make you a profitable servant of the Lord.

HELPS FOR REMEMBERING

The Lord knows that we are but dust, and we are sinners at that; he can tell us that we need to study his Word but that doesn't mean that we will remember to do it. So he gives us a little help so that it will be easier for us to study his Truth more regularly. He also knows that we have short memories. We forget things too easily, especially under times of pressure and trouble. Since we can't afford to forget the works of the Lord in such times as these (they will be our salvation if we would only use them!) he helps us with memory aids so that his truth will come to mind more easily.

In the days of the early Israelites he instructed the people to wear tassels on the fringes of their clothing – not for decoration, but ...

> You will have these tassels to look at and so you will remember all the commands of the Lord, that you may obey them and not prostitute yourselves by going after the lusts of your own hearts and eyes. Then you will remember to obey all my commands and will be consecrated to your God. (Numbers 15:39)

They were visual reminders to them of the commands of God. There were other visual reminders that God instructed them to use, such as the Passover Meal in which each part of the meal represented something in the story of the Exodus of God's people out of Egypt. Moses made a song after the Israelites escaped the Egyptians, and he instructed the people to remember it and sing it often as a reminder of how God worked to save his people. So it was duly recorded in Scripture for all time and for the whole Church. (Exodus 15:1-18)

Actually we don't have the time or space to go into all the memory helps that fill the entire Old Testament. The Jews have always been known as experts in educational methods, and it's probably because the Lord first used those methods on them to get them to remember his works. The Temple, for instance – every aspect of the Temple represents some reality of the works of God in saving, cleansing, forgiving, accepting, sanctifying and strengthening his people.

What about us? Are there memory aids that we can use to remember God's works? Actually the stories and lessons in the Old Testament are designed for easy memorization; if the whole Bible was a theological treatise like some of Paul's letters then we would have a tough time remembering it all! We need to appreciate the *form* that God's truth is in, because this form makes it easier for us to get hold of and keep hold of the information that we need about God and his works.

But there are specific things that God put in place to help us remember the Scriptures. One is a little-used device that would do wonders for the modern Church if people would only return to it:

Remember the days of old; consider the generations long past. Ask your father and he will tell you, your elders, and they will explain to you. (Deuteronomy 32:7)

Unfortunately ours is a country and a generation where the ideals for a good life are youth, strength, and looks. Aside from the fact that this is a foolish attitude in everyday life, it's a downright wicked attitude in the life of the Church. In God's economy the elders in the faith have the responsibility of caring for the younger ones in the faith – counseling them, instructing them, faithfully passing the truth on to the next generation so that each generation will have something worthwhile to pass on to their children. But almost nobody does this sort of thing anymore. Too often younger Christians despise the idea of going for help to the older ones in the faith. Everyone wants to make their own way, and everyone feels that they know enough about God without appearing that they need help from anybody. That's fatal for a church; when such an attitude prevails then each generation gets more ignorant about the Lord, not wiser. There are other countries where respect of and learning from one's elders is already a part of their culture; they already know how to do that when they become Christians. They put us modern, self-willed Americans to shame in following Peter's advice:

> Young men, in the same way be submissive to those who are older. Clothe yourselves with humility toward one another, because "God opposes the proud but gives grace to the humble." Humble yourselves, therefore, under God's mighty hand, that he may lift you up in due time. (1 Peter 5:5-6)

It isn't a mark of weakness when we go to those who are older in the faith and ask for teaching or help; it's a sign of wisdom, and it's God's will for you.

Another memory device that the Lord instructed us to use is this:

> Let the word of Christ dwell in you richly as you teach and admonish one another with all wisdom, and as you sing psalms, hymns and spiritual songs with gratitude in your hearts to God. (Colossians 3:16)

What is teaching but studying the works of God? And what do spiritual songs do but praise the Lord for what he has done for his people? Both teaching and worship are powerful memory devices to center our attention on the works of the Lord and to help us remember them through the day. They are gifts sent from God; no wonder that the Biblical writers urged us to hold up our elders and teachers in prayer and respect, because they are doing an important work for God's people when they bring us back to the old stories and draw lessons out of them for our spiritual growth.

On the other hand, however, we need to make sure that the teaching and worship that go on in a church actually do center on the works of the Lord! Too often they don't – they center instead on man and his works, and God's people go starving for lack of spiritual food.

Peter was concerned that his Christian charge would forget the works of God; we all tend to forget them when faced with the problems of life because God seems so far away and not very available to us. So he decided that, lest we forget God and his amazing works, he would take steps to put these spiritual realities under our noses again and again so that we wouldn't forget.

> So I will always remind you of these things, even though you know them and are firmly established

in the truth you now have. I think it is right to refresh your memory as long as I live in the tent of this body, because I know that I will soon put it aside, as our Lord Jesus Christ has made clear to me. And I will make every effort to see that after my departure you will always be able to remember these things. (2 Peter 1:12-15)

Don't be surprised, then, when certain people in your church do whatever it takes to drill the lessons of the Bible into your head – don't despise their efforts. It's hard enough to get people to take the Bible seriously, let alone use it when the need arises. The Spirit drives leaders to rehash the works of God over and over with the people with the hope that they will themselves turn to God in their time of need.

WHAT TO REMEMBER

One thing about remembering is that it can be either a conscious act or an unconscious act. Many times something will come to mind when we weren't looking for it; one thing leads to another and memories come rolling out in whatever order they please, entertaining us as they come, but not guided by us. It's nice when we think of the things of God like this – it shows that we have our heads filled with the right sort of thing instead of the junk of the world – but this isn't the sort of memory that we want to study right now. The sort we need to work on is the conscious act. Some memory is stored away for research purposes, so to speak, and will only come out when we go looking for it by name. We have to know what we are looking for and where to find it.

This is the kind of thing that the Scriptures tell us to do. "Remember such and such," it will say. What it means is that there is a specific thing to look for, some action that occurred in the past, that you need to look up and study. You need to find out all the details about it. When you do, its use will become obvious to you; until you do, it remains an unused memory that isn't doing you any good.

We ought to remember the whole Bible! But for starters there are places where the author tells us what to remember and why we should remember it. They break down into general categories of things to remember.

> ***Your former state.*** "Remember that you were slaves in Egypt and the LORD your God redeemed you from there." (Deuteronomy 24:18) One of the healthiest activities for a sick or ailing soul is to remember where you came from and how God brought you out from there. It can put so much needed perspective in your life; you can't very well despair of problems that you may have now if you remember back when the Lord pulled you out of death and gave you life.
>
> That was a thrilling thing, that original salvation of yours. Review the conditions a minute. You were, like other sinners, totally ignorant of the true God – perhaps not even interested in meeting him. You sinned against God and didn't care. Your friends encouraged you in your life of sin, or you were responsible for being a bad example for them. Perhaps people burdened you with hardships, petty fighting, jealousies, misunderstandings and by using you. You followed the ways of the world and yet you didn't find any real satisfaction in any of them. You were on your own then; nobody cared about you, really, because everyone was looking after themselves just like you were. You were sick at

heart and had no idea of what you had to do to be healed.

Then in stepped God – he came into your life, maybe even un-looked for. He came to claim you and to change you. He reached into your soul and took hold of it, never to let you go. He forgave you of all the sin you had committed against him. He gave you spiritual life so that you could see the kingdom of God, and so that you would have the hope of one day coming into the world where God lives, living with him forever. He called you "my son" or "my daughter." He pulled your heart away from the world so that you won't love it anymore. He alienated your friends against you – that was painful, but such company will only hurt you unless they also come over to your side. He replaced those old friends with new ones – people who love God and are concerned about holiness, who care about you and are willing to lay down their lives for you. He freed you from the trials of the world by making every trial a joy and an opportunity to witness to his amazing and ever-present strength. Now, how can you look back on that day and not take heart for today? If that's what God did for you then, don't you think that he's still just as serious about being close to you now?

The reason that it's important to remember how the Lord saved you is because you must appreciate what you were *then* and what you are *now* – and the Lord was responsible for the change. You were in the blackest night; you were "dead in sin" and "dead to God." You had no hope of ever seeing God or enjoying the benefit of salvation. Now, though, all that has been reversed and you have more than you could ever hope to imagine. The fullness of God! Eternal life! Perfect righteousness! Full understanding! The power of God! How did you come by all these impossible, out-of-reach things? It came by the person and work of Jesus Christ, the one who came to save you and bring you into the world of God. Perhaps, when you review the great changes that have come over your life, you will become curious about this Messiah who was able to do so much for you. Then (which is the whole idea of studying the works of God) you will go back and read (meditate on!) the story of Christ which was responsible for your spiritual rebirth and growth.

Of course this study of our beginnings goes way back in the Bible. In Genesis we find the story of the start of the human race – our duty, our miserable failure, our deadly sin, our path of death, our hopelessness. Then you will also read about the Lord's amazing and powerful works to rescue sinners from the hopeless condition they were in. It's all there – throughout the Old Testament and culminating in the New Testament – the works of the Lord to save not only others but you too. This is the history of your deliverance.

Big events. "Remember the Law of my servant Moses, the decrees and laws I gave him at Horeb for all Israel." (Malachi 4:4) This was one of the major events of the Old Testament – and the Lord never let the Israelites forget it. He was always reminding them of the time he gave them the Law.

Remembering the big events in the history of God's people helps to orient our thinking toward what's of primary importance versus what's of secondary importance. Let's use the example of the Law. When the Lord gave the Law to Israel, he did it with such great effect that the survivors remembered it all their lives. You would have too, if you would have been there!

> When the people saw the thunder and lightning and heard the trumpet and saw the mountain in smoke, they trembled with fear. They stayed at a distance and said to Moses, "Speak to us yourself and we will listen. But do not have God speak to us or we will die." Moses said to the people, "Do not be afraid. God has come to test you, so that the fear of God will be with you to keep you from sinning." The people remained at a distance, while Moses approached the thick darkness where God was. (Exodus 20:18-21)

The event was designed in such a way as to make an everlasting impression on the Israelites. However, as will happen with hard-hearted sinners, the succeeding generations who weren't there at the original occasion got a bit careless about the Law. That's why the memory of the meeting at Mt. Sinai was kept alive in the Scriptures and it was brought before the people's attention over and over again. "Remember the Law," said all the prophets and preachers down through the years. The original story was told and retold, with all its details, in order to keep the memory alive in Israel.

But another thing this story did was to help orient the people around the Law. The works of God, remember, are what he wants done – he does what he wills. He wanted the Israelites to live by his Law – so he set the stage for a magnificent display of his strength and awesome nature. It worked; they were terrified of him, which is exactly what he wanted to happen. (Deuteronomy 5:23-29) When someone fears the Lord, he's starting down the right path to obey him. It also makes that person aware that this is one thing that's very important to remember! Whatever else they may do in life, they had better take this Law seriously!

For all the works of God we can say the same thing. These are the important things in our religion. The things that God did in our world, through his power and wisdom, bringing about the impossible in the face of all odds against him, are the foundation stones of the Church. We need to be able to separate these primary works from our secondary works; we are here in the Church, with life and hope and joy, because of what he did, not because of what we do. His works are like stones lying across a creek where we can safely put our feet when crossing over. We may be interested in the other stones in the creek and bend over to study them, but these particular stones that we have our feet on are the most important ones for us – they have a practical value and fulfill our most important needs.

For instance, picking David to be king over Israel was a crucial event; you would think that it was a local political event to Israel, not very important for the history of the Church. But the rest of the Bible makes much out of this "local" event! All the following kings were compared to David, the prophets all predicted the King who was to come – the Messiah, the "Son of David" – and Christ himself covered himself with the aura of David and what he represented. So – study this work of God and you will find out what it means for your life; its importance extends to you too. It's the foundation of your faith.

The Lord in battle. "But do not be afraid of them; remember what the LORD your God did to Pharaoh and to all Egypt." (Deuteronomy 7:18) When times get rough, when certain people get overbearing, when you can't seem to win in the struggle of life, when it seems that the Church is going down in flames in the midst of a wicked world, remember that he who stands with God will have all the help that he could possibly want for any battle with any enemy.

The story of what the Lord did to Pharaoh and his country makes this point clear. It seems that the Lord wanted the story to be as rich and full of hope as he could possibly make it, so that the most discouraged of his saints would take heart from it. Remember that Pharaoh was the ultimate power in what was perhaps the most powerful nation of the world at that time. This job wasn't an easy pushover! It's no wonder that Moses had some grave doubts about the enterprise, and the Israelites themselves accused him of trying to get them into more trouble than they were already in. But they underestimated their God, as subsequent events proved. There is no power on earth that will succeed against the Lord Almighty when he decides to do something. His people can count on that.

Remember also the time when Hezekiah and his fearful city Jerusalem was surrounded by the hordes from Assyria. Sennacherib, the enemy commander, demanded arrogantly that they surrender the city, because ...

> Who of all the gods of these countries has been able to save his land from me? How then can the LORD deliver Jerusalem from my hand? (2 Kings 18:35)

But overnight his mighty army was dead in their tents, struck down by nothing other than the hand of the Lord whom he mocked.

Stories like these help encourage us when we are fighting the "fight of faith." Like Elisha, when we are surrounded by the enemies of our souls and things look hopeless, just a vision of the vast power and presence of the Lord of Hosts will put hope in us again. (2 Kings 6:8-23) God's people *will* prevail against all odds, because God *will* fight for them. That's why Jesus told his disciples, "In this world you will have trouble. But take heart! I have overcome the world." (John 6:33)

Miracles. "Remember the wonders he has done, his miracles, and the judgments he pronounced." (Psalm 105:5) Miracles are special things to remember because they remind us of one of the most important things about God's work: they are impossible from a human point of view. God does the impossible.

The Lord isn't interested in doing the possible, simply because that's in our realm. What we can do, he leaves to us to do. He prefers to take on the jobs that we can't do. Interestingly enough, the very things that we need to be saved and sanctified and prepared for eternity are jobs that we can't do – either God must do them or we are hopelessly lost. So expect to see miracles at every turn in the history of salvation.

Miracles fill the Bible from cover to cover. From the creation of the world to its ultimate destruction, God has been busy doing miraculous things that will bring about his will on earth. Salvation depends on these miracles. What would have happened to the Israelites if they were caught there by Pharaoh on the banks of the Red Sea? What if they would have died of starvation while wandering in the desert? What if the giants of Canaan would have succeeded in keeping the Israelites out of the land? On and on the list goes: the Lord worked miracles on behalf of his people so that they could be safe, happy, and fulfilled in a world full of barriers and enemies.

One of the points of Jesus' ministry was to work miracles; this was to be a sign that the Messiah had really come. When John the Baptist was himself wondering if Jesus was the Messiah, Jesus answered him like this:

> Go back and report to John what you hear and see: the blind receive sight, the lame walk, those who have leprosy are cured, the deaf hear, the dead are raised, and the good news is preached to the poor. Blessed is the man who does not fall away on account of me. (Matthew 11:4-6)

This answer shows how Jesus understood the situation: *God's* works are miraculous; that's a sign that it's really him at work. Others can claim to do God's work, but let them prove it by producing the results that *he* gets!

It takes a miracle to save us and build us up spiritually. Miracles aren't just for show or for entertainment; they are necessary if we are to be helped at all. It's going to take more than words in a book to turn sinners' hearts around from rebellion to total obedience and trust. It will take more than the efforts of all good men to convince unbelievers that there's a God in Heaven who is standing ready to judge them. It will take more than a little Bible study to put the eternal truth in someone's mind so that they turn away from this world and live for the future hope instead. The results and the goals are so demanding that nothing short of a miracle can fill the bill.

Even when we have become Christians, we need the miracles to keep coming in order to survive in this world. The Israelites were never free from the need for daily miracles, surrounded as they were by hostile neighbors and demanding temptations in a wicked world. Just like them, it's going to take the power of God to get us through the pitfalls of life and to the gates of Heaven in one piece. And somewhere in the Bible is the story of the miracle that you need to solve your present spiritual problems.

Glimpses of God's nature. "They refused to listen and failed to remember the miracles you performed among them. They became stiff-necked and in their rebellion appointed a leader in order to return to their slavery. But you are a forgiving God, gracious and compassionate, slow to anger and abounding in love. Therefore you did not desert them." (Nehemiah 9:17) Nehemiah, at least, learned something from the works of God: he saw what God was like in how he handled the sinners of Israel. This is a powerful use of the works of God, because it puts us in touch with this God whom we would otherwise know nothing about.

Knowing God is critical to our Christian living. If we knew nothing about God, we wouldn't know if we were offending him or pleasing him with our actions! We wouldn't know what his likes and dislikes are, or his ways, or what's on his heart. We wouldn't know if he's an angry "grandfather" God like the pictures make him out to be, or if he's an indulgent "grandfather" God like some other pictures paint him.

Christians have the great privilege of knowing God as he really is. They have the Spirit who teaches them who God is, and they have the eyes to see him – imperfectly now, but clearly at the end of time. But in spite of this mountaintop position of height that we stand on spiritually, we have to remember to look in the right direction for our image of the true God. It's as we study the revelation of God, the Bible, the history of his works on the earth, that we get our clearest view of him this side of Heaven. And it isn't as simple as reading the words and you'll get the point; unbelievers can read the same words and never see God in them. The Spirit helps us to read the accounts of the works of God and learn who God is.

For instance, we can read the words of Jesus that God is our Father, but that may not make as strong an impression on us as when we read about our Father *in action*. Who can fail to understand the heart of God when we see him accept such a determined sinner as Paul? God the Father accepted Paul in spite of his terrible history as the persecutor of God's precious Church; he simply put all that aside from his heart and welcomed Paul with open arms and no accusations. Paul himself was amazed that God received him so freely:

> Although I am less than the least of all God's people, this grace was given to me: to preach to the Gentiles the unsearchable riches of Christ ... (Ephesians 3:8)

From studying God's works we find out some important things about him such as these:

that he hates sin (he destroyed sinners from time to time, remember!); that he loves those who are faithful and trust in him; that he despises arrogance; that he feels great compassion for the downtrodden; that he has profound wisdom; that his power is unstoppable and overwhelming; that he intends to always get his way; that he has a goal in mind and he sticks close to the path that will take him and us to that goal. These are all personal matters that relate to his nature, to his personality, to what God is like. Again, how can we hope to please him if we know none of these things about him?

When we provoked God. "Remember this and never forget how you provoked the LORD your God to anger in the desert. From the day you left Egypt until you arrived here, you have been rebellious against the LORD." (Deuteronomy 9:7) This is a painful memory, but a necessary one nevertheless. We have been saved from sin, but we are still sinners. We don't *have* to sin now – we are no longer under its bondage – but we still do sin because our hearts look back to the old life and long for it sometimes. This always hurts God when we do this. After all, Christ came specifically to save us from that old curse; what are we doing wallowing in the mud again?

The Bible doesn't counsel you to remember your sin for no reason; it always shines the light of the Spirit on the matter and calls it what it really is: an awful offence against your Heavenly Father. You grieved the Spirit. You turned your back on your Savior who died for your salvation. You chose the old lusts and appetites of Egypt over against the hope of the Heavenly Jerusalem. If you can see what a terrible thing that sin is, that it's especially ugly on the Christian, then you will be more grieved yourself over what you have done. Like the prodigal son, you will be aghast that you have done such a thing against someone who loves you and gave you everything he had. You will be ashamed over your sin, realizing that you, a child of God, a king and a priest in the kingdom of God, a creature raised above all powers and dominions and the angels themselves, seated at God's right hand as one of the privileged few of the universe, that you have stooped so low as to touch what everyone else in the universe knows will offend God. Put in this light, the memories of our sins will serve to keep us more determined in the path of obedience and to trust in his salvation.

And if you can't be shamed into keeping your hands clean from sin, then at least you can remember the severe discipline that you received from God when you sinned against him and you will fear to sin again. Memory serves not only to remind us of what did happen, but it teaches us what will surely happen again if we aren't careful. We learned the hard way that God can't allow disobedience from his children; we are poor learners if we think we can get away with it this time.

The former times of righteousness and joy. "These things I remember as I pour out my soul: how I used to go with the multitude, leading the procession to the house of God, with shouts of joy and thanksgiving among the festive throng."

(Psalm 42:4) Celebrations and happy times are good times; we all enjoy them and look forward to them. But life can't consist of such things all the time. We jump along the mountain peaks of spiritual highs, but we have to come down after a while and earn our living and help those in need and relate to an apathetic world. The lows are never fun to live through; we prefer the highs. But here memory serves an important function in enabling us to relive those precious moments when life gets hard or boring.

Unbelievers think that we Christians are miserable creatures. That's because they see us suffering under pains that they don't feel, being spiritually dead as they are. But we are alive to the reality of human misery and the sin that causes it; and we are also alive to God, and we hurt that he hasn't come to make things right again. We live with hope in a hopeless world, and we wait for all things to be made new again.

But we needn't be miserable all the time. Think back for a minute on those glorious occasions when God drew close, when he was especially real, when prayer was like fire shooting up into Heaven, when your heart burst from the joy of living before the Lord. Everything went right back then; nothing could bring you down. Well, those moments live on in your memory so that you won't get discouraged in these dryer times. To keep you from losing hope, the Lord reminds you that things won't always be this bad; one day you will rejoice again just as you have in the past.

If we didn't have these precious memories of Christianity available to us, then we just may give up hope. People ask us how we are so sure of our faith when times are rough. We can respond by pointing to what the Lord did in the past – and the certainty we had of God's presence and power. Those are signposts, "witnesses" like the pile of rocks that Samuel set up and named "Ebenezer," to remind us that God does indeed exist and he rewards those who earnestly seek him. (1 Samuel 7:12)

It's worth a smile and a thrill in our hearts to go back over the record, like leafing through a photo scrapbook, and recall the high times of God's people. Like when Joshua led the Israelites through Canaan in conquest; they couldn't be stopped! And when Gideon routed the entire Midianite army with just a handful of men. And especially when Solomon completed the Temple – all the people turned out for this most momentous of occasions, and the Lord himself came down and filled the Temple so that the priests couldn't do their duty because of the heavy presence there. How about the time when Jesus spoke and brought Lazarus out of the tomb? That was a sweet foretaste of the resurrection to come at the end of time. These and other exciting moments in the history of God's work will keep us going in these dreary hours.

What was foretold. "But dear friends, remember what the Apostles of our Lord Jesus Christ foretold." (Jude 7) What did they foretell? That Christ would come, certainly, but more than that: that he would die, and rise again, and return to

God, and send his Spirit, and rule over his Church, and one day come back to gather his saints to live with him forever, and make a new Heaven and a new earth where there would be no more sorrow or tears or pain or sin or death. They foretold all sorts of things that we must remember and study.

History isn't over yet, not by a long shot. The wicked think that since God is long in acting on his promises that either there is no God or that he has changed his mind. Neither is true. As Peter tells us, God's longsuffering has only one goal: to give us more time to repent and so be saved. The end result of the wicked will be just as horrible as the Apostles and prophets said it would be in spite of the long wait. They would do well to remember how longsuffering God has been in the past with the wicked, and that it did no good then to ignore God's demands. Look at the time that God gave the Canaanites – he told Abraham that he couldn't inherit the land yet so that the present inhabitants would have more time to seal their doom, so to speak. Their end was just as he prophesied even though it took more than 500 years to happen. (Genesis 15:16)

On the other side of the coin, there are many prophecies and promises that God's people will gain Heaven if they only hang in there. Are the things of this world, the promises and gold and glitter, very appealing to us? Then consider what God has foretold for his people if they *wait* for their good things: everlasting life, perfect righteousness, love unbounded, pure light of knowledge, a position of power and authority reigning beside Christ, all the things that a human wants and needs but will only get when he comes to Christ. (Mark 10:17-31) The unbelievers can't wait for their good things – they want them now, and since the only things at hand are the things of the world, they immerse themselves in lust and physical comforts and earthly securities. But the people of God are willing to wait for theirs; they consider themselves to be no more than "strangers and aliens" in this world as they head for a better world. What gives them such confidence in the next world? What makes them despise the apparently satisfying things of this world and look to God for better things? Simply the old prophecies of what God promised to do for his people. They remember these things, and wait.

While you are looking for those prophecies, keep in mind that they are going to be found in more places than in outright prophecies. For example, the types that are used in the Old Testament are "shadows" of the world to come; they are prophecies in stone and wood and earth and flesh that teach spiritual truths. The Temple was a picture of the one in Heaven, we are told. David rewarded those who were willing to come out and help him set up his kingdom; when the kingdom came, he handed out important government posts to those faithful "mighty men." (1Chronicles 11-12; 27:5-6) Jesus raised people out of the grave with a word and healed the sick of their diseases; but such things are simply a picture lesson of what he intends to do for his people on the last day: death then will be utterly defeated in a glorious way, and we won't be sick with sin and surrounded by the diseases of spiritual darkness anymore.

WHAT NOT TO REMEMBER

The Scriptures also have something to say about what *not* to remember, which is just as important as what we should remember. Not all memories are helpful! We can spend valuable time daydreaming about worthless memories, or we can feed our pride or lust without having to wander outside of our minds to do it. Since the mind and its memory facility are so powerful, we can expect amazingly destructive things from this little powerhouse as well as helpful things.

Here are some of the things that the Bible warns us against when we go digging around in our memories:

> ***Don't dwell on memories of the "good things" of the world.*** "We remember the fish we ate in Egypt at no cost – also the cucumbers, melons, leeks, onions and garlic." (Numbers 11:5) The context for this verse is when the Israelites were wandering around in the desert, having just left their state of slavery under Pharaoh. Though they hated their slavery in Egypt, it seems that they hated losing the mouth-watering food of Egypt even more! They actually suggested going back to Egypt and slavery so that they could eat better!
>
> That attitude was complete nonsense. Back in Egypt they complained about their slavery, and none of them would have suggested such a foolish idea as staying there for the sake of the food. When a human being has to go through some dry and trying times he will often say stupid things without thinking about what he's saying.

The problem is our fickle hearts. We know full well that the Lord rescued us from death when he saved us; we know that our condition then, when we were lost, was "without hope and without God." (Ephesians 2:12) We couldn't have been any worse off than we were. Now, however, when we have to live on a Spartan diet and go without the comforts and securities that we have been used to getting from the world, we feel ourselves abused. We forget too easily the danger of sin and the wrath of God that characterized our lives before, and we foolishly wish we could go back to those more comfortable times.

"Remember Lot's wife!" (Luke 17:32) Lot's wife's problem was that she was reluctant to leave her life of ease. So are we at times; we wish that following the Lord wasn't so hard, that he would relax the standards a bit and let us enjoy what the world enjoys. But we may not remember those promises that God made about the world:

> But the day of the Lord will come like a thief. The Heavens will disappear with a roar; the elements will be destroyed by fire, and the earth and everything in it will be laid bare. (2 Peter 3:10)

> In the beginning, O Lord, you laid the foundations of the earth, and the Heavens are the work of your hands. They will perish, but you remain; they will all wear out like a garment. You will roll them up like a robe;

like a garment they will be changed.
(Hebrews 1:10-12)

The good things of this world will serve their purpose and then the Lord will do away with them all. The bad things of this world will be swept away and good riddance to them! Either way, it's no use setting our hearts on any of it. It won't survive Judgment Day, and it doesn't build up your soul in any way. You need some things to get along in life, and the Lord blesses his people as well as unbelievers with good things. But he separates the sheep from the goats with this test of materialism and longing after the things that this world offers.

Too often we long after those things. We remember when we used to earn twice as much as we do now; we remember when we had lots of friends and we used to go out every night and enjoy ourselves; we remember when people looked up to us because of our physical accomplishments or achievements in school or advancement in our jobs. We remember when we didn't have any supervision and could do whatever we wanted. We remember when we didn't have many responsibilities and were free to do our own thing. The trouble is that the more we dwell on these memories, the more inclined we are to return to them and forget our original commitment to God's ways.

The problem about all this is that we remember those "good old days" when the present days aren't to our liking. We long for the past when the present is hateful or troublesome to us.

It's when we are burdened with responsibility that we long for the days of irresponsibility. It's when the Lord is disciplining us to make us walk the straight path of obedience and faith that we remember the former days of no supervision. It's when we are nobodies, having to associate with nobodies, that we remember when we were more important.

We say all this as if the Lord doesn't know what he's doing with us! Doesn't the Maker of all things know whether those things will do you good or harm? He has your future laid out very carefully, and he knows what you need and when you need it. Like the Israelites, we sometimes need to go through hard times – times of doing without the enjoyments of the world – in order to strengthen us and give us hope for the realities of Heaven. Sometimes the Lord deals with us in this way because he knows we have yet to be weaned from earthly comforts and earthly riches; he can see that our faith is pretty weak, that we don't regard the things of this world as so much "dung" like Paul was able to do. (Philippians 3:1-11)

Remember Jesus' counsel to you about the riches of this world:

> Do not store up for yourselves treasures on earth, where moth and rust destroy, and thieves break in and steal. But store up for yourselves treasures in Heaven, where moth and rust do not destroy, and where thieves do not break in and steal. For where your treasure is, there

your heart will be also. (Matthew 6:19-21)

He knows what he's talking about. He could see the kingdom of God clearly and he knew that there was no comparison with this world, no matter what the glitter here looks like. He considered it a small, unimportant trial to go without good things now if he, by going without, gained an eternal inheritance. He considered the cross, as horrible as it was, a small price to pay for God's kingdom. He never had a problem about remembering the "riches and pleasures of Egypt," not since he had the kingdom of God clearly in sight.

Forget the sins of your earlier years. "So I will put a stop to the lewdness and prostitution you began in Egypt. You will not look on these things with longing or remember Egypt anymore." (Ezekiel 23:27) Another problem that the Israelites had was musing about the life of sin that they lived when they were in Egypt. Keep in mind that the Israelites were slaves in Egypt, but they were free to sin against God however they pleased; their morals weren't a concern to Pharaoh. And evidently they sinned against God while in Egypt, because we have some startling proofs of their immoral nature as the history of the nation unfolds.

We all sinned before God took hold of us and dragged us into the light. Paul says that you all "were dead in your transgressions and sins, in which you used to live when you followed the ways of this world and of the ruler of the kingdom of the air." (Ephesians 2:1-2) We were masters of sin; we loved our sin; we fought for the right to sin. Our natural tendency was to sin and it felt good. That old life doesn't leave so easily when we become Christians. For as well-trained as we were in the ways of the world, the new training under Christ's banner isn't going to happen overnight. The surprise isn't that we continue to sin as Christians, but that the Lord successfully prevents us from sinning as much as we would like.

The danger comes when we have need of our old tools of the trade. For example, when someone runs across our path and aggravates us, the thing that we instinctively reach for to deal with the problem is *anger*:

> My dear brothers, take note of this: Everyone should be quick to listen, slow to speak and slow to become angry, for man's anger does not bring about the righteous life that God requires. (James 1:19-20)

We have delicious memories of how effective anger was in the past for putting others in their places. But we can't dwell on those memories now. We aren't in the business anymore of putting others down, but in building them up and "considering others better than ourselves." We have to follow Jesus' counsel to "turn the other cheek" when someone irritates us, and Paul's counsel to be "long-suffering" and "patient" with those who may little deserve such gentleness.

Our old sins kept us in ignorance about God, but now they are poison to us. We are new creatures, created in the image of Christ, called to be holy and perfect like our Father in Heaven. Just the memory of how we used to live in our wickedness and impurity will stain our minds now! To relish those old thoughts, to rummage through the memories of when we used to be slaves of sin and following every whim of passion and self-will, is to leave ourselves open to a vicious attack of temptation from the enemy of our souls. We can't afford to run that risk. We can't afford to dishonor God by sinning against him and bringing hurt on God's people. So we have to stay away from the dangerous precipice of sin and not even wander near the edge anymore with our thoughts. We are still weak; we need God's grace every single minute if we hope to keep on that straight and narrow way to Heaven. It's understandable if our weak flesh responds to the power of sin's temptation; but it's foolish to willingly entertain the thought of sin – that's like drinking poison on purpose!

Don't ridicule what God has done. "First of all, you must understand that in the last days scoffers will come, scoffing and following their own evil desires. They will say, 'Where is this 'coming' he promised? Ever since our fathers died, everything goes on as it has since the beginning of creation.'" (2 Peter 3:3-4) This sounds incredible, but someone who claims to be a Christian may one day find himself mocking the very works of God. Out of the mouth that once praised God for his works will come scorn instead. And it isn't unthinkable that you yourself may be that person.

The Jews who crucified Christ once welcomed him into Jerusalem by the thousands. It turned out that the very people who laid their coats on the road for the Messiah, as he entered their city in triumph, turned on him in just a couple of days and shouted to Pilate for his blood! We can surely assume that many of those who "believed" in Jesus very soon afterwards mocked him in the streets of the city, recalling his words and his works in jokes and ridicule. (see John 6:66)

It often happens to Christians – I've seen it – that they get too sophisticated for the simple things of the Gospel. At first, when they enter the kingdom and everything is new to them, they love it; they wouldn't dream of having life any other way than a simple faith in the Lord, reading their Bibles, and testifying of the Lord's goodness to others. Christianity was good then in its simplicity. But as they get older and "wiser" they find out that there are "more important" issues to focus their thoughts on. They become politicians and social planners now. They wrangle with each other about church organization and function. They create theological distinctives that separate them from other theological positions. As their sophistication level rises, they forget the simplicity of the faith as it once was, and they will actually make fun of that former way of life. Oh, that's kid's stuff, they will tell us; you have to be pretty naive to live on that level all the time. The Lord wants us to grow up and tackle these more important issues.

What they are really saying is that they don't believe in the Biblical process of faith anymore. Faith is trusting God to do the impossible – waiting on him to do the miracles that he promised to do to keep us spiritually alive. Faith is a helpless dependence on God to save us from our sins, daily, constantly, faithfully – but they don't like to admit their weakness, their dependence, their sinfulness, nor that God is primarily interested in this matter of their sin. When they don't see life in such simple terms anymore, when they've built the issues of life into something more challenging to their own powers, then they will ridicule the simple Gospel.

What they are really saying is that they don't believe that the spiritual world and spiritual matters are of primary importance to a Christian. They don't like to divide up reality along those lines because they might lose what they like of this world in the process. Aliens in this world? Never! We are called to transform this world, to be masters of this world, to work out the "will of God" in this world. A fine challenge for the powers and wisdom of men. But the Lord called us *out* of this world, if we can believe what the Bible says about it; he has doomed this world with all its programs and issues and methods and goals. He has called us instead to focus our minds on "things above," not on things below. We have an inheritance waiting for us in Heaven, not in successful programs on earth. We should be about the business of preparing our *souls* for the last day, not our surroundings. The Lord is master here, not we, and he has reserved this world and all of its busy activities and issues for the flames. Our business is to escape from that coming judgment. Is this childish? Is this naive? Do we look foolish when we focus on the simple things of Christianity? Do we really need to grow up into more important matters? David was proud to look so "foolish" for the Lord before the world! (2 Samuel 6:20-22)

Beware of that "grown up" feeling that often comes over Christians who have been around a while. Our faith has always consisted, and will always consist, of the simple Gospel; we will never outgrow the need to sit at Jesus' feet and learn the ways of salvation. When we forget his counsel to be like "little children" in our faith, then we will start saying things about God's works that aren't at all good. We will begin to disassociate ourselves from that simple Gospel, from the plain and simple statements of the Bible, in an effort to look more respectable to the world, and we will eventually be like Peter who denied that he even knew the Lord. Fear that day.

TIMES TO REMEMBER

When does the Lord want us to remember his works? This is a pertinent question, because going back to those memories of God's works is like reaching for a hammer when you have a nail to drive. *You will not be able to do your work unless you remember God's works at the right time.* Unless you are alert, unless you are skilled in remembering the Lord's works when you need to, the opportunities that you have to obey God and honor his Name will float by you and you will be helpless to bring them back. You will have failed to do your duty because you failed to use the spiritual tools that he has given you.

When is the critical time for remembering what God does? ***When you are in the midst of battle.*** You have to remember that the Lord fights for his people or you will try it on your own – and lose miserably. You battle against the powers of evil, against the world, against the misunderstandings of unbelievers and family and friends, against the sin in your own heart. These are all areas where you have to turn to God if you hope to be delivered. If the Israelites went out to battle fully confident in their own strength and weapons, they lost the battle. If they pleaded with the Lord to fight for them and give them victory over their enemies, they won. It was that simple. They had to remember that the Lord fights for his people, that this is one of the works that *he* wants to do in their lives. "The LORD will fight for you; you need only to be still." (Exodus 14:14)

You need to remember the works of the Lord ***when you are fighting depression.*** Spiritual depression is like a slippery pit that sucks us down into hopelessness and despair. We become more and more convinced, the longer we struggle with our problems, that there is no answer for us from Heaven. We feel as if we have nobody on our side, no one to take up our case before God and man. We think that these problems will always dominate us no matter what we do. But it's precisely at that low moment in our souls that we need to remember the works of God. He rescues; he delivers; he changes things. David despaired of life itself as he sank below the waves of depression; he didn't think that there was any hope for him. But suddenly he remembered the Lord, what he was famous for in the past, and he cried out to him. You should read what happened to him when he did that! It was like taking hold of a lifeline in the nick of time. (Psalm 18)

You need to remember God's works *during the watch of the night.* When the Church is asleep and nothing is happening, when the battleground is quiet and the enemy is still, when you have time on your hands to meditate, spend that valuable time reviewing the works of the Lord. Make the most of every opportunity to learn as much as you can about how God does things. You will need that information later, and you won't have the leisure to study it then! You will be in the thick of battle then with pressing needs, and it will be important that strong and ready memories are available, not weak or incomplete ones. Now is the time for homework, while you have time on your hands. "On my bed I remember you; I think of you through the watches of the night." (Psalm 63:6)

And meditate on God's works *while you are young.* Far from being a study only for older and more mature Christians, the Works of the Lord is something that young Christians ought to be studying and getting skillful at. You need to learn good habits early; bad habits are hard to change later on. There are a lot of older Christians who don't want to learn this truth about God's works; unfortunately they have been spending all their time over the years putting together a structure made mostly out of their own works – their own efforts at righteousness and good works and things that they thought would please the Lord (as well as a lot of other useless stuff!). It's a rotten house that they live in, and Judgment Day will show it up for what it really is. Now they are too old and "wise" to be taught the truth about their works. But younger Christians have not yet laid the groundwork for houses of straw, and they still have the opportunity to learn God's ways and how God builds his own house. "Remember your Creator in the days of your youth, before the days of trouble come and the years approach when you will say, 'I find no pleasure in them.'" (Ecclesiastes 12:1)

And you must remember the works of the Lord *when you are scattered like sheep across the nations.* It's the Lord's work that binds all of God's people together; we would be totally helpless and without hope if we didn't have the encouraging news that the Lord is still putting his kingdom together. It seems to us, when we are surrounded by the world and by people who don't care about the things of God, that we are divided and conquered, and the work of the Lord has failed. Sometimes we find ourselves completely on our own, and those times are the most discouraging. But remember Jerusalem! "Though I scatter them among the peoples, yet in distant lands they will remember me. They and their children will survive, and they will return." (Zechariah 10:9) "You who have escaped the sword, leave and do not linger! Remember the LORD in a distant land, and think on Jerusalem." (Jeremiah 51:50) Someday all the injustices in the world will be reversed, and God will fix everything that is wrong. Someday the works of God will shine in the open so that everyone can see them. Someday the salvation that we long for will happen, and the new day will dawn. This is our hope, and this is what keeps us going when life seems so hopeless and so dark. Though we are aliens in this world, someday we will go home for good – to our God who calls us to him – to *our* Jerusalem.

RESULTS OF REMEMBERING

Although we've seen this already in what we've studied, we need to look more closely at the fact that remembering brings results. Too often we underestimate the power of our spiritual weapons. They have the power to bring down strongholds! (2 Corinthians 10:4) Things happen when we remember God's works; things change. And conversely, things also change when we *don't* remember his works. Either way we can't afford to ignore this subject.

Let's take the negative first. When you don't remember the Lord's works, aside from the fact that you miss out on all the good things that the Lord would otherwise do for you, the worst possible thing that you can imagine will happen: he will come and take away your witness to him.

> Yet I hold this against you: You have forsaken your first love. Remember the height from which you have fallen! Repent and do the things that you did at first. If you do not repent, I will come to you and remove your lampstand from its place. (Revelation 2:4-5)

Not remembering God's works leads to the unthinkable. We may be satisfied in our spiritual lethargy, but the Lord is never satisfied. He wants profitable servants, not unprofitable ones! And he's going to get his way. Though we think that he would never treat us so harshly, he isn't going to change his rules just to suit our personal preferences or to save our honor. It's an unpleasant thing to see a Christian who has lost that original fire, that zeal of testimony, that interest in spiritual things. When his own works take precedence over God's works then he has become, by order of God, useless and worthless in the kingdom. God won't give him important work to do because he's undependable now. He spends the rest of his days working on things that don't matter to God or to God's people. It happens all the time, and it happens to people better than you and me. Take warning.

On the positive side, remembering the Lord's works will inevitably result in comfort, hope, encouragement, inner strength, more faith, holiness and obedience. That's a lot to claim from a simple exercise! But it's true, nevertheless, and for a very simple reason: it puts us in touch with the God who has done all these things that we remember. We come close to him because he comes close to us. When we honor him with our thoughts, he honors us with his presence.

We proclaim to you what we have seen and heard, so that you also may have fellowship with us. And our fellowship is with the Father and with his Son, Jesus Christ. We write this to make our [or *your*] joy complete. (1 John 1:3-4)

Remembering the Lord's works is one of the most life-changing things that a Christian can do.

Conclusion

This has been a long study, but hopefully it has been a fruitful one. What we would expect from studying the Lord's works is that our own works take on a special power and meaning as we begin using materials from God's world for a change. It's time we put less stock in things of this world, things that won't last the ravages of time and sin, and started using the eternal realities of God's kingdom. If we do that then we will find that our works will follow us into Heaven.

You may have noticed that this study has been pretty "off balance" in this regard. We have plunged deeply into what the Lord does, but we haven't gone as deeply into man's works. Isn't this a shortcoming? Don't we need to find out exactly what God wants us to do so that we can live in obedience to his will?

But I don't apologize for the method taken here. Unfortunately there is little enough said in today's literature about what *God* does, and *too much* said about what man does. It's about time we swung the study over to the other side for a while. It's nice to just think about God and keep man out of it until we are ready for him. Besides, we won't truly understand what it is that man is supposed to do until we get it firmly in sight what God does. We can't run off in "obedience" too soon! We run the great risk of trying to do God's works for him; what makes it worse is that man's sinful heart would rather do God's works for him because we feel it's too risky to let God do his works for us – we might lose our sin in the process! So don't trust the impulse to quickly review the works of God and then go off to do your own thing; sit at the Lord's feet for a period of "meditation" on his works and build a solid foundation for your works that will come later. We have alluded to what man's works should be in light of God's works.

What have we learned about the Lord's works? We've learned, **first** of all, that they are special works that achieve what God is after. Man has tried for thousands of years to bring about a "perfect" world – perfect according to his definition, at any rate – and he consistently fails. God, however, has set about the same job and succeeded amazingly well. His works are quite capable and very suitable for the job of creating righteousness, justice, love, wisdom, joy – all the things that go into the kingdom of Heaven.

Second, we've learned that *only* God can do those works. It's a mistake, and a damaging one at that, for us to even attempt to try to do God's works for him. We need to stay out of his way when he does these things. There are things that he wants us to do, and he will hold us accountable for our duties; but he never asked us nor did he expect us to do his work for him. He alone has the power and the wisdom and the determination to build his kingdom, in all its many facets.

Third, we've learned that his works are his will. What he does, that's what he wants. We often wonder what God's will is, and we really shouldn't; his will is right under our noses in the record of what God has done. We should never run short of material for our prayers. We should be praying not for what we want, but for what God has done in the past – because these things are the same things that he wants to do for us now. God's will is plain to see in what he does.

Fourth, we've learned that his works teach us who God is. He didn't think it sufficient to sit in Heaven and send news down to us about his nature, about his ways, about his likes and dislikes. He came down personally and took matters in hand. He showed us graphically what he's like. There's no mistaking his message when he backs it up with action. His works teach us who he is, and should be a valuable resource of information about him.

Fifth, we've learned that the Lord's works are specially designed to support, hold up, encourage, and help his people. Others will miss the point, and the soil of God's works will kill an unbeliever because of its other-worldly harshness. But we thrive in his works. They are literally our salvation and our hope; if God would stop working then we would all die spiritually. We just don't realize how dependent we are on what God does for us.

Sixth, we've learned that we must remember the Lord's works when it comes time to remember them. Life is full of trials, struggles, temptations, sorrows, confusion, warfare, and many other things that gradually wear a human being down to death and the grave in defeat. There is no more powerful weapon that we Christians have in hand than the memory of God's works. In recalling what he did in the past, we turn to him for those same things in our own lives – and he comes through every time. Without the Church's collective memory of the Lord's works we would get discouraged and sit down defeated; but when we go back and research these things, then we find ourselves fully armed from a Heavenly arsenal, ready to take on any problem.

We need to remind ourselves of one last point. One of the most important reasons that we study his works is so that we can identify them; when something claims to be a work of God, then the principles that we've learned about his works become valuable resource material. Check to see if those claims are true. If the "work" in question doesn't line up with what the Bible says that God does, you can safely dismiss it as a work of man and not a work of God. What we want is God's works; we need what God does to base our lives upon. We can't afford to believe everything that we hear simply on the basis of its own merits – *even if it means that we have to examine what we ourselves are doing in God's Name.* We want to get things straight; we want to find out the truth about what God does and what he expects of us.

We too are one of the works of the Lord, if we believe in Christ for our salvation. His work in us will produce more fruit as we help to build his Kingdom. May this Scripture be true of us as we ponder the works of the Lord and become wiser workmen ourselves:

> For we are God's workmanship, created in Christ Jesus to do good works, which God prepared in advance for us to do. (Ephesians 2:9)

NOTES

NOTES

NOTES

www.ingramcontent.com/pod-product-compliance
Lightning Source LLC
Chambersburg PA
CBHW022102150426
43195CB00008B/231